**Petero Civoniceva** is among Australia's most honoured and beloved sportsmen. In fifteen years of top-line rugby league he played with distinction for Australia, Queensland, the Brisbane Broncos and the Penrith Panthers. Now retired from the game, he lives in Redcliffe, Queensland, with wife Bonnie and children Tallulah, Ruby, Kaden and Jacobi.

**Larry Writer** is the author of the Ned Kelly Award-winning *Razor*, *Bumper: The Life and Times of Frank 'Bumper' Farrell*, *Newk*, *Pleasure and Pain*, and *Never Before, Never Again*, the saga of the record-breaking St George rugby league team of the 1950s and 60s.

# PETERO
## MY STORY

**PETERO CIVONICEVA**
WITH LARRY WRITER

MACMILLAN
Pan Macmillan Australia

First published 2012 in Macmillan by Pan Macmillan Australia Pty Limited
1 Market Street, Sydney

National Library of Australia
Cataloguing-in-Publication data:

Civoniceva, Petero.

Petero: my story /
Petero Civoniceva (with Larry Writer).

9781742611334 (pbk.)

Civoniceva, Petero.
Rugby League football players–
Australia–Biography.
Rugby League football–
Australia–Biography.

Other Authors/Contributors:
Writer, Larry.

796.3338092

Typeset in 12/16 pt Sabon Roman by Post Pre-Press Group, Australia
Printed in Australia by McPherson's Printing Group

Papers used by Pan Macmillan Australia Pty Ltd are natural, recyclable
products made from wood grown in sustainable forests. The manufacturing
processes conform to the environmental regulations of the country of origin.

# CONTENTS

# FOREWORD

## *by Wayne Bennett*

Cyril Connell loved him from the very beginning, the way Cyril did with the kids he'd discover for the Broncos on those back roads around Queensland. He was excited when Darren Lockyer was coming, and with Steve Renouf before him . . . with so many young guns. And when your trusted recruitment officer tells you this guy named Petero is coming, the tone in his voice suggests you should be excited too.

Petero Civoniceva was a centre three-quarter. I knew he was there, and I'd see him now and again, though I couldn't see anything much in him. He was big, but I'd seen bigger kids. Had a little step. He'd do something, not much, then wander around the field for a while doing nothing at all.

'What do you see in him?' I'd ask Cyril.

'Just be patient, Wayne,' the wise man would reply.

So patient we were.

The next time I really noticed him, he was playing in reserve grade against Cronulla in 1997 and this big fella from the Sharks was taking the ball up. Taking the ball up hard.

Petero hit him. One of the biggest hits I've seen to this day. The big Sharks forward didn't know if he was Arthur, Martha or General MacArthur.

I remember thinking, *So that's what Cyril saw.*

Still, we brought him along at his own pace and by '98 he was in the first-grade squad, playing in the second row alongside a couple of other young blokes in Shane Webcke and Brad Thorn. They were to become great mates.

Petero? He was the club's rookie-of-the-year in '98 and played off the bench in the grand final win. He became the rock for the Broncos, Queensland and Australia, the centre-piece in the toughest part of the field. He was the Broncos' player-of-the-year in 2004 and again in 2006.

You look at him today, at 36 years of age, and you marvel at a true statesman of our game, both as a player and person.

He's always been there for everybody. If you're having a bad day, go and sit next to Petero, because you're going to walk away feeling a whole lot better. He's not going to kid to you, or tell you what you always want to hear, but he's going to be real and caring, and he's never going to let you down. Year by year, week by week, day by day.

Petero Civoniceva makes the grand final of the toughest players I have coached. No one ever wanted to get tackled by him.

In 2008, I was helping out New Zealand when they played Australia in the Centenary Test at the SCG and I remember talking afterwards to a concussed Roy Asotasi. I asked the Kiwi prop what had happened out there.

He said, 'Petero got me again.'

He got him good.

Years ago the Broncos were playing the Warriors at Lang Park and they had a professional boxer in their forwards, a bloke named Monty Betham. Betham had been voted the player rivals least wanted to pick a fight with. He'd had 53 pro bouts, but not against the likes of Petero.

That night at Lang Park, he hit Petero in the head with everything he had. Petero didn't even flinch. Didn't look at him, acknowledge him, nothing. Just got up and played the ball.

Monty Betham left the field. He had broken his arm in six places.

Back in Petero's rookie year, we were in Melbourne playing the Storm at Origin time, so missing many of our senior players and struggling. When the players came in at half-time, Petero told the club doctor his arm didn't feel right. The doc had a look and, sure enough, it was broken. He still went back out and gave us another 15 minutes before we could get him to agree to come off.

In 2007, Petero left the Broncos for the Penrith Panthers. Not often in life have I wanted to have my time again – and you can't – but we all felt the pain. If I could have my time again, it wouldn't have happened. He had earned the right to be a lifer at the Broncos, deserved it, and I'm so glad he got to go back and finish his career where he always belonged. With the hunger, honesty and humility good ol' Cyril Connell saw from the very beginning.

# PREFACE

# Home

Ismelled the salt air of Redcliffe and I knew for sure that I was back, and it felt so good. It was a humid Queenslander of a late spring afternoon in 2011 and my wife Bonnie and our children, Tallulah, Ruby, Kaden and Jacobi, had just returned to my hometown of Redcliffe on Moreton Bay on the peninsula north of Brisbane. After four tumultuous years captaining the Penrith Panthers in Sydney's west, and still buzzing from the recent State of Origin series, in my opinion the best ever, I had returned to play out my career with my old club, the Brisbane Broncos.

We were gathered at Suttons Beach at Redcliffe and as the dusk came on we were joined by our family, all of whom live a walk or a quick drive away: my mother, going grey now, loving and gentle and always smiling, and father – grey, too, but still a huge, fit man – and my sisters Lusi and Lily, Bonnie's mum and dad and her siblings and their partners and kids. In the Fijian-Melanesian way, we all tucked in to a feast that gave us energy for all the catching up we had to do and the swimming and cricket and footy games we'd play until it got too dark.

All around us, other groups were picnicking too. There was a Thursday Island wedding party going on down the beach with island songs sung to the accompaniment of soft guitars. Jacobi, who was two, ran over and flung his arms around my legs, in tears because he had taken a tumble. I picked him up and hugged him until he settled down, then he broke free to take more tumbles.

I went for a swim. I swam out a way and then just floated and wallowed for a while, allowing the salty sea to work its magic. Maybe it's my heritage, but immersing myself in the ocean makes me feel good and at peace. I could never live far from the water.

My decision to return to play for the Brisbane Broncos for my swansong season in rugby league was, I knew now for certain, a good one. There's no place like home.

Earlier in the afternoon, before I had collected Bonnie and the kids from our home – which had been rented out during the four years we were in Sydney – I took time to drive around the neighbourhood to reacquaint myself with the place where I grew up and lived until the harsh realities of modern rugby league banished me to another part of the world. Although I truly grew to love the Panthers and the people of Penrith and did my very best there, I was never able to shrug off my longing for home, family and friends. It was the same for Bonnie and the children.

It's funny – when Bonnie and I were teenagers we always told each other that when we were adults we'd leave Redcliffe and move to the Big Smoke, Brisbane. That was our dream. Yet here we were, in our mid-thirties, and Redcliffe was where we wanted to be after all, now and forever. I guess, after living around here for so much of our lives and then moving away, we both appreciated what a special place it is, what a perfect place to live and bring up our kids.

The Redcliffe of today is different in many ways to the place where I rampaged as a kid. It was sleepier then. There's more bustle and noise and a lot of jackhammer development going on now. A home costs many times what it did back in the '70s and '80s. A place by the water may cost a million dollars. The old jetty, Redcliffe's great land-mark, has been replaced by a sturdier, if less romantic, structure. The shopping centre, once a little strip of mum-and-dad shops with a weekend market, is now a sprawling commercial complex. The infrastructure has grown to accommodate Redcliffe's population explosion.

And why wouldn't people want to live here? The best of Redcliffe survives. The pine tree-lined beaches where we swam as kids, the parks where we played footy, are still there. Some of the old wooden Queenslander homes – set on stumps and with their wide-verandas – survive in the area. There's a view to Bribie and Moreton islands on a clear day. The friendly people seem imbued with a laid back holiday spirit 52 weeks a year; and the seafood is still always fresh.

Redcliffe is named after the red ochre clay cliffs all around the peninsula, which, when we were kids, were great places to play and make cubby houses (but that red clay was hell for mothers to try to wash out of school uniforms). The cliffs are still there and something else that hadn't changed and which took me back to my childhood was the cooling, salt-smelling sea breezes. The first thing we noticed when we got back from Penrith was the sea breeze.

On my drive that afternoon, I was hailed down by a bloke in a truck who coached a local kids' football team. He happened to have some footballs with him and asked me to sign them. As someone who was a footy-loving kid here many years ago, I was glad to be asked. The man explained that he'd been a teammate of Matt Gillett, who is, like me, a former Redcliffe Dolphin now a Brisbane Bronco. I'd never laid eyes on the man before, but we chatted for a bit about footy, the weather and kids. 'Good luck at the Broncos, mate,' he said, and we went our separate ways.

I looked across Moreton Bay to Moreton Island, which was the holiday spot for Redcliffe families. Bonnie and her family holidayed there. I remember camping trips, walking on with our gear, watching cars drive onto the ferry at the Scarborough boat harbour and we would chug across to the sand cliffs at Bulwer on the north-west tip of Moreton Island or to Bribie Island, north of which is the Sunshine Coast.

Across Moreton Bay to the right, you can see the docks and the cruise liners in the Port of Brisbane at the mouth of the Brisbane River. In the terrible Brisbane floods of December 2010 and January 2011, debris was swept down the river and across the bay from there and washed up on the Redcliffe beaches.

I pulled up by the Redcliffe Leagues Club. I played my first senior rugby league for Redcliffe, the home club of Arthur Beetson. When I was a kid, before the land on Ashmore and Klinger roads in Kippa-Ring was developed into the club premises and Dolphin Oval, the area comprised acres of mangroves and my pals and I rode through the bush on our bikes and swam in the waterholes there until the blokes who owned the land chased us off their property.

I drove past the Scarborough Hotel, where Dad used to work. Not long back a storm hit and the pub was badly damaged and it's still closed for business. I hear it's been bought by a developer who'll turn it into high-rise apartments.

There was Jamieson Park with its spectacular views of the Glasshouse Mountains. Bonnie, Mum and I had taken the kids there that morning for a play.

I came to the Ambassador Hotel, where I once had a part-time job in the bottle shop. I remembered that Dad had worked there as a bouncer. The first time Bonnie met my father was when she and I, young sweethearts, walked in the front door of the Ambassador just as Dad was tossing some troublemaker out. She will never forget how that poor man hurtled through the air and landed in a heap on the footpath. What an impression . . . Right after, when I introduced her to Dad, she was tongue-tied with shock.

I drove past our old house in Anzac Avenue. We rented different houses around Redcliffe, but this is the place I remember as my home because we lived here longest. Everything was a five-minute bike ride from that house. I had so many mates, many living at nearby Kath Walker Hostel (named after the nurse, writer and activist whose indigenous name was Oodgeroo Noonuccal). Aboriginal and Torres Strait Island kids came from all over Queensland to stay there and go to school in Redcliffe. There were some terrific athletes among them and, with their speed and ball skills, they were in demand for any park or beach football game.

Also a short ride away, by Humpybong Primary School, was Langdon Park, where we played all our school football games and the athletics carnivals were held. I went to school at Humpybong. (As did writer and actor William McInnes, who also grew up here a few years before me. Some of his books capture the spirit of that old Redcliffe, the Redcliffe I love.) On the beach near Humpybong Primary School – Humpybong is Aboriginal for 'dead shelter' – was where Europeans first landed in Queensland and in the nearby creek we fished for eels just as the indigenous locals did for thousands of years. I played league for Humpybong, under the Moreton Bay fig trees.

As a complete contrast, just near our house on Anzac Avenue was the notorious intersection known as Crash Corner, because the road that passed through it goes all the way up the Redcliffe Peninsula and was the local drag strip. A hot rod magazine named it one of the great drag spots of Queensland. Back in the day, young blokes in their V8s would all line up at the lights and the light changing from red to green signalled the start. From my bedroom on the top left of the house facing the street, I would hear the screech of tyres on the road and smell the pungent burning of rubber. I'd look out of my window and thick smoke would be hanging in the air. One night I saw a bunch of guys pouring oil on the road from the tray of their ute, then spinning their wheels in the slick. I don't know how many times Mum had to ring the coppers. Those drag-racing days are long gone in today's Redcliffe.

For better or worse, that Redcliffe is my heartland. The place where my life and rugby league journey began . . .

# 1

# Junior years

I was 18 months old when I arrived in Australia with my family from Fiji in 1977. I was a big little boy. Size is a Civoniceva trait. Today, my father, Petero Snr, is 1.98 metres (six feet six inches) tall and weighs 130 kilograms, five centimetres (or two inches) taller and 20 kilos heavier than me. Petero Snr was one of Fiji's most promising young rugby union players – he was a hard-running and tough-tackling second-rower – when in 1977 the Redcliffe Demons rugby club invited him to join them in the Brisbane competition to stiffen up their pack. He considered the offer a chance to give himself and his family a better life, and he brought my mother Tima and me (called Junior by my family to distinguish me from Dad) to live in Australia. I've often wondered how life for all of us would have worked out if Dad hadn't taken up the offer. It was much more than a chance to play rugby in Australia; it was the offer of a lifetime, because it was an opportunity to give his family a better life.

I have no memories of being a baby in my homeland . . . all I have are photographs that Mum took of me, in our village by the sea. After we moved to Redcliffe, Mum tried to maintain our Fijian heritage. When they first arrived in Australia, she and Dad spoke Fijian in the house, although they didn't insist that my sisters (Lily was born in 1978, Lusi in 1982, both at Redcliffe Hospital) and I learn the language. We could talk with my parents and understand what they were saying, but we've never been fluent. I'm proud of my heritage, but before long Mum and Dad embraced Australia and its culture and thought it best to speak English at home.

I never really knew my grandparents on Dad's side, as he had a tough upbringing, but Mum's parents played an integral role in my young life, when we visited them in Fiji or they came to stay with us in Redcliffe. Virisilia and Saloisa's life revolved around church and family. Just by being themselves, they set a good example for my sisters and me. They were loving, sweet-natured people, like my mother. They were very supportive for Mum when her world collapsed in 1983 when Dad went to prison.

My grandfather Saloisa worked for the council and was a coach and administrator in Suva rugby union. He took a shine to Dad when he played in the provincial Suva rugby union competition, and it was through Saloisa that Dad met Mum at a rugby function. My grandparents were extremely fit. Cancer took Saloisa a few years back, but Virisilia is still going strong and runs a market stall in her town of Lami.

Mum's strong nature is not all she inherited from her parents. People can't believe how fit she is for her age, which is approaching 60. She does hard physical work in her long-time job as a cleaner at Redcliffe Hospital, and also takes classes at the local gym.

Dad's battered football rivals would have been surprised

to know it, but at home he was gentle, loving and funny. Early on he worked as a bouncer, then he managed bars and bottle shops around Redcliffe. He trained and played for the Redcliffe Demons rugby union team in his spare time. To help him provide for us, Mum slogged long days at the hospital, starting at 6 am.

Dad would have played for the Fijian national side had he not come to Australia, and he took up where he left off at the Demons. No doubt about it, he had an aura. There was his immense size, the rampaging runs he made and the tackles that skittled the opposition. His reputation as a hard man was justified.

I was seven in 1983 when I told Dad I really wanted to play rugby union like him and, against Mum's wishes, he got me a game with his club's under-12s. I was the youngest kid on the field by about five years and although I was tall for my age, I was a midget compared to the other players. Naturally, I was picked where they stick all the little kids, at halfback. At training just before my first match against the reigning premiers, Everton Park, my teammates kept talking about the opposition's best, biggest and baddest player. They were terrified of this kid.

I wish I was able to tell you that I took him on and came out on top. Unfortunately, that didn't happen. From the kick-off, he singled *me* out. The match was only minutes old when he ran at me, over me, and slammed the ball down between the posts. I picked myself up, humiliated, busted and spitting clumps of dirt and grass, and burst into tears. Dad, standing on the sideline, thought this was hilarious. When he stopped laughing, he sternly motioned to me to stop bawling and get back into the game. I was intimidated by the tough guy in the other team but totally terrified of my father, so I did.

I guess Dad figured that it was better for me to learn sooner rather than later that rugby is a hard and unforgiving game. I learned something else that day: that I loved playing football.

ONE RAINY winter's night that same year, 1983, Dad was driving me home after I had watched him play when our world disintegrated. Dad was obeying the speed limit, which seemed to annoy the driver of the car behind, who began blasting his horn and flashing his high-beam headlights. Dad didn't panic and stayed right on the speed limit. Next thing we knew, the car had knocked into our back bumper. My father pulled over and stopped the car. The vehicle behind stopped too. Dad got out, and so did the driver and his passenger.

We learned later that it was a middle-aged man and his adult son. There was an argument, push and shove, and a fight broke out. Dad was protecting himself and me and the two men were treated in hospital for broken bones, cuts, bruises and concussion.

However, they pressed criminal charges on the grounds that he had used undue force on them. In a court case that was front-page news because of Dad's football fame, he was found guilty and sent to jail for two years. This tore our family apart and left Mum to raise three little kids alone. Dad being in prison was extremely hard on Mum. She worked her usual long hours at the hospital and did overtime as well to earn a little more to feed and clothe us and pay the bills. We were able to see Dad in jail because of the generosity of his boss Michael McCaffery. Michael would give up his weekends with his own family to drive us up to the prison for visits. To repay his kindness, Mum asked if she could do Michael's housekeeping once a week. Michael said this would be all right, then still paid her for her work (and often gave her more) as his way of helping Mum financially.

We counted the days until Dad was released and could come home to us, but when he did he had changed. It was as if all the fun and sweetness that we loved had been beaten out of him. He was very quiet and introspective and distant with Mum and us children. He rejoined the Redcliffe Demons, but he also began working as a bouncer at hotels and clubs and not coming home until the early hours. Security can be a tough job. The pubs could be wild.

I loved my father very much and was very happy to have him back with us, even if he was different from before. I always went with him to watch him play for the Demons on weekends. The Demons' home ground was Dalton Park at nearby Clontarf, and there and at the other rugby union ovals of Brisbane I saw some wonderful players at their peak, such as the Wallabies' Roger Gould, Michael Lynagh, Andrew Slack, Rod McCall, and, a little later, Tim Horan and John Eales.

Before and after the main game, all the kids would charge onto the field and play touch footy. For a time I was the Demons' sand boy. I was so proud to run out onto the field with my little tin can of sand so the goal-kicker could tip some onto the grass and build a mound from it. That's to say, I *was* proud, right up until the moment when, in the dying moments of a tight game, I ran the sand out to the kicker for the match-winning penalty kick but tripped so that both I and the sand went flying. As I tried to put the sand back into the tin, I could have dug a hole right there on Dalton Park and crawled in. Thankfully, the penalty kick was successful.

My friend Rupert McCall, who is a poet and staunch Redcliffe rugby and rugby league man, has a regular column in *U On Sunday* magazine in Brisbane's *Sunday Mail*. In August 2011, he reminisced about the old days watching the Redcliffe Demons play at Dalton Park, when my dad packed down in the second row and Rupert and I, both of us about seven or eight (Rupert a bit older than me), were entrusted with the glorious job of working the scoreboard. There are bits of Rupert's article that are far too kind, but he captures better than I ever could the way it was:

I sat next to the kid called Petero on that old scoreboard, our eyes fixed firmly on the action. With every addition to the match tally, he'd leap down from our perch, land gracefully on those big feet of his, locate the correct number, then hand the tin square up to me for display.

Sunday afternoon in suburbia and a modest crowd had gathered to watch the Redcliffe Demons take on Teachers Norths. We were the boys on the scoreboard. The kings of our castle, keeping rugby followers informed for the lucrative sum of a steak burger and a Coke. Club stalwart 'Bushy' Mann reckoned that was fair enough for a young fella and nobody argued.

We played rugby for the local team although he was a few age groups below me. Having said that, when A-grade ended and youthful swarms flocked to the field for their touch footy ritual, 'Junior' carved them up no matter how old they were.

He was a halfback then but those feet. Those gigantic flippers. When he grew into them, you knew he'd be conversing with mountains. Just like the man he was watching now. The man who thundered through the Dalton Park dust like some sky-scraping behemoth. The man who brought a wife, a son and two daughters from his island to this peninsula. His father.

There was something about the kid. Like he understood the qualities that made his dad excel as a fiercely talented and loyal competitor and adopted them.

But not the temper. That warrior trait required cooling.

For a beautiful kindness that conveyed the warmth of life regardless of the situation, he drew from his mother's well. He became the best of both of them and humility was his compass, the same as his sisters. Destined to lead, he was elected school captain in his graduating year.

The next time I saw him, his physical prophecy had been fulfilled. His body was now a match for his feet and he'd changed codes.

Whispers filtered through Dolphin Oval from the snow cone van to the can bar. The kid could be anything.

Such murmurings always sound good and yet so many of them end up in the waste basket. Muscle is one thing. Mentality is another. The muscle to continually catapult your body into the rock wall. To bend it back and thereby lay a loyal foundation for your arrows to penetrate. To hold the fort, week in, week out, year after year, season upon season.

The mentality to ache but continue. To learn from mistakes and answer critics. To get back up. To confess when you're not at your best and drop yourself from the team, even if it costs you a national anthem.

The last time I saw him he was being honoured by his peers at a post-match function. Teammates had judged him their players' player that night and for the entire series. From a side that had just won six Origin titles straight, the rap was epic.

His dad was at the game as well. The man he is named after. His wonderful mum Tima, and two proud sisters Lusi and Lily. His schoolyard sweetheart now wife, Bonnie, stood devotedly, flying the flag for his children. They were all beaming. Family is everything to the big man. And there he was with a smile to match.

My father was in his element, for club rugby in Brisbane in the '80s and '90s was a war. When there was a fight, and no game was complete without a few, it was a *real* fight. Among the most furious brawls were those that erupted when the Redcliffe Demons and Brisbane Brothers played. Brothers was a prestige team bristling with Wallabies, Queensland representatives and Nudgee College old boys, while the Demons were the battlers, assembled on a shoe-string from locals, other teams' cast-offs and the odd Fijian. Quite a few of the sons of that generation of Islander players have gone on to be prominent players in rugby and rugby league.

On the field, my dad was a wrecking ball. He was the kind of player other teams' players and fans loved to hate. Because of his short fuse, vigorous play and having been in jail, he was the most feared player in that Brisbane competition in an era of tough guys such as Stan Pilecki, Tony Shaw, Chris Handy and Rod 'Sergeant Slaughter' McCall, a big Wallaby lock who would play 40 Tests for Australia and pack down in the Wallabies' 1991 World Cup victory.

Dad always seemed to be in the centre of a blue or being cautioned or sent off, usually as a result of defending a smaller team member, or when he was baited into losing his temper by the likes of Tony Shaw or Rod McCall. In a 1988 pre-season trial, there was a skirmish at a lineout and my father clashed with McCall. It was a very short fight. Dad punched Rod McCall so hard that the Sergeant was unconscious before he hit the ground. He went down in a dead fall and landed so hard he dislocated a bone in his leg. McCall was stretchered from the field and Dad was sent off and later suspended for a record seven matches. Rod was out for 10 weeks while his leg healed and he had plastic surgery to his smashed lip.

He considered legal action against Dad, but not for long. Next time they played, all was cool between them. After that game, Rod years later told *The Australian*'s sports writer Wayne Smith:

Petero [Snr] came up to me and said, 'I think I owe you a beer'. So we had one . . . or two. He was a gentle giant. You just didn't want to be within arm's length of him when he snapped. There are no ill-feelings. I probably did the same thing to other people in my career. I just didn't have the same punch.

Today the knockout is Brisbane rugby lore, and, true to the spirit of rugby, and rugby league for that matter, when the old protagonists are reminded of the stoush each recalls it with a grin.

Although I have inherited my father's physique, my temperament, on and off the field, is more like my mother's. I play football hard, brutally hard at times because that's how forwards must play, but I have a placid nature and my discipline is good. I don't like conflict. Perhaps as well, and despite my pride in his exploits, seeing Dad getting into all that strife, being hated and booed, turned me off being a similar type of player. In 2006, Dad told Wayne Smith, 'I had a short fuse. It was the main weakness in my game. Young Petero is totally different to me. He's very disciplined. You have to have that tough mental approach to survive at the level he has.'

I am not a saint. I *can* get angry out on the field, and have done so, but unlike Dad, who preferred the Island way of resolving a dispute with his fists, I prefer to channel my frustrations into hard running and tackling. Anyway, you're no good to anyone cooling your heels in the sin bin or, even worse, in the showers while your teammates battle on a man short.

DESPITE PLAYING rugby union early on, at around age 10 rugby league won my heart. Everywhere I went I carried a league ball, making believe that I was a big-time player with the local team, the Redcliffe Dolphins.

It was when playing for Humpybong in the local primary school competition that my passion for rugby league took root. I lived and breathed that game, and I was good at it. You'd never know it today when I weigh 110 kilos, but right up until I was 18 or so, I was tall and skinny as a reed, a fast, side-stepping centre with ball skills. I hated being so thin. I felt that somehow I was letting Dad down. I wanted to be huge like him. He would tease me about my lack of bulk, and I suppose this was his way of toughening me up. If someone had told me back then that I would play front row for Queensland and Australia I would have been incredulous.

Basketball and tennis were my summer sports. Tall, thin and agile, I was built for basketball, and Dad imparted to me his love of tennis. We lived across the road from a Catholic school which had a tennis court. The priest who looked after the grounds opened the gates to let Dad and Mum and my sisters and me and other local kids onto the court. Mum was a competitive netball player who played the game for years. For as long as Dad played rugby, and that was well into his thirties, Mum played local netball.

Redcliffe is one of the great Australian rugby league clubs. When I was young, my heroes were such Dolphins stars as Arthur Beetson (who returned to Redcliffe in 1981 and would play a role in my later career), Chris Close, Bryan Niebling, Steve Bleakley, Mitch Brennan, Wally Fullerton-Smith, Trevor Benson and Ian 'Bunny' Pearce, who would die too young in 1993. The Dolphins' home ground was just down the road from my house.

After I left primary school, I juggled my schoolwork at Redcliffe High with a part-time job at Coles. I kept out a small amount of my wages for pocket money and gave the rest to Mum. She never moaned about her bad fortune but I knew she was struggling. We carried on in our little weatherboard home in Anzac Avenue just down the road from Crash Corner. Our sleep was regularly interrupted by the revving of V8 engines and the screech of brakes.

The beachside community of Redcliffe was a wonderful place to grow up. I have lasting memories of long hot days and muggy twilights playing and swimming at Suttons Beach. Growing up it felt like so many kids lived in Redcliffe. There was always something to do and someone to do it with. I was a regular participant in the pick-up footy games in the parks and on the sand. I swam and fished and played tennis, cricket and basketball, I ran and I rode my pushbike around Redcliffe and up to Scarborough and all over the peninsula. I can think of no better life on this planet for my own kids.

I remember jumping off the famous Redcliffe jetty into the cool and refreshing sea and treading water while I watched to see if my mates could make as big a splash. The Redcliffe *Herald* was always grumbling that the local children were risking their lives hurling themselves off the pier. Naturally, that made it all the more fun. When I was 13, and just after some child had hurt himself leaping off the pier, Mum said to me, 'Junior, do you promise me you don't jump off Redcliffe Jetty?' I looked her in the eye. 'Mum, I give you my word that I would never, never, ever do that.' Next week's edition of the *Herald* had a spectacular front-page picture of a skinny teenager throwing himself off the jetty and into the water as his mates cheered. The kid was me.

That was a bad one . . . but generally I was a well-behaved boy. I was always mindful that I had a responsibility in my family and trying not to disappoint Mum or let her down. My worst regular crime was coming home late after swimming or playing football in the park. I could never drag myself away from footy. It was always 'one more try . . . one more try . . . last try wins . . .' and suddenly we'd realise we were playing in total darkness. If I close my eyes, I can still hear Dad's voice, before he went away, booming out through the gloom, 'Junior, come home!'

### TIMA CIVONICEVA

He had a lot of energy and was always going at 200 miles an hour. He had his moments and mucked up like all kids, but he was always a good and very responsible boy. I never doubted that he understood and was grateful for the sacrifices that were made so he and his sisters had a good life. They got on well, and stuck up for one another. The only problem for Petero about Lily and Lusi was that they were girls. I think he resented not having brothers to play footy with in our backyard and the park, on the sand and at school. He once told Lusi, 'No offence, Sis, but I really wish you were a boy.'

When I was 14, in 1990, Dad chose to leave us. Mum, my sisters and I had to fend for ourselves. I grew up fast and became the man of the house. It was in those days when I learned that taking responsibility and caring for your loved ones was the mark of a man, more so than being a tough guy. I was determined that when I grew up and became a husband and father, I would treat my wife and children differently than Dad had treated us.

After my father walked out, there were long periods when I didn't hear from him. I missed him badly because I loved him and, besides, a boy needs a dad. Mum was mother *and* father to us, and she did a wonderful job. Today I see Dad, we might talk once a week, he'll call me or I'll telephone him. He turns up sometimes to family gatherings, and he dotes on his grandchildren. I have never asked him if he has regrets about leaving us. I suspect he does. When he has a few beers and lets his guard down a little, he tells me things that lead me to believe that if he had his time again he might make different decisions.

Today he and I are mates. I think I have made him proud, even if I don't always take his advice when he rings me before a game. In the bar at his home, he has hung two large pictures: one is of Muhammad Ali, and the other is of me on the charge for the Broncos.

I ATTENDED Redcliffe High School until grade 10, when I left to go to Frawley College in Scarborough, where my friend Marcus Riley went. For a while then, I was considering playing grade rugby union, like Dad, and Frawley College would develop my talents. Somehow, I'll never know how she managed, Mum always came up with the school fees, right on time.

I completed grades 11 and 12. My schoolwork improved and my rugby gamble paid off. I hadn't played the code since I was nine, but I joined Marcus in trying out for the junior rep sides and, amazingly, as a lock and flanker, I made the Brisbane side. Marcus and I were then both selected in the Queensland under-16 merit team.

I'd known Bonnie Chisholm from school athletics. She lived in Scarborough, a few kilometres up the peninsula, with her parents and four younger siblings. Her father Peter ran a successful drilling business and her mother Terri worked at the local ANZ Bank. Bonnie was a fine all-round athlete who made various state athletics, netball and softball teams, as did her sisters Kasey, Chelsea and Ellie. Her brother Zac was a top young league player who would play rugby league with Redcliffe and junior grade with the Brisbane Broncos.

Like me, Bonnie went on to attend Frawley College and when I saw her at orientation I remembered her. While I worked part-time at Coles, Bonnie had a weekend job at Chandlers electrical and music store. We always said hi at school and in the street. I was very keen on her. One day, midway through grade 11, I summoned the courage to ask her to meet me for lunch. She said yes. We got on. For a while, we were just good friends, with neither of us really thinking our friendship would blossom into romance.

In grade 12, Bonnie and I were appointed the captains of our school. She was excellent academically and at sports and a model citizen in the school community, so thoroughly deserved the honour. Me . . . I'm not so sure. I was an enthusiastic kid at school, and enjoyed it, and I could play rugby union, but I was average academically, an upstart from a public school who had only been at Frawley a year. I think quite a few of the students were having a gee-up when they proposed me as school captain.

I couldn't believe it when the votes were counted and my name was read out. Kids with greater claims to the school captaincy than me, brainier kids, kids who had been groomed to be leaders, were, I reckon, justifiably disappointed. Bonnie backed me all the way, and made it clear she thought we'd be a good team. That cemented our relationship. We started dating. We didn't tell a soul. As the year went on, I guess it was obvious to everyone that Bonnie and I were together.

### BONNIE CIVONICEVA

The first time I was aware of Petero was when we were kids competing at athletics carnivals around Redcliffe and Scarborough. We became friends when we were in years 11 and 12. What struck me was how all the girls had a crush on him, a sweet-natured, skinny boy with the biggest smile. It was a complete shock when he took me out to a Sizzlers and he held my hand. I had no idea he liked me. He confessed that he'd had a crush on me for quite some time but hadn't had the courage to tell me. Clearly that night our relationship moved to a higher level.

It took him a while to meet my parents. Dad would see him standing out on the street or just happening to jog past and say, 'When will that boy come in and say hello?' Eventually he did, and they fell in love with him. Petero was always a little worried about the black–white thing and how my parents would react. That has never been a problem for me or my family. Back then he was always imagining that when we were out together people were wondering what a dark-skinned boy was doing with a white-skinned girl.

I will never forget the first time I met Petero's father, Petero Snr. Petero and I had just turned 18 and could go to pubs, and we went to one where Senior was bouncing. We walked up the steps, then I heard heavy footsteps inside, the front door burst open and a huge man was ejecting a poor man who flew through the air like a cartoon character and landed in the street. Petero said, 'That's my father.' I was terrified. Senior, of course, was warm and gentle. He has that incredible mix of gentleman and warrior. Petero has it too.

I did well enough academically in year 12, considering the fact that I was playing rugby for the school on Saturdays, rugby league for the Redcliffe Dolphins juniors on Sundays and training most days in between.

As well as the Queensland representative rugby team, I was picked in the Queensland under-17 rugby league team. This meant a lot to me, because when I was younger I had always missed out on representative selection. I was so envious of the kids who had been picked when they swanned around with their maroon kitbags with the big Q on the side. I wanted one of those bags so bad. Making the state sides at age 16 was a dream come true. Here's a lesson I feel qualified to pass on: never give up. I coped with disappointment and persevered, and learned my trade.

When I was in the Queensland under-17 rugby league team in my final year of school, we played New South Wales under-17s at the Sydney Football Stadium as a curtain-raiser to a State of Origin match. I decided I'd stalk the Queensland Origin side to get all their autographs. After the game, a couple of us followed our heroes to the bright lights of Kings Cross and, even though we were under-age, we were big kids and looked older and were able to duck into the Studebaker Bar where the Maroons were celebrating. I gatecrashed their gathering and my heroes signed my napkins and coasters . . . Wally Lewis, Peter Jackson, Allan Langer, Trevor Gillmeister . . . I got them all. Mum still has them at home.

On weekends, right after playing junior league, I would go to watch the Redcliffe Dolphins play. They were my team, and I planned to play for them some day. I also admired the Southern Suburbs side. Souths were the number one team and their champion centre Mal Meninga was my favourite player. Someone bought me a copy of Mal's autobiography, *Big Mal*, and I kept that dog-eared book in my schoolbag for a year as inspiration. It will come as no surprise to tell you that today I'm still a huge fan of Big Mal, as Queensland coach and as a man.

There's a funny side to my relationship with Mal Meninga. I guess, somehow in my mind, I have turned him into a father figure. When I see Mal, I see my dad. They have both influenced my life and they look a bit the same: both huge, dark-skinned men with big bushy eyebrows and an imposing aura. When they walk into a room, heads turn and the joint goes quiet.

It's amazing to think that I have a strong bond I hope will last our lifetimes with the man I once gazed at in awe from the grandstands when I was a boy. To think I played under his coaching in some of Queensland's greatest State of Origin triumphs. To think that we're mates. To this day, when I see his name come up on my mobile when he is on for a chat or when he singles me out for a one-on-one talk in Origin camp, it gives me a thrill. Memories of being a kid with his book in my bag come flooding back.

## MAL MENINGA

Petero being the guy he is has never told me how
he felt about me when he was a boy. Now I know
about the autobiography in his bag, and how he
considered me a father figure from afar, I can only
say I'm happy if in any small way I have played
a part in that boy growing into the man he has
become.

Naturally, I'd caught the State of Origin bug and back
in the late 1980s and through the '90s, while watching
the action on those wildly exciting nights, I dreamed like
all Queensland kids that I would one day follow in the
footsteps of Mal, Wally, Alfie Langer, Gene Miles, Rowdy
Shearer, Greg Dowling and the rest. A maroon jersey
became my Holy Grail. As with most things in life, vow-
ing is the easy part, making those dreams come true is a
whole lot harder.

# 2

# Cyril Connell's love child

When Cyril Connell died on 9 June 2009, the Queensland rugby league world was shattered. We knew the great talent scout had cancer, yet his passing came as a shock to me and many, many others including Darren Lockyer, Shane Webcke, Wendell Sailor, Justin Hodges, Darius Boyd, Steve Renouf, Karmichael Hunt, Brad Thorn, Sam Thaiday, Corey Parker, Brent Tate, Carl Webb, Ashley Harrison, Tonie Carroll and Lote Tuqiri. We had all been discovered by the humble, soft-spoken little man who in his rich life had been a Queensland and Australian rugby league halfback, a coach, a fine teacher and second-in-charge of Secondary Education in the Queensland Department of Education.

In 1993, Cyril saw me playing weekend rugby league with Redcliffe juniors while I was at school and noted down my name as a kid to keep an eye on for the future. I was a skinny back-rower centre then who liked to carry the ball in one hand. Unbeknown to me, Cyril went to Wayne Bennett, coach of the Brisbane Broncos, and told him that he'd seen a tall Fijian boy at Redcliffe who was a likely prospect. Wayne checked me out and wasn't impressed. Cyril persisted, 'No, I'm telling you, Petero has got what it takes to make it.'

Wayne, against his better judgement and probably mainly to please Cyril, awarded me a Bronco scholarship. The club would contribute to my schooling costs and monitor my progress with Redcliffe and later at Brothers, where they got me a start. Then, if I was still on track, I would be brought into the Broncos' fold. Even then, when I was running around in the Broncos' lower grades, Wayne saw me playing and was still unable to share Cyril Connell's opinion of me, grumbling to Cyril, 'I don't know what you see in him. This bloke must be your love child.' Cyril told Wayne, 'Hang in there, he'll come good.'

The Broncos were not the first team to show an interest in me. The year before, in 1992, when I was 16, Arthur Beetson – who began his senior career at Redcliffe Dolphins and then won every honour in the game and became an Immortal of rugby league – was a talent scout for the Sydney Roosters. My dad and I knew Artie, who ran the Moreton Bay Hotel and had often watched me play, and his son Mark was a good footy and athletics friend. Artie wrote to me inviting me to Sydney to take part in a Roosters' development camp. I was about to accept when the Broncos got in touch asking me to attend *their* juniors camp. I chose the Broncos over the Roosters because they were my local team and I wanted to save Mum the cost of my travelling to Sydney and my accommodation expenses.

When I learned that I had won a Bronco scholarship, I was proud for myself and also because my ability to play rugby league had eased the school fees financial pressure on Mum. My short flirtation with rugby union was over and I was ready to throw myself into rugby league exclusively. Since they were established in 1988, the Broncos have been a huge part of Brisbane culture. In that inaugural first-grade side were players who became household names: Wally Lewis, Allan Langer, Willie Carne, Steve Renouf, Michael Hancock, Glenn Lazarus, Trevor Gillmeister and Kevin and Kerrod Walters. In 1992, when the Broncos won the comp, beating St George 28–8 in the grand final at the Sydney Football Stadium, I watched the game on TV, sitting on the edge of my seat till the final siren.

Suddenly, football went from being fun, to fun *and* the opportunity to make something of myself. Before the Brisbane Broncos gave me their stamp of approval, I had dreamed of playing for them, Queensland and Australia. Now Cyril and Wayne had put the ball in my hands. It was up to me to run with it.

At 18, I played under-19 Colts for Redcliffe Dolphins. My coach was Steve Bleakley, one of the Redcliffe Dolphins' favourite sons. Steve told me that the Dolphins' first-grade coach Ross O'Reilly was impressed by my performances and I was close to being selected in the top grade, which was the best team in the Brisbane competition. I was a reserve for the firsts a few times, but never made it onto the field. I didn't care; warming that bench on the sideline, I felt on top of the world. The year 1994 was a memorable one for the Dolphins. We won the Colts grand final, as did our reserves and first grade. I will never forget the celebrations afterwards with all teams on Dolphin Oval.

Redcliffe was lucky to have two rugby league legends among its administrators. Dick 'Tosser' Turner had played and coached at Redcliffe, managed the Queensland State of Origin teams from 1982 to 1996 and the 1987 Kangaroos to England, and was a Redcliffe stalwart until his death in 2006. Des Webb, who died in 2011, was the Dolphins' president. They were both Redcliffe institutions and pillars of our community. Tosser and Des were always friendly and supportive of a nobody kid like me. Tosser, I felt, always had a soft spot for me as a fellow 'Fin' but his cheeky and generous nature made everyone feel special. When the Broncos offered me a contract, Redcliffe was demanding a fair amount of money from them that could have jeopardised the deal. Dad went to his mate Des and they sorted it all out. I will always be indebted to Des for helping me to take the next step in my senior football career.

The following year, 1995, I was called up to the senior Broncos' squad. In 1996 I played the entire season in reserve grade, locking horns with bigger, stronger opponents. Travelling to Sydney was a buzz as well. Playing on grounds I had only seen on TV seemed so surreal to me. The challenge of making it into first grade still seemed a long way off as our team was stacked with players who had had first grade experience already. I was determined to keep chipping away.

That was when my education as a forward began. I was not a player like Darren Lockyer, whose prodigious brilliance even as a teenager saw him slot seamlessly into first grade. I needed to learn my job as a forward, to bulk up, get tougher, grow used to the collisions.

Season 1997 was make or break for me. I had now put on more bulk to tip me over 100 kilograms. I had already played a full season of reserve grade. This was the year I had to make my mark or be thrown on the scrapheap. I did enough to see me through. By then, rugby league had been torn apart by the Super League war, and the Broncos, who had aligned themselves with Super League, were in a competition with the Cronulla Sharks, the Canterbury

Bulldogs, the Canberra Raiders, the North Queensland Cowboys, the Auckland Warriors, the Penrith Panthers, the Western Reds, the Hunter Mariners and the Adelaide Rams. (Contesting the rival ARL competition were the South Sydney Rabbitohs, the Sydney City Roosters, the Western Suburbs Magpies, the Balmain Tigers, the Parramatta Eels, the St George Dragons, the Manly Warringah Sea Eagles, the Newcastle Knights, the Gold Coast Chargers, the Illawarra Steelers, the North Sydney Bears and the South Queensland Crushers.)

I have to be honest and say that I didn't give much thought to the ramifications of the terrible rip in the fabric of our game. All I wanted was to make the most of the chance the Broncos had given me and play football.

It was a privilege being a part, even a bench-warming part, of the first-grade Broncos side in 1997. What a team we fielded for the Super League grand final against the Sharks, which we won 26–8 at ANZ Stadium. Twenty-year-old Darren Lockyer was fullback, Wendell Sailor and Mick De Vere were the wingers, our centres were Steve Renouf and Anthony 'The Man' Mundine, Kevin Walters was five-eighth, Allan Langer was halfback and captain, Darren Smith, locked the scrum, Gorden Tallis and Peter Ryan paired in the second row, Andrew Gee and the giant Brad Thorn were the props, and Johnny Plath was hooker. I was on the bench in very distinguished company: Tonie Carroll, Shane Webcke and Mick Hancock.

One of Wayne Bennett's many qualities as a coach is that he tries to relate to every player differently, according to their temperament. He can give a bloke a savage bollocking one day, then put his arm around him the next. He decided that I needed tough love. He had seen me playing and observed me at close hand with the Broncos squad.

He had concluded that, while I wasn't as hopeless as he had at first thought, I was an inconsistent player. As usual, he was right. I would play a strong game and then, without ever consciously slacking, be barely noticed in the next two matches. Wayne ripped into me, told me to lift my game or forget all about playing in his first-grade side. I was hurt and embarrassed, but, of course, Wayne's needling was exactly what I needed.

Time and again in my career, I have taken criticism very personally and responded to it positively. Jamming my critics' opinions down their throats has always been a prime motivator for me. Back in seasons 1997 and 1998, I was determined to prove Wayne Bennett wrong, to show him that I could play this game at a high standard week in and week out.

Wayne is a coach who believes in discipline in football and in life. He has standards that his players must meet on the field, like going hard for the whole game, playing smart and defending well; and off the field, such as dressing well and conducting yourself with style and class. He insists that players should be employed or studying. I was offered a hospitality industry traineeship at one of the pubs that sponsored the Broncos.

I also had a role as a sports and recreation officer and co-ordinated sports programs for boys at the Sir Leslie Wilson Youth Detention Centre in Brisbane. Being with those kids opened my eyes and humbled me. You think you go through hardships in your own life and then you meet youngsters who have committed crimes after really doing it tough. I was shocked that drugs and domestic violence played a role in derailing so many of the inmates' lives. My job was to give them a bit of normality through sport. I organised games of basketball and touch football, and conducted gym sessions to keep them physically active while they were at the detention centre. Being a rugby league player gave me cred and helped me connect. Working at the detention centre taught me about life and about myself. I think that as much as can be expected under the circumstances we all had fun and got a lot out of the experience.

I STARTED my first-grade rugby league career comparatively late. I was 21, about to turn 22, at the start of '98. I was now a two-year veteran of reserve grade. In a reserve grade trial against South Sydney I was on a mission not to be discarded. I ripped into a Bunnies pack stacked with first graders. I was told after the match that Wayne Bennett had been watching from behind the goal posts and he'd been impressed by what he saw of me. I was told to report to first grade training for the final trial, against Cronulla in Ipswich. I could not believe it. My perseverance had paid off. I played off the bench in the first six rounds and completed my first full first-grade game for the Broncos in round seven, against the North Sydney Bears at ANZ Stadium. When Wayne told me I was in the run-on team, I was as excited as I had ever been and beamed like a kid, despite trying hard not to. It was all my boyhood dreams come true.

My debut match against North Sydney was made even more special when I found myself opposing one of my real idols, former Queensland great Gary Larson. I had to pinch myself that I would be playing against a bloke who I had willed on as a kid to keep tackling and driving the Maroon pack forward. In Origin he played against more illustrious opponents, yet he gave as good as he got and never let anyone down. That's what I loved about him. I was in awe.

### GORDEN TALLIS

Petero made an indelible impression on me in his full first-grade debut, against Norths. He smashed a bloke named David Fairleigh. Dave was a huge man and a current New South Wales State of Origin forward. Pet hammered him. He toyed with him. I thought, 'This quiet kid has more self-confidence than I thought.' I was especially impressed because in my debut match I came on after playing a second-grade game and I was unprepared for the speed and intensity of first grade and I was off the pace. I dropped the ball. I was driven back in tackles. In a game a couple of weeks later, Pet proved that he was a first-grader to stay when out of the blue he passed the ball magically right around his back. It was beautiful to see and so graceful. Then he broke his arm and lost much of his ability to offload. As a kid, his offloading ability was unbelievable.

In 1998, the Super League war wounds had healed, superficially at least, and the two competitions, Super League and the Australian Rugby League (ARL) were combined and run by the newly-formed governing body, the National Rugby League, the NRL, with some input from various vested interests. To arrive at a 20-team competition, the Western Reds, the Adelaide Rams and the South Queensland Crushers were made extinct. In the years ahead, there would be more rancorous rationalisation as more teams, such as the grand old Rabbitohs (who of course would be reinstated) and the Bears, were cut, and others, like St

George and Illawarra and Wests and Balmain, merged to survive.

Right from early pre-season training sessions in season 1998, there had been intense discussion in the Broncos' camp about proving ourselves the best team in the united competition. We vowed to beat the ARL premiers, the Newcastle Knights, in the competition rounds and then, to put the bragging rights issue beyond doubt, we would beat the Knights or whoever we came up against in the grand final to win the premiership.

We hit the ground running. We walloped the Sea Eagles, the Bulldogs, the Panthers, the Chargers and the Cowboys, copped a wake-up call hiding from the Sea Eagles the second time we played them, and thrashed Gary Larson's Bears 60–6 in my debut game. Winning six out of seven matches put us in the right frame of mind to play the Knights with their star-studded team, including the Johns brothers, Andrew and Matthew, and Paul 'Chief' Harragon. I did enough in the Bears game to hold my spot in the starting pack, and my friend and mentor Andrew Gee took my place on the bench.

I knew I'd be packing down against the Chief, and I was nervous as hell. He was a hard, uncompromising international prop whose rip-and-tear battles with Mark 'Spud' Carroll are always featured in big hit highlight reels. There I'd be, in just my second full game, at the Newcastle International Sports Centre in front of a full house of Knights fans hoping to see Chief, the leader of a champion pack, dismember me and the rest of the Bronco forwards. What a great battle it was to be.

All week before the game, the papers were buzzing with the prospect of the two best sides in rugby league going head to head. Peter Sterling wrote a newspaper column profiling each of the players. He raved about Locky ('showed champion qualities'), Wendell ('the best broken field runner in the competition'), Alf ('a true champion'), Andrew Johns ('superb . . . the man the Broncos must control'), and he lauded the Chief ('for his disregard for personal safety').

As for me, as far as Sterlo was concerned, the jury was still out: 'Looks a likely athlete, especially for a prop, but is obviously very inexperienced. Didn't feature particularly prominently in last week's landslide [against Norths] and won't find things anywhere near as comfortable in this match.'

It was a tough, grinding game played in the wet and we overcame injuries to win 26–6. The Chief, as I knew he and his front-row partner Tony Butterfield would, tried all game to separate my head from my shoulders. In my first hit up I got smashed so hard that the contact lens in my right eye was dislodged. Coping with that, and the pouring rain and the mud, I survived – just. I was beginning to understand that first grade was going to be hard, like this, every week.

I thought I'd played well against the Knights, and I confess I was a bit swollen-headed . . . right until the moment Wayne got his hands on me in the team's video review session the Tuesday after the match. The coach pressed 'Play' and screened footage of me missing a tackle and he roasted me in front of the team. In a flash, my head reverted to its normal size. I was devastated. All I could think was that I was a failure and in the days afterwards I moped around hoping I hadn't blown my opportunity and that Wayne would retain me in first grade against the Roosters next weekend and give me a chance to make amends. I look back now and think that giving me a serve when I least expected it was Wayne's way of dragging me down out of the clouds and revving me up for the Roosters. It worked. Time and again in my career playing under Wayne it would be driven home to me that he had an ability to understand his players, their personality, what made them tick. He knew when to scold and when to praise to get the most out of you. He treated each player differently.

That year, if any of the senior front-rowers – Shane Webcke, Andrew Gee or Peter Ryan – were injured, I'd start the game, and if they were in the side I'd come on from the bench. In the grand final Wayne, perhaps feeling I was still a bit green, dropped me from the bench altogether, and I was only reprieved when Peter Ryan got himself suspended.

Nothing prepared me for grand final week. It was a surreal time of new experiences, sheer enjoyment and camaraderie and nervousness about the looming match. All week, the vibe in Brisbane was electric. Fans in their thousands rocked up to our training sessions early in the week and the city and suburbs were swathed in maroon and gold. We arrived in Sydney on the Wednesday night and checked into the Swiss Grand Hotel on Bondi Beach. We attended the grand final breakfast the following morning. After that, we trained a bit and did some sightseeing before locking out the public and media for our final training run on the Saturday. Mick De Vere, Phil Lee and I had our photo taken under the Harbour Bridge. It was then, standing with my teammates under the famous landmark, that all the hype and fanfare fell away and it hit home that this grand final was the biggest moment of my life.

I came off the bench and played around 35 minutes. Many guys who have participated in a grand final tell you that time seems to speed by at a faster rate than in normal games. That's true, it does; and the same, as I would find out, applies to State of Origin. Before I knew it, the final siren had sounded and we were doing a lap of honour of the Sydney Football Stadium.

We won that grand final against the Bulldogs 38–12, after being down 12–10 at half-time. I was happy with my limited contribution. I did what was expected of me in attack and defence and didn't stuff up by turning over the ball or being caught out of position in attack or defence. I had a fierce tussle with the Bulldogs prop, a fellow named Steve Price with whom I'd be having a fair bit to do in the years to come. Gorden Tallis pipped Tonie 'Tunza' Carroll for the man of the match award.

After the match, when I went to place the premiership winners' ring on my finger, it was two sizes too small. I do have big hands. There was no way I wasn't going to wear it, so I jammed it on and despite it being very tight I kept it on through too many days of heavy celebrations and cut off the circulation to my finger. After a while, I couldn't have taken off the ring if I'd wanted to because my finger was swollen and hurting. Also, my entire hand was tender and had blown up. I realised this was not good, but I figured it would all come right and ignored the pain.

After three days of celebrating with the team and everyone in Brisbane (or so it seemed), I awoke at Bonnie's parents' house to find that my finger had turned dark purple, the colour of an eggplant, and it wasn't hurting anymore because it was numb. 'Bonnie, I can't feel my finger!' I panicked. We both tried to prise off the ring but couldn't. The only thing to do was to go to the emergency department at Redcliffe Hospital. How embarrassing was this! Suddenly, to my relief, I was surrounded by doctors and nurses, although it occurred to me that they were more interested in having a close look at my grand final ring than removing it from my finger. In the end, a nurse cut it off – the ring, not the finger. Sweet relief. In time, my finger regained its feeling and returned to its usual colour and size. I had the split ring mended and today it's as good as new.

At the Broncos' end-of-season dinner, I was named Rookie of the Year. The former New South Wales and Australian front-rower turned-commentator, Steve 'Blocker' Roach (who I remember booing loudly when he was bashing Queensland forwards), named me one of the finds of 1998 in *Big League* magazine: 'I think he could be anything. For a young bloke to come into first grade at prop and show skills straight away is a great effort. He is obviously a player who listens to his coach . . .'

When I was first selected in the Broncos' top side I watched and learned and kept my mouth shut. I spoke only when spoken to and sometimes not even then. It certainly wasn't my place to initiate conversations. I felt out of my depth and in awe of my more illustrious teammates. I was intimidated by these legends until they accepted me and encouraged me to regard them as mentors and friends. Then, nothing was too much trouble for them, whether it was teaching me the tricks of the front-rower's trade or including me on an outing, or being welcoming to Bonnie at functions.

As far as the Broncos' inspirational leader and resident court jester, Allan 'Alfie' Langer, was concerned, I knew he thought I had passed muster when he began making me the butt of his practical jokes. At training, Alfie would tell me to stand with the backs, knowing that when I did Wayne would bawl me out for being in the wrong group. As Wayne was ticking me off, I'd look and see Alf doubled over with laughter way off in the background.

•

MY GAME changed for the better and forever in 1998. As a centre in my junior football and then a running back-rower with the Broncos' lower grades, I ranged wide in attack and used one-handed off-loads, speed and a step to break up a defence. Wayne, however, earmarked me for the front row, so, by now weighing 106 kilograms, I found myself undertaking Andrew Gee, Peter Ryan, Shane Webcke and Brad Thorn's prop's master-class. They taught me that a good front-rower in the modern game is a player who in attack provides relentless go-forward, who can defy exhaustion and pain to hit the ball up again and again, relentlessly storming across the advantage line and bending it back and so sapping the sting from the opposition's defence.

Every bit as important as carrying the ball is defence. A prop's job is to physically and mentally overcome his opponent by tackling him hard, knocking from him his strength, energy, wind and confidence. Repeatedly tackling 110-kilo men charging at you from 10 metres away is energy-sapping. Andrew, Peter, Brad and Shane made it clear to me that there was a responsibility to the team, to provide momentum and to stop the opposition's. They all had a hard edge, a ruthless work ethic of always looking to be the one who made the next run or tackle. I thought it best to forget about flash and flair and play a no-frills power game. This was how I could best benefit the team. Also, they said, telling me something I already knew very well, Wayne Bennett had no tolerance for mistake-prone players, and there was less chance of error when I played it tight.

I remember my first gym session with the senior Broncos' forwards and how I was nervous as hell at having to lift weights and do the endurance work alongside these guys. I had nothing to worry about. We did the work together.

They were all no-bullshit blokes on and off the field – hard, rugged and straight down the line. If they had to lay down the law to me, they did so as they pushed me hard to reach their level. Shane Webcke, who became a Bronco a couple of years before I did, has told me how Peter Ryan, Brad Thorn and Andrew Gee helped him along too in his early years. In my final season, when I was the senior Broncos forward, I tried to be a positive influence in the training and on-field form of Ben Hannant, Josh McGuire, Scott Anderson, David Hala and Dumanis Lui and the other young blokes, just as Andrew, Peter, Brad and Shane were for me.

From such men as them – and Wayne, Gorden, Alf, Kevvy and Kerrod, Kevin Campion and Darren Lockyer – I learned what it took to win. I learned to play hard and relentlessly and to never give up.

I had to be mentally stronger, dealing with pain and fatigue, which is part of every game as a front-rower. I learned early on that if you are going to be any good at this game you have to play when you are hurting. I took very seriously my role in the team and I didn't want to be the guy who let his teammates down by not being there to do his job. I had to improve and push myself to the limit.

I WAS a little sad that Bonnie wasn't there for much of 1998 to see me become a fully-fledged first-grader. She was in London as part of a six-month working holiday, and the hundred dollars or more a week I spent telephoning her reflected just how badly I missed her. Happily, the Broncos had just increased my contract money to keep at bay other NRL clubs who were sniffing around me, and I could just about afford the phone bills. Instead of doing a Solomon

Haumono (the Canterbury Bulldog and future boxing champ who famously took off to London mid-season to be with his girlfriend Gabrielle Richens), I was happy to sock away money to take Bonnie on a holiday to Fiji when she returned from England. She made it back in time for the grand final.

Bonnie had taken time out from our relationship after we experienced a rough patch when I became a Bronco. Being so focused on the Broncos and my teammates and being in the media spotlight and recognised everywhere I went by football fans was changing me, maybe making me a bit big-headed. I admit that. You don't want to think that the bright lights and the pats on the back change you, but they did.

Bonnie believed she was no longer as important to me as when we were growing up and dating and dreaming our dreams. She thought I valued football and my football mates more. Things were changing between us, so even though we loved each other and wanted to be together, Bonnie thought it would be best if she gave us both some breathing space by heading off to realise her own dreams of travelling and working overseas. When Bonnie and I holidayed together in Fiji, she met my mum's family, but she still wasn't con- vinced that she meant more to me than football and my footy mates and she wisely kept her distance.

In fairly quick time, I understood that she was the one I loved more than anything in life. I kept at her, trying to convince her that I was worth a second chance. I'm glad to say that my persistence wore her down and we fell into each other's arms again and our relationship, because I had grown up and come to my senses in the meantime, was stronger than ever.

## BONNIE CIVONICEVA

We were 16 when we first started going out together, so by the time we were 22 we had been together for six years. This was just when he was establishing himself as a footballer, and I felt that I was taking second place. I wanted a little more commitment. Football meant we couldn't have late nights, go away for the weekend camping, or travel overseas. He was the boyfriend who was never there. I understood the situation, yet I had dreams of my own. I went overseas. I cried all the way to Hong Kong. Then I went on a Kon Tiki trip around Europe and had a ball. I worked in London, toured Scotland and Ireland. He rang me and I sent him a postcard every three days.

After six months away, I came back to Australia to be a bridesmaid at a girlfriend's wedding, intending to return to Europe right after. Instead, I realised I'd got travel out of my system and when Petero asked me to go with him to Fiji to meet his family I thought this was a step in the right direction and we had a lovely holiday there.

Then, back in Brisbane, the demands of football reared up again. I could see how happy Petero was being with the boys at the Broncos, and we broke up. I took a job taking phone reservations at an airline. Meanwhile, I guess he realised how much we meant to each other and kept ringing me. After six months, we were back together

A healthy and in-form Allan Langer was vital to our team, but in the 1999 season Alf suffered a mystifying form slump and, not prepared to play at less than his best, he announced his retirement mid-season. (He would have a rethink and play for the Warrington Wolves in England in 2000, then make a sensational re-entry to Australian rugby league for Queensland and the Broncos in 2001 and 2002.)

When Kevin Walters took over the Broncos captaincy from Alf at the halfway point of the comp, without Alf's guile and flair, with injuries to Mick Hancock and Steve Renouf, and with rival teams lifting to beat the reigning premiers, we were struggling. 'Struggling' is an understatement. We lost our first five matches of the season, and eight of our first 10. After 10 rounds we were running 17th in a 17-team comp. Under Kevvy, we came home with a wet sail, won 11 straight and squeaked into the semis in eighth spot. This was a remarkable achievement, and it was also as far as we would go that year. After our string of wins, we simply had nothing left in the tank when it mattered most. In the qualifying final, we were walloped 42–20 by the Sharks.

The old gang was breaking up. At season's end, we lost Steve Renouf to Wigan, Peter Ryan defected to rugby union, and Andrew Gee bowed out. That year was a frustrating and emotional one for us as we fell to earth with a resounding thud after our stellar 1998. Season 2000 could only be better, and the general consensus was: Bring it on.

Quite apart from all this doom and gloom, I sat out most of the second round of the 1999 competition with my arm in plaster after I went to tackle an Auckland Warrior in our round-19 match on 10 July at ANZ Stadium; he ducked and my forearm broke when it collided with his skull. I heard the crack and figured I might have busted my arm, but I played on. When I came off the field at the end of the game, my arm was throbbing and getting sorer by the minute. I listened to Wayne's post-match talk and then went for an X-ray that confirmed the break and the need for a plate to be inserted. My season was over. I was inconsolable. I had never played better than in the past few weeks. Once again it was rammed home to me that despair has a way of following triumph in this game we play.

# 3

# Making the grade

In 2000, I was a wide-eyed kid in the land of gods. I had such respect for my Bronco teammates and coach that I sat back, grateful to be included, hanging on their every word and trying, with varying degrees of success, to emulate what they did on the field, at training and in life.

Maybe more than anyone, I modelled myself on Shane Webcke. In a game – for the Broncos, Queensland and Australia – and at training he knew only one speed: full on. Top gear was the only gear he had. When Steve Irwin came to a training session, he thought it might be fun to be tackled by Shane. Shane didn't hold back and smashed Steve who, to his credit, picked himself up off the ground with a grin and a 'Crikey!'. Shane was an uncompromising and supremely tough player who knew his role and carried it out every game he played. He taught me to go as hard in the 80th minute of a match as in the first. He didn't need rubbish in his game. He was a fair player who carried his life principles onto the paddock. He was kind to me, and took the time to show me the front-row ropes.

Seeing how we stuck together, Wayne Bennett called Shane, Brad Thorn and me the Three Amigos. Brad had been a Bronco since 1994. From the start, he was one of my best friends in the side and today, 12 years later, I still count him as a close mate. At the age of 36, he starred for the All Blacks when they won the 2011 Rugby Union World Cup. I wished him well and watched all his games on TV. He has won multiple premierships with the Broncos, State of Origin matches for Queensland, and represented Australia in rugby league. He has won Super Rugby titles, a European rugby grand final and he is a World Cup champion with his native New Zealand rugby side. Imagine the strain on his family trophy cabinet! To sum up Brad's game, he used his 1.96-metre (six feet five inches), 115-kilogram frame to run hard with the ball and demolish guys in defence. He had skills and, like Shane Webcke, he was uncompromising and competitive, never packing it in until the final siren, no matter what the score. Also like Webby, Brad was a clean player. When you're Brad Thorn, there's no need for cheap shots.

I knew him when we were up-and-coming teenagers and I remember him playing for Western Suburbs as a 19-year-old and easily holding his own in what was a very rugged and experienced Wests forward pack which went on to win the 1993 Brisbane rugby league grand final. I thought, 'Jeez, this bloke is a tough bugger.' When I started out at the Broncos where he was already an established player, and packed down alongside him, I realised that my first impression was spot-on. I've never known such a hard-arsed competitor.

We were great mates on and off the footy field. A beer or two was routine after a game. Then in 2001 he found God and embraced religion and it made him a better person and a better footballer. He still had fun, just looked at life and footy differently, more seriously, and dedicated himself to being as good as he could be in both. I reckon that as gratifying as all the trophies, grand finals and Test matches are, Big Thorny would always say his greatest achievement is his family. He and his wife Maryanne have four kids, as Bonnie and I do. We've both taken a similar journey from being young knockabouts to responsible husbands and fathers. Well, we like to think so. (Is that the sound of our wives' laughter I can hear in the background?)

Gorden Tallis was another Broncos forward and the most aggressive player I have ever played with or against. His rage on the field – and *rage* is the right word – was infectious. He was not one for cheap shots, just super-vigorous and played on a heightened emotional level. Occasionally that emotion bubbled over and sparked some memorable stand-up stinks, notably with the young Ben Ross and Wigan forward Terry O'Connor. What Gorden Tallis did on the field, you can't coach. He would make a ferocious run, knocking defenders out of his way or dragging them along with him, or a huge tackle, and you'd bust your gut to do the same. When we needed a lift, Gordie provided it. Off the field he was a jovial, friendly guy, always joking, great to be around. It's just that he left his smile in the locker with his street gear.

Gorden was the benchmark for intimidation and, like the legendary gunslingers of the Old West, he was singled out by young guns keen to establish themselves as hard men. In a late '90s Test match against Great Britain, the young Adrian Morley took Gordie on, and the two belted each other all day. At the end of the game, they swapped jerseys and not long after a very impressed Artie Beetson signed up Moz for the Sydney Roosters.

Late in my career, Jared Waerea-Hargreaves tried to make his reputation at my expense. Come to think of it, I did exactly the same thing against the top veterans of my early years. I didn't always come out on top against Chief Harragon, Mark Carroll and David Fairleigh, but I made sure they knew I was on the field.

Kevin Campion was small in stature compared to forwards like Thorn and Webcke, which didn't stop him being one very tough nut. Kev was a no-nonsense footballer who made as few mistakes as he made headlines – the reliable type every successful side needs. Wherever he played, he was held in high regard; be it at the Broncos or the Warriors, he always gave 100 per cent and was a genuine tough man. His former teammate Shane Webcke found this out the hard way after Kev left us to join the Warriors. The pair had an on-field blue, which Kev won.

During one season, Kevin suffered a deep cut to his chin. The doctors didn't want him to play, because they said there was a high risk that the cut, which was refusing to heal, would become infected and could permanently disfigure his face. Kev took no notice and played on, the wound getting bigger, deeper and nastier. Every week it re-opened and drenched his jersey in blood. Kev said it would have plenty of time to heal in the off-season. He still has the scar to show for it.

Darren Lockyer is a freak. Back in 2000, he was a brilliant young fullback, slight of build but tough, unflappable and brave, and already showing signs of the magnificent leader he would be in years to come. I was in awe of the way he casually plucked a high ball out of the air and, despite a herd of defenders rushing at him, managed to evade them and make a long dash. He was mature beyond his years.

Wendell Sailor, our winger – what a character! He was dynamic for Brisbane, Queensland and Australia and later

St George–Illawarra, and a human headline off the field. Even more than a decade ago, in 2000, Del was talking about himself in the third person, reminding me of some big flash and brash American sportsmen like Muhammad Ali, Michael Jordan or Carl Lewis. His ego and self-belief were huge, and he endlessly talked himself up – only occasionally tongue-in-cheek. The irritating thing was that what he boasted he would do, he usually did. The first time I encountered him I was playing for the Queensland under-17 side and he was in the under-19s. I was in awe of this big dark guy, this awesome athlete. He was everything I wanted to be, but I was just too shy and way too slow. The whole time we were at our junior rep teams' camp at Gympie, he took on the most challenging fitness tests and blew us all away. He was the coolest guy I'd ever seen.

As I MENTIONED in the last chapter, Shane Webcke, Peter Ryan and Andrew Gee gave me a master-class in what it takes to be a rugby league forward. From them I learned to play with pain and never give up, to bust my guts running and tackling for as long as I was conscious. They were real men, who talked about the special privilege of being a forward, and who walked that talk each week. They had an immense work ethic, in a game and at training, a determination never to shirk. Like Wayne Bennett, they could be scathing on slackers. They were hard men physically and mentally, ultra-professionals who played to a consistently high standard and demanded that standard of their teammates.

It was part of my makeup, to the end of my career, to try never to let anyone down. Aiming up to meet, and exceed, expectations made me feel good about myself and it motivated me. It pushed me to succeed and it was a big part of me. It was reinforced for me in 2000 by my fellow Bronco forwards Shane, Andrew, Gorden, Brad, Kevin Campion and Luke Priddis. I would have died before I let them think I wasn't pulling my weight. This sense of responsibility became the source of my work ethic.

A result of not letting others down can be consistency and intensity. As Wayne never got sick of telling me in 1998 and '99, I was an up and down player, a stand-out performer one week, average or poor the next. Even in the course of a single game back then I might do something that would get me noticed, then, to the fury of Wayne and the frustration of Shane, Gorden, Brad and Kev, be invisible for the rest of the match. In 2000 I got my head in the right place and started sustaining top form, intensity and concentration for 80 minutes and stringing good games together. I now regularly made the starting team. In one match, I managed to make 40 consecutive successful tackles. I reduced my errors significantly. I was finally accepted in the side.

I would beat myself up for days on end if I did something dumb on the field, made a lazy play, missed a tackle or dropped a pass. Wayne, of course, would berate those who made mistakes. Being told off by Wayne in front of team-mates is not a pleasant experience, and avoiding getting a bollocking was another motivating factor for me.

IF A young fella came to me today and said, 'I want to play prop, what's my role?' I'd reply, 'Where do I start?'. Yet summing up the essentials I'd say: work ethic, endurance and a good motor, strength, intelligence and desire.

Prop is the most physically demanding position on the field. The demands on a front-row forward have become so heavy in the modern game that being rested during a match and interchanged is essential for all but a handful of supermen.

A front-rower's job is to hit the ball up time and again into the teeth of the opposition forwards, and bend the defensive line back to provide forward momentum and a strong platform from which the faster and more elusive players can attack. Scores of times in a game, props stand back 10 metres and take that ball up as hard and fast as possible. The defenders are back 10 metres too, so you have men weighing 110–120 kilos colliding at speed. It's said that the smash-up is the equivalent to the impact of a car prang.

A prop has to work harder than any other player on the football field and be able to keep going in situations when he is exhausted and hurting bad. It's a simple fact: if a front-rower can dominate his rivals, his team is on the way to a win. I learned the hard way that a soft run would see me get hurt. Wayne helped me simplify my goals. They were:

In attack: run to hurt and be aggressive in every carry and stay in motion.

In defence: line-speed and have a mongrel aggressive attitude when I make contact.

In general: keep trailing the play.

These were my starting points, my flags or cues to help me focus on my job. If I did these my game would fall into place.

Early on, I battled with fatigue. A lazy effort hampered my performance too often in my starting years. I had to learn to push through the fatigue. I tried to reach exhaustion as soon as possible in a game so I could progress to the next level of fatigue and then get my second wind. You have to hit the wall and then break it down. I knew that if I didn't reach that stage of secondary fatigue I wasn't having a go. So, in the early part of a match, I hit the ball up twice in a set of six tackles. That was a battle that I waged in every game and training session. In my final years that battle got harder to win.

Football is very much a mental game, as well. You have to consciously defy your burning lungs and aching muscles, the voices in your head telling you to take it easy and let someone else do your work for a bit because you're so damned buggered. It's a choice.

Cardio fitness is essential in defence, as essential as strength and tackling technique. To continually run 10 metres, tackle your opponent, run back 10, run up again . . . again and again, takes stamina. This is when talk among teammates, willing each other on, can help you lift. Sometimes just the act of talking to each other can help distract the brain from negativity and tiredness. Positive words of encouragement help break down the wall of fatigue and push through it.

Front-rowers are members of a special club. They belt each other on the field, asking for and giving no mercy, yet mostly respect and like each other. If you ask me, anyone who plays in the front row is special. In my long career, I packed down with and against some wonderful props, too many to mention, though among those opponents, a few made an extra special impression on me, in more ways than one. Ruben Wiki, Adrian Morley and my teammate Shane Webcke were cut from the same cloth.

And there was Martin Lang. Martin, who played with Cronulla, Penrith and Queensland, was a terrific opponent, a rampaging, direct runner who charged, head up, chin thrust out, knees pumping high, straight at you. With him, every hit-up was personal. Unfortunately, his fearless upright running style led to him suffering a number of head knocks and he was knocked out a few times. Self-preservation was something Big Marty did not understand. It was that mentality that made him tough. I remember the 2003 grand final playing for the Panthers. The Roosters, with their feared forward pack led by Adrian Morley, tried to bash and intimidate Marty. But he refused to relent for the 80 minutes. He continually trucked it up until the Roosters pack were beaten.

I particularly recall one time that I was responsible for KO'ing Martin. In the third-round clash with Cronulla in 2000, we started out the game yapping at each other. He yelled, 'Civoniceva, what have you got?' I yelled back, 'Plenty.' 'Yeah? Well what shoulder do you want me to run at?' I grinned at him and patted my left. I tried to make my tackles on Martin sting. He always picked himself up, dusted himself off, and stampeded at me again. In the 10th minute he hit it up in my direction and I lined him up. At the last moment, he ducked his head . . . right into my swinging forearm with which I'd planned to collect him high on his chest. The sweat sprayed from his melon and down he went in a heap.

Referee Steve Clark put me on report and I was charged with making a grade two careless high tackle. My case wasn't helped when Martin's father, John, the Cronulla coach, said: 'The NRL has to devise strategies so no one is repeatedly copping high shots. I'm not really concerned what penalty Petero Civoniceva gets and I don't think he's a dirty player. I think he's a tall guy who needs to work on his tackling technique.'

I pleaded guilty to the charge and escaped suspension because of my good record.


IN SEASON 2000 I was so glad to be back in action, healthy and fit, after my broken arm had sidelined me for much of the previous season. My enthusiasm was rewarded when the Broncos offered me a new two-year deal, which I gratefully accepted. My determination to make this a year to remember was spurred on when I was selected, at age 24, in the Emerging Queensland State of Origin squad. To know I was close to selection sent my confidence into orbit. My childhood dream was to play Origin and that dream was a step closer to coming true.

Wayne put us through one hell of a pre-season camp at an army base at Canungra in the Gold Coast hinterland. The bus stopped 10 kilometres short of the camp and we were made to run the distance lugging heavy ropes with tractor tyres attached. It got worse . . . After some torturous bush-bashing and night manoeuvres, Gorden Tallis and Lote Tuqiri passed out with exhaustion and Wayne was convinced by Michael Hancock's angry glare that Mick was tossing up whether to kill – or just maim – him. On the first morning, my feet sprouted blisters the size of 20 cent coins.

This wasn't the last time we pre-seasoned at Canungra. The following year it was far more gruelling, and I'll come to that. Even so, Gordie attributed our successful 2000 season to that first camp: 'After that, no one was going to beat us. It didn't make us better footballers. It wasn't going to make us run over a bloke or tackle harder, but it made us tougher mentally. After going through the bush for 15 hours straight, the 80 minutes it takes to play a game of football didn't seem all that long.'

Gordie said that we thought we knew our limit of endurance before Canungra, but after surviving that camp we all realised that our limit was a long way further down the track.

At the Broncos that year, Wayne changed our style a little. Making the most of his powerful forward pack, there was a greater emphasis on grinding, no-mistake footy upfront, to provide room for our brilliant backs. We forwards played with more structure and less ad hoc razzle-dazzle than we had in past years. Wayne kept emphasising to us that we were one of the biggest and best packs in the competition and to take on other teams in the middle of the park.

Typically, though, he gave us free rein to use what ball skills we had *after* the hard metres had been won. Journalist Peter Badel nailed our new role in *Big League* magazine after we'd beaten Parramatta in round two: 'Gorden Tallis and back-row cohort Brad Thorn scored the side's three tries with powerhouse displays, while front-rowers Shane Webcke and Petero Civoniceva laid the foundations with relentless go-forward and stinging defence.'

We were undefeated in our first eight games.

By the middle of the second round of the competition, I was still happy with my form. The Maroons had been beaten again by the Blues in State of Origin 2000 and I dared to hope that if I continued to play well I might be a member of the premiership-winning side and, if changes were to be made to the losing Origin side, be awarded a maroon jersey in 2001.

Then disaster. In round 16, against the Melbourne Storm at ANZ Stadium, I broke my arm again. Just as my arm had shattered the previous year when an Auckland Warrior ducked into it as I went to tackle him ball and all, a Storm forward's knee connected with my arm and I knew straight away that I had re-broken it. After I'd had a plate inserted in my arm in 1999, the doctors warned me that when I played again its most vulnerable spot would be right at the end of the plate. That is exactly where my bone snapped. The arm guard I wore had made no difference. Even though in that match I knew my arm was gone, our bench was depleted through injury, so I pretended that I was okay to play on. I told myself I could catch and tackle with my good arm and a broken arm wasn't going to prevent me hitting the ball up. During an interchange spell, I was making out that all was fine, while a doctor who had been watching me closely and suspected what had happened tried to make me quit. I protested that I was okay and there was no way I wasn't going to play on. 'Prove it,' he said. 'Do some push-ups.' So, despite the pain, I peeled off 10. He allowed me to return to the field and play out the match. Yes, it hurt, but I knew I couldn't do any more damage to my arm than I had already done, my adrenalin was running, and I simply didn't want to let the boys down.

After the game, when the realisation hit that I had played my last match for 2000, I was pretty emotional. The rug had been pulled from under my feet again. I had been living my dream and now for the second year in a row a broken arm had ended my season.

So I was missing when the Broncos won the minor pre-miership and then defeated the Roosters 14–6 in the grand final in front of more than 94,000 people at Stadium Aus-tralia. I was glad for my teammates and for our supporters, but could not believe my bad luck. It was devastating to miss out. I felt like an outcast and an impostor and I played little or no part in the end-of-season celebrations because I didn't believe I had the right.

Thankfully the club found things for me to do, and my enforced lay-off in 2000 turned out to be one of the most rewarding periods of my life. I conducted coaching clinics in Cairns, Roma, Mt Isa, Rockhampton, Emerald, Tamworth and on Thursday Island. I got a sense of how important rugby league is to the kids, just as it had been to me when I was growing up so starry-eyed. I met many passionate and decent people whose lives are enriched by playing and following our game. I'm sure I learned more from these folk and the kids I coached than the kids learned from me. Being a Broncos ambassador made my lay-off from football bearable . . . well, almost.

SEASON 2001 was when I graduated from being a club player to a State of Origin and Kangaroo Test regular. The only downside to the season was the Broncos' disappointing campaign. We were unable to win back-to-back premierships and bowed out of the competition in the preliminary final after a dreadful second half of the season.

We all believed we were good enough to be premiers. I'd worked so hard in the off-season to get my arm right and reach a level of fitness I'd never attained before. The disappointment of breaking my arm again and then missing the grand final win had focused my mind on making 2001 a season to remember.

There was a glitch when we were beaten by St Helens in the World Club Challenge in England. St Helens was a fine side, but it's a fact that our hearts were not in the match, because just the day before, Broncos' founder Paul 'Porky' Morgan died suddenly of a heart attack. His larger-than-life personality and business acumen had made him a beloved character in our club, and we were stunned by his passing. Andrew Gee put on a stink in the game . . . maybe for Porky's sake, maybe because he was furious at the baiting and heckling by the local crowd. The loss to St Helens was ancient history by the time we returned to Australia and the team mood was 'Onward and upward'.

•

In 2001, the Queensland State of Origin team had plenty to prove. New South Wales had won the 2000 series by an embarrassing three games to nil, scoring a total of 104 points to our meagre 42. The folks down south were saying that Origin had all become too easy and the concept was dead, because the Maroons simply couldn't compete with New South Wales anymore. There wasn't one of us in the Queensland squad who didn't use that talk as motivation.Playing for my state in this wonderful series was everything I thought it would be. I'd spent most of my life living and breathing State of Origin – praying for Queensland wins – and suddenly here I was. I'd never experienced anything like the intensity of the build-up. There was so much pressure on us to stop the rot and stick it to the Blues. The whole state *needed* us to win. There was so much riding on the team and Wayne, who was the Queensland coach, made some bold selections. With 10 newcomers, he was taking a big risk. Making their Origin debut in Origin I at ANZ Stadium were Broncos Lote Tuqiri, Kevin Campion, Carl Webb, Brad Meyers, Chris Walker, John Buttigieg, John Doyle, Daniel Wagon, Chris Beattie and yours truly.

Origin camp was a revelation. The team trained hard and thanks to Wayne and all the former Origin greats who joined us we became convinced that we were capable of winning the series. We learned to believe in ourselves. To a man, defeat was not an option. We also had a lot of fun. I got to know the non-Bronco guys for the first time, know them as mates and teammates rather than opponents. We were, for a little while at least, united by the maroon jersey. There wasn't one of us who didn't try to live up to the principles of State of Origin: Trust; Effort; Aggression, Mateship – the acronym for which is TEAM. I listened spellbound to the yarns of the former players. They told us of the mighty deeds of Origins past, and gave us insights into their experiences. They left us in no doubt about what it takes to be worthy of playing for Queensland. We first-timers enjoyed hearing that even men who went on to become the greatest Maroon legends had the dry retches when they made their debut.

The only fly in this heady ointment was an article under the by-line of former Queensland centre Mark Coyne in the Gold Coast *Bulletin* which was reprinted in the mass circulation Brisbane *Courier-Mail* in which he doubted that I could cope with Origin pressure. 'I hope he measures up,' wrote Coyne. 'Personally, I don't think he can adjust and take the step up. For Queensland's sake, I'll be happy to be wrong.' I would use the article to drive me to prove that I *was* up to the task, but it rankled.

I called Mark and he explained that his ghost-writer on the newspaper had written the story without consulting him and he hadn't had time to check the copy. He apologised and assured me that my selection was justified. 'I'm distraught about the way it came out,' he said. 'I wouldn't criticise any player. I copped enough criticism in my day to know how hurtful it can be. It was a terrible misunderstanding . . .' I accepted Mark's apology and moved on. This would not be the last time criticism lit a fire under me in Origin.

Before the opening match at Suncorp Stadium, Wally Lewis revved us up with a speech that Winston Churchill would have been proud to make and he handed the newcomers our jerseys. It was an overwhelming moment.

I'll never forget running out onto the field wearing the maroon of Queensland for the first time. It was magic. I looked into the crowd and imagined myself, aged six or seven, sitting on the terraces cheering on Wally, Gene Miles and Mal Meninga, and it occurred to me that somewhere out there in that vast throng my now-retired childhood heroes were sitting, their hearts in their mouths, cheering *me* on.

Origin is 15–20 per cent faster and more intense than a normal club game of rugby league. It just is. The emotion supercharges the players and everyone lifts. This is why there have been so many classic games down the years. In Origin you don't give up, so there have been numerous miraculous come-from-behind wins.

Origin I in 2001 started at warp speed. We came out hard and fast. In only the second minute, Darren Lockyer sent Lote Tuqiri away on a long run, then backed him up to score the try. Carl Webb brushed aside Jason Croker and Jamie Ainscough and carried Croker and Matt Gidley over the line for a remarkable solo try. Then successive tries to John Doyle, John Buttigieg, and Chris Walker put us ahead 34–4. The final score was 34–16. Buttigieg played a blinder and Gordie (who was injured in the match and didn't play again that season) pipped Locky for man of the match. Pleasing to me was the way we battered the Blues forwards.

New South Wales, as we knew they would, came back at us in the second match, at Telstra Stadium in Sydney. This time, inspired by Freddie Fittler, they smashed us 26–8. I was very impressed by the strong game of their prop Mark 'Shrek' O'Meley. 'Mad Dog' MacDougall, the Blues centre, was put on report and later suspended for lifting his knees into me as I tackled him. There wasn't much in it.

With the series tied and the decider looming, our half-back Paul Green was ruled out with injury. It was now that Wayne produced a coaching masterstroke. I was standing with a group of the Queensland boys before the team assembled at QRL headquarters at the Gabba when a cab pulled up and out jumped Allan Langer. We were gobsmacked. We all thought he was in England playing for Warrington. He said he couldn't say anything, but the look on his face told us he was here to play. His addition to our team had been top secret. He had even travelled to Australia under an assumed name. As shocked as his team-mates were to see him, it was nothing to the shock, mingled I'm sure with horror, the New South Wales boys felt when they realised they'd be up against this little master.

Spurred on by his own pride and, perhaps, Phil Gould's jibe that it was a shame that Queensland's playing stocks were so low that we had to resort to 35-year-olds to beat the Blues, Alf let nobody down. He was unstoppable that night. He had a hand in our first three tries and scored a solo try from close to their line in the second half. The Langer–Lockyer combination picked up from where it had left off at the Broncos in mid-1999 and that pair tore the Blues to shreds. We won the match 40–14, and took the series 2–1.

Nobody south of the border was saying Origin was dead anymore. After the match, Wayne hugged us all, but his biggest embrace, quite rightly, was for Alf Langer.

Playing well in that victorious series made me realise that I could hold my own against the best players in the game. I had more than survived my greatest test. To be honest, before the series I probably had doubts about whether I had the ability to play at Origin level. After helping beat New South Wales, I knew I could cut it.

BEING THRASHED 44–0 by the Newcastle Knights in the first post-Origin club game was a savage dose of reality.

Wayne had warned us that an ambush was on the cards, because he could see our Origin players had still not come down off the victory. We tried to lift against the Knights. We couldn't.

Nevertheless, I was selected in the Australian team to take on the Kiwis in Wellington in a one-off Test. How did I feel? Huge pride is the best I can put it. Mum, my sisters and my dad were just as happy as me. It meant so much to us as a family, especially my parents. My career, and now playing for Australia, was proof that their decision 20 years earlier to migrate to Australia was the right one. I was determined to do the green and gold jersey proud, and not let down my teammates or all the legends who had worn the jumper before me. I wasn't that nervous, having just come through State of Origin . . . just determined to play well and hopefully not be a one-Test wonder. Making their Kangaroo debuts, too, were fellow Broncos Lote Tuqiri, Brad Meyers, Dane Carlaw, and Newcastle's Danny Buderus. I came off the bench, and did what was required of me. We won 28–10.

People have asked me what it is like to stand there before a game as the Kiwis perform the haka. I have to say it is one of the great football experiences. Growing up I was always in awe of the haka, whether it was the Kiwis rugby league team or rugby's All Blacks performing it. It is intimidating – that raw emotion of the warriors of New Zealand. With their eyes rolling and tongues hanging out of gaping mouths, every vein protruding, it is their call to arms. It makes me feel respect for my opponents and the Maori culture. But for me there is no greater feeling than singing Advance Australia Fair in your green and gold jersey, ready to take those Kiwis on. You can't help but get fired up.

After the Broncos' loss to the Knights, we lost seven of

our next eight club games. The many Queensland players in the team were experiencing a syndrome that we came to call 'post-Origin slump'. Because we had given our bodies and souls to winning the Origin series, we suffered a let-down. Wayne warned us and we all thought we could get back into a premiership frame of mind, but as a team we couldn't adapt. Even in years to come when I was a seasoned Origin player, it took me two or three weeks to get over the mental and physical demands of Origin and I had to really push myself to maintain my Origin form.

One of the most dismal points of the year came in round 25, when we were destroyed 40–18 by cellar dwellers Canberra. Wayne accused us of not having a go, and that hurt. I told *The Australian*'s reporter Brian Burke after the match:

It was terrible out there today and I was one of the ones responsible. I didn't think the good times would end. The new blokes to the [representative] scene let ourselves down when we came back into the normal [NRL] fixtures. We forgot what got us [rep honours]. You can't afford to flirt with form. You put in a couple of average games back-to-back and all of a sudden you find yourself in a situation where it is hard to get back into the zone where you were before. It has been a bad year with injuries and losing someone like Gorden Tallis, who can lift you when you're down, was a huge blow.

We'd accumulated enough points in the first half of the season to scrape into the finals, but after beating St George–Illawarra 44–28 in the semi-final (in which, after inspiring pre-match addresses by Pat Rafter and Gorden Tallis, I scored two tries in the first six minutes . . . when usually even one in a season is a rarity), we crashed out 24–16 to Parramatta in the preliminary final.

WHAT BETTER way could there have been to get over the Broncos' disappointing year than hearing my name read out in the Kangaroo team for a seven-week tour of England? Fellow Broncos Darren Lockyer, Shane Webcke, Gorden Tallis, Brad Meyers, Dane Carlaw and Lote Tuqiri were picked too. I was genuinely shocked by my selection. I knew that I was a chance after Origin and having played for Australia against New Zealand, but feared that the Broncos' premature exit from the comp would cost me my place. I was overjoyed to be recognised by the national selectors to represent my country in the northern hemisphere.

For a while, the tragic and terrible events of September 11 put the tour in doubt, especially when some team members withdrew fearing terrorist attacks on foreign soil. Not Jason Ryles. He declared that he'd be happy to play in Afghanistan if it meant wearing the green and gold of the Kangaroos. I'd have joined him. There was no way I was withdrawing from the side. No terrorist was going to stop me from playing for Australia. Bonnie backed my stand. She was over the moon for me, although probably a little worried by all the media beat-ups that we'd be targeted by al-Qaeda. She knew how much it meant to me to play for Australia.

I have memories of being a boy watching the great Kangaroo tours, the Invincibles of 1982, the Unbeatables of 1986. I set my bedside alarm at 3.30 am to get up and watch the Second Test, at Old Trafford, in 1990. Great Britain was leading with minutes to go when Ricky Stuart cut through and passed to Mal Meninga, who was backing up like a steam train and scored the winning try. My yells of joy just about lifted the roof off our house. That win locked the series at one win apiece, and Australia won the decider at Leeds the following weekend.

Twelve years later, it was an equally tense series against Great Britain. They had a strong side, with Andy Farrell and Jamie Peacock and the tough and skilled lock or five-eighth Paul Sculthorpe. They shocked us 28–8 in the First Test at Wigan, inspired by a once-in-a-lifetime performance by Sculthorpe; but we regathered and with Locky, Brad Fittler and Andrew Johns leading the way we won the remaining Tests and the series. I got my share of game time and loved the toughness of Test match rugby league.

# 4

# The front-rowers' union

Every player counts the hours until the start of the new season, but *nobody* looks forward to pre-season training. Usually it is devoted to regaining peak fitness after the letdown of the end of the previous year's campaign and a couple of months of inactivity, topped with the excesses of the festive season. Running sandhills and long distances on the road and lugging heavy weights is what it is about, rather than fine-tuning speed, skills and tactics. At the Broncos, we were known for horror pre-season camps, but at the onset of season 2002, Wayne had a welcome surprise for the boys. Thinking that a happy frame of mind might erase memories of season 2001, he organised a pre-season training trip to Fiji.

When we returned from our tropical paradise, Wayne got our minds back on the job by working us hard in the weeks before the premiership kick-off. We were happy to be flogged, as we were all keen to do better this year. Yet for some reason – a severe shin injury? Or maybe too much kava in Fiji? – I took time to find form.

We were bolstered by the return of Andrew Gee, who had missed 2001, and the great Allan Langer, who at 36 was having his swansong year. He would play 18 games for the Broncos in 2002 and all three State of Origin matches. As well as his skill and guile as a player, he was valued for his irrepressible and wicked humour. No one was safe from Alf's wit, least of all me. He was the only bloke who could get away with taking the piss out of Wayne. He was the court jester who could crack up the most serious team meetings. Alf was the ultimate team man and everyone loved him.

After 14 rounds in 2002, we had suffered just two defeats and recorded massive wins over the Rabbitohs (42–16), the Northern Eagles (50–12) and the Cowboys (42–6 and 52–8). After State of Origin, however, we lost more than we won, and our season ended with a 16–12 defeat by the eventual premiers, Ricky Stuart's Sydney Roosters, in the preliminary final.

In 2002, I found myself in the headlines for the wrong reasons when in a 20 April match against Penrith at ANZ Stadium I tackled a rival head-high. Unbelievably, the bloke I hit was good old Marty Lang, whom I'd accidentally knocked out when he was playing for the Sharks in 2000 and who had transferred to the Panthers. Once more Marty's father John, now the Penrith coach, went ballistic and demanded that I be banned from the game, and the media put a sensational spin on what was no more than another ball-and-all tackle that went wrong. My natural instinct was always to keep a low profile and just do my job on the field. Now I had a taste of being under the media microscope.

As usual, in the opening minutes of our match Martin and I had been having a ding-dong but fair battle. I would hit it up and he'd smash me, and I'd return the compliment when he had the ball. There was no animosity. It's just what props do. And with Martin and me there was extra spice because we were both vying for selection in the Queensland State of Origin pack.

Anyway, this time Marty came at me hard in his usual style, knees pumping and head high. I raced in, aiming to hit him in the chest, knock him over and hopefully dislodge the ball from his grasp. Again he lowered his head, this time when tackled by our hooker Michael Ryan. I couldn't pull out and instead of getting him in the chest I hit him in the head with my bicep. Down he went, unconscious. He was carted off with severe concussion and after a CAT scan he spent the night in QEII Hospital.

I was not penalised or placed on report by referee Shayne Hayne – who had said, 'It was not high, it was around the shoulders' – but Marty's teammates and the Penrith supporters let me know what they thought about the tackle in no uncertain terms. What made it worse was that the game had been close until Martin's injury and right after he left the field we scored two tries and scooted away with the match. I was upset that I'd hurt Marty and checked on his condition on the field and then in the dressing sheds afterwards.

I was cited and charged with a grade three careless high tackle. I told reporters who suggested I might be facing a suspension: 'I have a good record, which hopefully will hold me in good stead. I'm not the sort of bloke who goes out on the field to hurt anybody. It was an accident and I hope the judiciary can see that.'

The atmosphere became even more explosive after Broncos' management accused the NRL of discriminating against us. In recent times, Bronco players had received what our head office believed were heavier penalties than their offences warranted, certainly in comparison to lighter sentences dealt to players from other clubs for similar offences, especially clubs in New South Wales. That may have been so, and there also may have been a bit of the old Broncos' siege mentality at work. To thumb their nose at the NRL, the Broncos ran a clip of my hit on Marty in a TV commercial . . . and were ordered to cut it.

When John Lang and Penrith's CEO Shane Richardson continued to attack me in the press, our CEO Shane Edwards accused them of 'evoking hysteria' to get me suspended. Yet perhaps the most inflammatory comments came from, of all places, New Zealand. Selwyn Pearson, the outspoken chairman of the NZRL, wrote to the NRL judiciary to say:

> The gutless attack on Martin Lang was inexcusable. I do not see it as a grade three careless tackle. I see it as a grade-103 intention-to-maim. Martin Lang is a wonderful young man and a great ambassador for our game and he does not deserve the disgraceful treatment he received last week.

I ignored Pearson, but many were outraged when he stuck his nose into the furore. Journalist Barry Dick in the *Courier-Mail* lambasted the hapless Kiwi: 'Three questions spring to mind immediately: Who is he? What on earth does it have to do with him? And what is he on?'

Dick agreed that Marty was a 'wonderful young man' but added:

> Well, Sel, ditto for Petero Civoniceva . . . He certainly does not deserve a misinformed attack from across the Tasman. Civoniceva's tackle on Lang happened straight in front of referee Shayne Hayne and touch judges Mark

Oaten (an experienced first-grade referee) and Brett Meredith. Video referee Eddie Ward, a veteran of about 500 first-grade games in Brisbane and Sydney, had the benefit of three replays while Lang was being treated. None of those officials, all of whom would know more about the game than Selwyn Pearson, saw fit to penalise Civoniceva or put him on report.

Pearson . . . seemed to indicate the tackle was a deliberate attempt to take Lang out of the game. Apart from being an unfair slur on a very fair player in Civoniceva, that is ridiculous. If you wanted to 'take out' any player in the Penrith team it would not be Martin Lang. Fine, brave player that he is, Lang is never going to hurt the opposition. He doesn't have a sidestep and rarely passes the ball, so rival forwards line up to tackle him. Keeping him on the field is good for their stats.

Let me tell you, it's a confronting and nerve-racking experience to face the judiciary. It's all deadly serious, the lawyers for the prosecution and the defence really go into battle, and the protocol and their use of legalese is bewildering to a layman. In the days before the hearing, I spent plenty of time with our legal eagles planning what we believed was a legitimate defence.

I testified:

First contact in the tackle was my left shoulder with Lang's left shoulder before my bicep struck his head. I was setting myself for a ball-and-all tackle when Lang deviated late in his run. He was heading in my direction and at the last moment he headed towards Michael Ryan. Ryan affected the tackle down low first and Lang's height had changed. I had a split second to change the tackle I was trying to effect. Normally, Lang has a very direct style, he rarely deviates from the direction he's going. It's very much an upright style.

It was all for nothing. I was found guilty and suspended for one week. Frustratingly, the game I would miss was our top-of-the-table clash with the Knights.

Wayne and the senior players tried to help me cope with my sudden notoriety. It hurt to be painted as a dirty player. I played hard and it happened that rivals sometimes came off second-best when we clashed on the field. That same year in the preliminary final against the Roosters I accidentally clashed heads with Roosters hooker Simon Bonnetti and while his melon was split open and his eye and lip swelled to Elephant Man proportions, mine was unscathed.

Meanwhile, I was working overtime with extra defensive sessions, to lower my point of contact and to avoid any more appointments with the judiciary

I FEARED that my suspension might prejudice the State of Origin selectors against me, so when they again named me in the Maroons' second row for Origin, I told reporters:

After having the experience last year, it's a case of stepping up this year. But when the team was named on Monday I was as nervous as ever. Mate, the butterflies are still going. I'm stoked to be named in amongst these guys and playing second row with Gordie Tallis. I'm looking forward to it so much.

Had I known how the series was going to pan out, I'd have been even more stoked. State of Origin 2002 was the tightest series ever. At the end of three fierce games, the honours were shared. I have no excuses for our 32–4 loss in the first game, in which I suffered a grade two medial ligament tear. Under new coach Phil Gould, the Blues were focused and energised and they blew us off Telstra Stadium.

Much as Queensland is always motivated by the beltings we received in pre-Origin days when New South Wales teams comprising Queenslanders playing in the elite Sydney comp routinely thrashed Queensland teams picked from the Brisbane and Queensland bush competitions, the Blues in '02 were out to get square for our series victory in 2001. The New South Wales selectors chose a team filled with a mix of established champions such as Andrew Johns, Ben Kennedy and Nathan Hindmarsh and young blokes with plenty to prove: Danny Buderus, Jamie Lyon, Luke Bailey, Timana Tahu, Matt Gidley, Steve Simpson, and the mercurial lightweight fullback Brett Hodgson.

Brett carried the ball for a record-breaking 390 metres that night, yet it was Joey Johns who won man of the match. Like most players of my era, I rate Joey a genius. He was the complete rugby league package. He could make a break, set up a man, kick goals and kick in general play with pinpoint accuracy, and he tackled like a forward. His control of a game was unbelievable. No player has ever steered his team around the park like Johns. He could seem laid back but, believe me, he was a driven competitor whose intensity was infectious. He *hated* to lose.

The pressure of State of Origin is unrelentingly brutal and the game is strewn with the carcasses of rookies who have been singled out for special attention by the opposition and found wanting. Few who saw Justin Hodges in his debut game, on the wing for Queensland in the second Origin game of 2002 at ANZ Stadium, would credit that he would go on to be the mighty player he became. In the 27th minute, with the Blues pounding us in our quarter, Johns kicked over our line on the fifth tackle. Justin skittered to retrieve the ball but instead of running it back into the field of play himself or forcing it for a goal-line dropout, he had a brain explosion and flung a speculator pass to Darren Lockyer. The ball never reached Locky and Blues five-eighth Braith Anasta fell on it for a try. Justin hung his head. Then 34 minutes later he did it again. This time, their second-rower Luke Ricketson scored.

Coach Bennett hooked Justin from the field. Justin was so distraught that he drove back to Sydney, where he was playing for the Sydney Roosters, rather than take the flight with the other New South Wales–based boys.

Many a player would have been destroyed by the nightmare. Not Justin Hodges. He put the events of his disastrous Brisbane match behind him and today is a star for the Broncos and a Queensland and Kangaroo regular, a skilful and tough centre not above applying fairly scary pressure to rookies himself. It takes a special man to face down an experience like that and show the world what he is really made of. Today, Hodgo is arguably the best centre in the world.

We owed our 26–18 win in that match – which I missed with my medial ligament injury – to a strong game from centre Chris McKenna, Lote Tuqiri's three try/three goal effort, and a Gorden Tallis–led forward display.

Has any other sporting series provided such thrills year in, year out as State of Origin? The desire and intensity and sheer skills on display guarantee that remarkable things happen regularly. The 18–18 draw in game three, in front of 74,842 baying Blues fans at Sydney's Telstra Stadium, could not have been scripted. The forwards waged pitched warfare. Every tackle hurt. Such was the pace from the kick-off that every player's lungs were burning after five minutes.

There were many memorable moments, such as Gordie grabbing Brett Hodgson by the collar and rag-dolling him over the touchline. Then there was Gordie again, going off his rocker when he spotted a hateful sign in the crowd that was directed at his family. There was a wonderful team try that resulted in Blues winger Jason Moodie scoring to put the Blues ahead 18–14 with three minutes to go and seemingly winning them the series. Then, just one minute later, big Bronco second-rower Dane Carlaw ran 50 metres for the try that drew us level at the end. Lote uncharac-teristically missed the conversion that would have won us the match and the series, but because we had won the year before we retained the shield.

We did not win, yet rarely have I felt so proud after a match as when I sat quietly in the dressing-room with Shane Webcke, both bruised and bleeding, reflecting on our performances, and on our ferocious battle with our New South Wales counterparts Jason Ryles and Luke Bailey. We had all put some serious shots on each other. We faced a tremendous New South Wales forward pack and came out on top and were very, very proud. I had had very little game time in the lead-up to the match because of my medial liga-ment tear and it was good to have got through the game.

Gorden Tallis was a man possessed in that classic Origin encounter. It was always guaranteed that Gordy would be fired up to play. But as a passionate man who loves his family deeply, that sign set him off, with damaging results for New South Wales – not that any of their guys would have con-doned such a cruel and offensive sign. Fans are entitled to their opinion. Criticism is part and parcel of our game and players have to perform at a high standard and be prepared to

cop it on the chin when we're not up to scratch. Yet as someone who has suffered racial abuse from fans (and much more
about that later), I often wonder why people feel compelled
to overstep the mark by brandishing hurtful and slanderous
signs and by over-the-top barracking. What does it say about
their lack of respect for others and for themselves?

By all means, people who pay their money at the gate
can boo and cheer and poke fun, but they should keep it in
perspective. Vicious and personal baiting of the opposition
has nothing to do with supporting your team. I guess to me
the yardstick is that a so-called fan should never direct a
comment at a player from the safety of the grandstand that
he would not be prepared to say to his face; or if it's on a
fan blog site, put his name to.


AROUND THE middle of that season, I started getting nibbles from other NRL clubs' management who knew my
Broncos contract was expiring at the end of the year. I was
also contacted by the Queensland Reds and ACT Brumb-
ies rugby union sides. I was happy in league and, though
honoured that rugby union was interested, did not seriously
consider switching codes.

The North Queensland Cowboys were in the vanguard
of the rugby league clubs courting me and they made me
an offer that, 26 by now and no longer a kid, I found very
hard to refuse. Bonnie and I thought long and hard about
whether we should accept it and move to Townsville. The
Cowboys were offering me a three-year deal at $350,000 a
year, money far in excess of what I was being paid at the
Broncos. The sum, in fact, blew Bonnie and me away. It
would have been madness for a young couple planning to
marry and have a family not to consider it.

Yet money wasn't the only reason I was tempted to head north. The Cowboys had good facilities and a passionate and partisan bunch of supporters. Peter Parr, their CEO, who had been at the Broncos and whom I knew as a good man, was very keen for me to join them. He thought I had plenty to offer on the paddock and as a club man and mentor off it. Billy Johnson was there as club trainer and the former Bulldog and boxer was someone I'd worked with in rep sides and respected a lot. Obviously, too, the Cowboys, though struggling on the ladder then, were assembling a strong side including Paul Bowman, John Buttigieg, Josh Hannay, Glenn Morrison, Tim Brasher, Matt Bowen, John Doyle, Micheal Luck and Matt Sing. It was a real opportunity to establish myself as a senior forward leader, while at the Broncos guys like Gordie and Shane held down the senior, and therefore, and quite correctly, the most highly paid spots.

On the other hand, I felt truly at home at the Broncos and was devoted to the club and my teammates and coach. The Broncos had given me my chance, developed my talent, and it was as a Bronco that I had made the rep sides. Some of my best friends were at the club and it would be hard to play against blokes like Shane, Darren, Brad and Gordie. And there was Wayne Bennett, whom I had come to see as a gruff but caring father figure. My respect for him was immense. Bonnie had also just begun a job with Qantas in Brisbane, so she would have to resign if I joined the Cowboys.

Still . . . they were offering so much money. I truly didn't know what to do. As I always would have done before reaching a decision, I requested a meeting with Wayne and told him of the Cowboys' offer, which would set Bonnie and me up for life, and admitted that I was tempted to head north to Townsville. Wayne gave it to me straight. He informed me that the Broncos could not match the money that the Cowboys were offering me. Not now, anyway. But in a couple of years when Shane Webcke and Gorden Tallis retired, I could, as a Broncos' forward leader, state and Australian player, expect to receive the top money that they were now earning. I put my faith and trust in Wayne and took his words as a promise that if I remained in form and became leader of the Broncos' pack when Shane and Gorden retired, I would be paid what they were.

I took Wayne's words to heart, and those of my manager David Phillips, and most of all Bonnie, and I stewed for a week. I hardly slept. To stay or go? This was such a big decision. Finally, I decided: I would remain with the Broncos, forsaking the big bucks now in the knowledge that my opportunity to earn something like the Cowboys had offered would surely come in the not-too-distant future. I called Peter Parr and told him I wasn't going to be a Cowboy. He was disappointed but said he understood. Broncos' CEO Shane Edwards released a press statement:

> We were always quietly confident that Petero would stay with us because he was weighing up a whole range of issues. If this was a money issue with Petero, he would certainly have signed elsewhere. By re-signing with the Broncos, he has displayed his respect for the club, for coach Wayne Bennett and his fellow players.

JUST AS I felt that I had come of age as an Origin player in 2001 and 2002, this was also the year when I started to believe in myself as a top-class front-rower, a fully paid-up member of the props' union. If you wanted to test yourself against some of the best front-rowers ever to play the game, 2002 was an ideal year. There were Mark O'Meley and Steve Price at the Bulldogs, Jason Ryles and Luke Bailey at St George, John Buttigieg at the Cowboys, the Sharks' Jason Stevens and Chris Beattie, Melbourne's Robbie Kearns, Adrian Morley as a prop at the Roosters after making his name in the second row, and Martin Lang at the Panthers. What these guys had in common was that they were great competitors who played the game with intensity. They did not compromise. They were tough and self-preservation was not a concern. Their job was to smash the opposing forwards and help lay the platform for their backs to score tries. Each would do whatever it took to win. Every match against them was a war. There was respect between us and, after the game, a genuine liking.

A few fleeting impressions . . .

I was responsible for injuring Jason Ryles a couple of times in 2003 when he went to tackle me and got his timing wrong. Said Jason afterwards of the Origin II incident which put him out of the game for six months: 'I guess I didn't time my hit as well as I should have. My shoulder went into his hip and basically fell apart. My rotator cuff is 80 per cent torn and they are still working out the damage to the nerves.'

In spite of that, we roomed together on a Kangaroo tour of England and hit it off. He has a wonderful sense of humour and is a lot of fun. On the field, not so much.

Luke Bailey is another guy I respect a lot. For a while, he and Ryles were forward leaders at St George and for New South Wales in State of Origin, and I knew if I'd done well against them then I'd done well indeed. Bull plays it tight, no frills, the ultimate front-row tradesman. As I had with Jason, I roomed with Luke on tour and we had plenty in common. Conversation came easy. He is a family man and we approach league and life in a similar way. You get to know a lot about a roomie.

Steve Price has my respect and friendship. Our battles before we were paired in the Queensland front row were ferocious, born of a genuine liking for each other. He was an incredibly strong player and relentless all game. He had a tremendous motor and a huge heart. He's a very decent man. In years to come we would pack down many times in the Queensland and Australian front row, and that is a highlight of my career.

Adrian Morley epitomised toughness. Moz's aim was to inflict as much pain on opponents as possible and he didn't care if he damaged himself in the process. He was strong, very fit and agile and hurled himself at you like an Exocet missile. Like Gorden Tallis, he was a friendly and charming bloke off the field who went into a destructive zone on it, for the Roosters and Great Britain and England. He intimidated. He was capable of taking apart a rival team and for that he was feared. He added steel to a top Roosters pack including Luke Ricketson, Craig Fitzgibbon, Mick Crocker, Bryan Fletcher, Craig Wing and Jason Cayless and turned it for a time, until their high-impact tackling and running style took its toll, into the fiercest pack in the comp.

For all my footy success, far and away the best thing to happen to me in 2002 was marrying Bonnie. It nearly didn't happen. We had been together since school and things were going great. Then I was a first-grade footballer and the demands of this – the training and the media and fan attention and the constant travelling – drove a wedge between us. I also enjoyed a beer or two with my teammates. For a while, football, not Bonnie, was the most important thing in my life. She became a bit frustrated by my lack of commitment and rightly figured that life was too short and went overseas on a working holiday to experience travel, something that was out of the question for me.

I feared that might be the end of us, but instead time doing our own thing made us both realise how much we meant to each other and that we did not want to be apart. Football was fleeting, Bonnie was forever. We loved each other, and we were also great friends; I believe it was our friendship that allowed us to survive the pressures that football brought and, after a few more break-ups and reunions, took us to the level where it was right that we were married.

Early in '02, when I decided that I wanted to spend the rest of my days with Bonnie, I went to her mother and father and asked them if I had their blessing to ask her to marry me. They said that nothing would make them happier. Terri and Peter are like my own parents, and Bonnie's siblings – Kasey, Ellie, Chelsea and Zac – are like my own brothers and sisters. They've been very good to me. When my dad left us and I had no male influence, I turned to Peter because he is a strong and wise man who has made a success of life. He was a father figure to me, and in many ways he remains one today.

I took Bonnie out for dinner at a restaurant in the Brisbane suburb of Rosalie, then we drove up to nearby Mount Coottha lookout. I had a new digital camera in my pocket, which was the source of my excuse to go up there. When we were at the picturesque spot overlooking the night skyline of Brisbane, I handed the camera to a passer-by and asked him to take our photo. As he was about to press the button, I dropped to one knee and asked Bonnie to be my wife. She said yes. That photo is one of our most precious possessions.

We were married at the end of the football season, on 2 November 2002, on the beautiful white sand beach at the Outrigger resort in Fiji. Originally we planned a small wedding, just our immediate families and a few close friends, but of course it grew, and we ended up having a large celebration. People came to the wedding and stayed for a Fijian holiday; it worked perfectly. My best men were Mick De Vere from the Broncos, whose partner Olivia is a great friend of Bonnie's, my childhood friend Marcus Riley, and my cousin Moses Raulini. A few of the Bronco boys came with their partners. The big day was one enormous party and the week before and after was celebration time too.

Our wedding is right up there with the best times in our life. Bonnie looked beautiful in a mint-coloured gown and I wore a formal suit. We had a choir from a nearby village to sing for us, and there was a guard of honour of Fijian warriors in traditional dress to escort Bonnie and her father down the aisle, which was covered in frangipani petals.

After the reception, Bonnie and I flew by helicopter to Castaway Island, a private island 15 kilometres off Fiji with fabulous beaches, coral reefs, a rainforest and luxury accommodation. Our few days there were amazing and very romantic. Trouble was, we knew that our loved ones and friends were all partying on Beachcomber Island, and though we were making the most of our romantic seclusion, we kind of missed the fun and got a bit lonely. What made it worse was that we could stand on the beach at Castaway Island and actually see Beachcomber Island on the horizon. We thought we should pay everyone a visit and asked a local fisherman to take us over in his boat. We surprised everyone, and ended up staying at Beachcomber.

Bonnie and I made the decision to have a year together enjoying being a married couple, then we would start our family.

•

FROM HEAVEN to hell! Just weeks after our Fijian wedding I was back in harness for season 2003 and the happy times in Fiji were a distant memory. It was back to Canungra army base for another pre-season team-building camp. Last year, pre-season training in Fiji was fun. This year it became immediately obvious that Wayne and the military guys had decided it would be a good idea to break us down by dropping us into hell. They divided us into two groups, each under the stern command of an officer. Each group had to do intense bush-bashing, carrying heavy packs and following GPS co-ordinates through thick jungle in steep terrain. One lot had to do it on a starvation diet, but was allowed to rest at night. The other bunch, my group, was given a few ration packs to share, a small amount of food, but denied rest. Wearing night vision goggles the officers pursued us, and when they caught us we had to run to the next set of co-ordinates which were being radioed through to us from the command post. We were kept moving all night and if any of us did manage to doze off we were woken by bursts of machine-gun fire.

No one came out of that three-day camp the person he was when he went in. It was a superb team-building exercise because we had to pull together to survive. It pushed us to physical and mental extremes (I didn't realise what effective torture sleep deprivation was until Canungra) and took us out of our comfort zone – the traditional football training regime.

The day I passed out was a scorcher. We were only allowed a small supply of water. Cramps have always been an issue with me because of the amount of sweat I lose when I exercise. Being out in the bush without much water, I became dehydrated and my legs started to cramp up by mid-morning. I did what I could to prevent it, eating as much food as I was allowed and emptying my water canteen. The cramps got worse. We progressed through the day, still doing the tough challenges.

There was one infamous exercise in which five of us had to figure out a way to push up a hill a fully-loaded trailer with one wheel missing. We strapped a pole to the axle and started shoving. When we finally made it to the top of the hill, 20 jerry cans of water were added to the load and we were ordered to push the barrow up and over the *next* ridge. I have never taken on a harder physical challenge – that barrow was so awkward and heavy and the hill was so steep.

I collapsed. My legs, my arms, my chest, seemingly every muscle in my body, was in complete cramp. After a bit the cramps subsided enough for me to make it down an embankment to the edge of a lake. We were instructed to float the trailer using our gear. Suddenly I was on the ground and couldn't move. I was panicking, terrified, not knowing what the hell was happening to me. The boys did everything they could to alleviate the cramps. They poured water down my throat. I was in great pain.

Luckily, an army ambulance was in the region and they picked me up and got me to the base medical unit. There, they immediately put me on a drip and covered me head to toe in ice to cool down my core temperature which had sky-rocketed dangerously. The doctor told me that I'd come close to doing some serious damage to myself. Because of the seriousness of my condition, I was then taken by ambulance to a Brisbane hospital, where I spent the entire night on a drip, trying to replace the lost fluids. My blood test came back and it showed that I had damaged my kidneys. It took two weeks of bed rest and medical treatment before my body, and blood tests, returned to normal. I missed pre-season training and a trial game before I was passed fit to play.

### GORDEN TALLIS

That camp was so hard. We were crying, broken physically and mentally, suffering sleep deprivation, being woken at 2 am to carry our 20-kilo packs up steep mountainsides. Petero is a big sweater and lost too much body fluid and he was hurting, but he never once complained. He was so mentally tough. He must have known his body was breaking down, yet he never even said a word, never said, 'I'm sick', never took a lighter load, never shirked, just kept going until he collapsed convulsing on the ground with his arms and legs right out of control. He was obviously terrified but remained calm, and never complained or demanded special treatment.

He had to be taken to hospital where he pulled through. It was the same when he broke his arm in a match and didn't say a word about it and kept on playing. Wayne, who, like the rest of us, never even knew Pet's arm was broken, got up him when his busted arm bounced right off the blokes who ran at him. Pet stood there and took it and didn't say a word in his own defence. Afterwards, when Wayne realised what had happened, he was deeply sorry he'd spoken to him that way.

The year before, the Broncos had experienced a form slump after State of Origin and history repeated in 2003. We won nine of our first 11 games, then post-Origin we fell apart and lost 10 of our last 11 games. It was a humiliating fall from grace. Our lowest point was a 40–4 thrashing by the Bulldogs, whose terrific pack, with Steve Price, Willie Mason, Andrew Ryan and Mark O'Meley, had them vying with the Roosters and the Panthers for premiership favouritism.

Our strong start saw us amass enough points to sneak into the finals, but once in we went nowhere and fell 28–18 to the eventual grand final winners, Penrith, in the qualifying final. I missed that game, suspended again, for two weeks, after I pleaded guilty to another accidental high shot.

People often asked me about the Broncos' post-Origin slump. To me there is no secret. The highly physical, highly emotional event that is State of Origin takes a toll on those who play it and when so many Origin players are chosen from a single club, that club obviously will suffer more than a team with no or only a couple of Origin players on its books. From time to time, the Broncos had as many as seven guys playing for the Maroons and others, such as Mick De Vere, played for the Blues.

Wayne and the team would attempt to devise ways to counter the negative effect of Origin on the Broncos but sometimes, as hard as you try, your plans don't work out. That was certainly the case in 2003. It's mental and physical fatigue, it's the letdown after Origin intensity, it's re-acclimatising to the very different style of club footy after the particular demands of Origin. To win consistently in the weeks after Origin, things have to go your way.

Speaking for myself, I do feel depleted after a State of Origin match, and I try to compensate for that by giving the next club game 120 per cent. That has worked for me.

It's a fact, too, that other teams know what Origin players are grappling with and, like sharks, they smell blood in the water and rip in all the harder. I have always believed that the NRL should give a break in the draw to teams like the Broncos and the Storm with a disproportionate number of Origin stars. Perhaps they should grant them a bye the week after to give the players a chance to recover. Perhaps the NRL should stop playing Origin mid-week and hold the games on stand-alone weekends to give the players a week's breather instead of having to back up two days later.

Because of the Origin factor, I rate the Broncos' best win of 2003 our 10–8 victory over the reigning premiers the Roosters, played just two days after our shellacking in Origin II, with Shane, Gordie and me all backing up. I have had many sweet moments in rugby league but one of the very sweetest came at the end of that wonderful match when Shane sent me in for the winning try under the posts.

STATE OF Origin rolled around a few weeks after I'd been suspended for a fortnight for a high shot against one of the Warriors, and once more I was a little concerned that my enforced lay-off might jeopardise my selection. Adding to my anxiety was a statement to the press by Maroon great Gene Miles, who put it out there that I would be wise to lift my game and that my place in the team might not be as safe as most thought:

> There's some good young forwards coming through and there is plenty of competition in the pack. The Broncos have not been setting the world on fire and that has not helped the claims of some of their forwards. Petero is coming back from suspension and he has a month to prove he must retain his position. I'm pretty sure he will do it,

because he has the right attitude. But he is not as devastating as he has been in the past.

I heard you loud and clear, Geno. Immediately things fell back into place on the field. I strung together a number of good games, notably notching a man of the match performance against the strong Bulldogs forwards. Did Wayne Bennett put Gene Miles up to making his comments to motivate me? Stranger things have happened.

As it turned out, I was pleased with my Origin form, though not with the result. New South Wales smashed us in the first two games and we won the consolation dead rubber. This series belonged to our old nemesis Andrew Johns, who was fired up by press reports of a falling out with Blues coach Phil Gould. Gus noted publicly that Johns seemed to have lost his self-confidence and, understandably, Joey took exception and newspapers ran photos of the pair engaged in what the captions insisted, but which Gus and Joey have always denied, was 'heated discussion'.

For whatever reason, Joey was pure magic. In Origin I, which the Blues won 25–12 at Suncorp Stadium, Johns cut us to ribbons. With 10 minutes to play, it was 12–12 – anyone's game. Joey proceeded to set up a try for Craig Wing, kick a field goal, then score a try himself. He was on another level to anyone else on the field.

In Origin II at Telstra, won by New South Wales 27–4, Johns set up a number of tries, kicked seven goals and another field goal. That field goal came at the end of a virtuoso passage of play by Joey. From a restart on his quarter line, he dropkicked the ball far upfield and into touch. The Blues won the ensuing scrum and he hoisted a towering bomb on our quarter line. The ball landed, was knocked back to him by a Blue, and, cool as you please, he kicked the field goal.

We took some heart from our big 36–6 victory in the dead rubber Origin III, and I was very pleased with the way our forwards got square for the pounding we'd taken in the earlier games. That game was also made notable by being the first Origin appearance of Cameron Smith.

I WAS picked on the bench for Australia against the Kiwis in the one-off Test on 25 July in Sydney, which the Kangaroos won 48–6. I was also in the Kangaroo team that toured New Zealand, France and Great Britain at season's end under the captaincy of Darren Lockyer. We won the series against Great Britain 3–0, but the Tests were close and hard-fought, finishing 22–18 (after Adrian Morley was sent off after just 12 seconds for decking Robbie Kearns), 23–20 and 18–12. Any series win is a good series win, but it's so much sweeter when the opposition gives you a tough, grinding contest.

Despite our less than satisfactory season in 2003, I was happy at the Broncos. I felt wanted. At the end-of-season awards night, I was named most consistent player of the year. I believed I had made the right decision to stay.

I had been a little surprised when, mid-year, our new CEO Bruno Cullen announced that because so many players were coming off contract at the club in 2004, players would have to take pay cuts if we were to keep the team together. Still, I remembered Wayne's promise to me that I would be paid what a forward leader deserved if I hung in there, and didn't worry too much.

In fact, I told the media:

I'm one of the old men now at 27 and I want to play the rest of my footy at the Broncos. Hopefully I will secure a contract for the seasons to come, but I will have to work hard to keep some of the young blokes out of the front row. I'm just glad to be at the Broncos. They gave me my start, so it would be pretty hard to turn my back on them.

ONE OF the best things about rugby league is the people it attracts. For every pest and drunken yob who gives our code a bad name, there are a thousand good and big-hearted souls most people never hear about. These are the players who live their lives quietly and decently, those who visit children's hospitals and raise money for the ill, the mums and dads who sacrifice their time to volunteer as coaches, referees, administrators, drivers, gear-washers, line-markers, who fork out for jerseys and boots.

Let me tell you about one of the good guys. I met Dean Clifford around 1996 when he was a kid, and he would be about 30 now. He was born with *Epidermolysis bullosa*, a disease of the connective tissues of the body that makes the skin incredibly fragile and sensitive and causes separation of the skin and painful blisters and sores, notably on the hands and feet, though they can occur all over the body. It can also cause muscle deterioration. To avoid contact, a sufferer has to be, as the saying goes, wrapped in cotton wool, and so Dean is known as 'the cotton wool kid'.

In spite of this terrible condition, despite the constant pain, this strong man lives a busy and productive and inspiring life. He is a tremendous motivational speaker who has addressed school kids and prime ministers; he has written a book about his life; and is business and marketing officer at Ken Mills Toyota. He is also national ambassador of ACE (Australia's Disability Employment Services peak body), helping promote employment awareness to businesses and communities for people with disabilities. In 2000 he carried the Olympic torch for a 600-metre leg near his hometown, Kingaroy. Just being around this guy, who doctors said would be lucky to see six years of age, enriches my life. This is the bloke who can bench-press 130 kg. Under the tutelage of Brad Thorn and then Nick Kenny, he would turn himself into a powerhouse in the gym. He is truly an inspiration. It's been good to reconnect with him as a regular at our weekly team BBQs, which he comes to to show his support.

Typically, Dean says we Broncos inspire him and that rugby league gives him release from his pain. Let me tell you, if we inspire him, it's a two-way street. Every time I'm with him I think that, sure, players go through pain and adversity in a football game but that's nothing compared to what he contends with every single minute of every day. If I find myself doing it tough, I remember Dean and pick myself up and get on with it.

It hurts to hear people trash rugby league ignorantly and indiscriminately when I know there are fine people like Dean Clifford on the scene.

# 5

# The hardest head in rugby league

Every child is special. Your first-born changes your life forever. Our first child Tallulah was born in 2004. Bonnie and I had always planned to have a family, and after we were married we set about making it happen. Joy, excitement . . . terror, all came rushing when I first laid eyes on our beautiful daughter and lifted her high. We christened our daughter Tallulah because Bonnie and I loved the name, and it was also the name of the bobsled in one of our favourite movies, *Cool Runnings,* about a group of Jamaican bobsledders who surprised the world by competing in the 1988 Winter Olympics. We had other names picked out, but once we laid eyes on her, we knew no other name was suitable.

Bonnie, Tallulah and I were featured in the papers, with the Gold Coast *Bulletin* congratulating us then adding, 'Don't take it the wrong way, Petero – but we hope Tallulah looks like mum!' There was a baby boom at the Broncos in 2004: Gorden Tallis, Ben Ikin, Michael Ryan, Tonie Carroll and I all became dads.

I felt a heavy responsibility to give Tallulah a secure and happy life, and I thought once again how I would be a different type of husband to Bonnie and father to Tallulah than Dad had been to Mum and me and my sisters when he left us. No one knows how things will pan out – life happens and the best-intentioned plans often come unstuck. I'm quite sure my father had no intention of breaking up our family. I know that I would never hurt mine.

Both Bonnie's and my parents – including Dad, who is a big softy around his grandkids – were overjoyed when Tallulah was born. A constant stream of family and friends flowed into our house to see her.

As it happened, I had just been picked to play for Australia against New Zealand in Newcastle – it was my first time in the Kangaroos run-on side – but I had torn my medial ligament again in the previous match, against the Cowboys, and was ruled unfit to play. I was bitterly disappointed, but glad to stay home instead and be with Tallulah in the first days of her life.

I TURNED 27 in 2004 and was well and truly a senior Bronco . . . although still behind Gorden and Shane in the forwards pecking order. This would be our captain Gordie's final season in the NRL and also the season when, after the teenage fullback sensation Karmichael Hunt came into first grade, Darren Lockyer moved permanently from fullback to five-eighth, a position where he could better exert his authority. Wayne's plan was for Locky to succeed Gorden as skipper in 2005. To give an idea of the lie of the land in 2004, our back line, as well as Locky and Karmichael, boasted Brent Tate, Mick De Vere, Craig Frawley, Shaun Berrigan and Benny Ikin. Packing down with Gorden, Shane and me in the forwards were Tonie Carroll, Carl Webb, Brad Meyers, Casey McGuire, Neville Costigan and Corey Parker.

Corey made his debut in round three . . . in sensational circumstances. When he replaced Shane Webcke, who'd been KO'd by the Tigers' Bryce Gibbs at Campbelltown, Corey ran onto the field before Shane departed. We won the game but were stripped of our two premiership points for having 14 men on the field. Sanity prevailed and we were given them back two weeks later.

On the verge of first-grade selection that year were David Stagg, Tom Learoyd-Lahrs and a 19-year-old wild-haired tearaway forward named Sam Thaiday.

The rugby league world knows what a fine coach Wayne Bennett is, and I'd like to say here that he was responsible in so many ways for my development into an elite club, state and Australian player. He was fair but demanding and didn't praise cheaply, so when he kept picking me in the run-on side and giving me added responsibility on and off the field, I knew I was going well. I understood that he hadn't been convinced about me early on, back when he was calling me Cyril Connell's love child. He just couldn't see what Cyril could see in me. By persevering, learning, improving, I gradually changed his opinion, and without knowing exactly when it happened, he accepted me. I wasn't the reticent and awkward kid anymore. I had paid my dues. Such was my respect for Wayne that I played my heart out for him every week. He created an environment of excellence at the Broncos, as he has done at every club he has coached. Most who have played under him are better players and men for the experience.

I had always been one of the shy guys in the team, maybe the shyest. I was happy to take a back seat while the more confident players drove. In 2004, because I had earned the confidence of the coach and my teammates, I was invited to take more of a front seat and be a co-driver, with Gorden, Shane and Locky, of the team. I began speaking up at training and offered my opinions on the field.

Rugby league links communities. Even before the 2004 season began, the fans left us in no doubt that a repeat of 2003 was not acceptable and that they expected us to, first, make the semis and then win the premiership. We attended a fan day in the Roma Street Parkland, and hundreds of Bronco supporters decked out in maroon and gold were there. These fans have no qualms about telling you what's on their minds, and what they were demanding of us was a memorable season. The weight of expectation was heavy on our shoulders all year and got heavier as the semis loomed. It's always an uneasy feeling you have after a loss. You feel like you have let down so many people. When you win, everyone rides the high with you. It's not just at the Broncos. The late great coach Jack Gibson once said that when he coached Parramatta, absenteeism in the district would rise 20 per cent on the Monday after a defeat. The supporters who lived and breathed their rugby league team were simply too depressed, or hung-over after drowning their sorrows, to drag themselves out of bed to go to work. That's the price of being a true fan. The highs are stratospheric, and the lows are very low.

It's history that we didn't win the comp that year. We had a largely successful season, if any season when you don't win the premiership can be classed as successful, with 18 wins, seven losses and a draw, before bowing out with two straight losses in the semis.

My start to the year was hampered when I suffered a grade two medial ligament strain in a trial against the Storm. I returned to the field, probably sooner than I should have, for the season opener against the Warriors.

In that opening match of the competition proper, a 28–20 win for us over the Warriors at Suncorp, Monty Betham broke his arm on my head. Monty was a more-than-competent, if occasionally hot-tempered, hooker for the Warriors and the Kiwis, and when I was struggling with two or three tacklers, he saw his chance to race in from behind and stiff-arm me. *Crack!* Monty's five-week suspension gave his shattered arm a chance to heal.

The natives were restless at that stage of the season. After the opening round alone, as well as Monty, Matt Utai, Mick Crocker, Paul Gallen, Luke Bailey and Micheal Luck were all charged with on-field indiscretions.

In round five, against the Roosters, came another unfortunate incident. I hit the ball up from the kick-off fast and hard. Their forward Ned Catic led the Roosters' defensive rush. He lined me up. I stepped. Ned didn't have time to adjust and his head hit my knee. He was knocked out and I was upset to see Ned, a wholehearted player, convulsing on the grass. Thank God he recovered.

Sometimes things like this happen in a heavy contact sport such as rugby league. Pretty much the same thing that happened to Ned would take place in the Indigenous All Stars versus NRL All Stars game in 2011 when I trampled over Indigenous centre Beau Champion, his head hit my hip and he was KO'd. There was zero malice. I aim to run hard. If a tackle is properly completed, it's rare for the defender to get hurt.

There was nothing I could have done to prevent the injuries to Martin Lang, Ned Catic, Jason Ryles, Monty Betham, Simon Bonnetti and Beau Champion. Still, I continued to get into strife with refs when I accidentally hit a guy in the head when I was making a tackle. Our defensive coach, Peter Ryan, attempted to limit the damage I was doing to rivals by adjusting my defensive technique. I'm a tall man, 1.93 metres (six feet four inches), and if an attacker ducks when I'm about to tackle him I am likely to catch him around the head rather than the chest, as intended. Peter had me hitting lower, so that even if a player fell into the tackle at worst I'd connect high on his chest, which is legal.

It was a mark of my new standing in the team that I had graduated to be taking the first hit-up in a set of six now. In an early 2004 match, my hit-ups gained 200 metres of ground, the most I had ever made in a game. When a reporter asked me about my increased work rate, I replied: 'As a front-rower there is not too much to it, work hard and push through the fatigue. I am a senior player and it is up to me to show intensity and lead the way. I know Webby will always turn up and take the work rate, so I have been trying to match him.'

As I mentioned, just as Tallulah was born I was due to play for Australia, my first time in the starting line-up, but a recurrence of my medial ligament strain in our win against the Cowboys in round six meant that that elusive honour would have to wait for another day. Steve Price took my place. It was a testament to the Broncos' good form so far that six of us were selected in the Kangaroos team: Locky was five-eighth and captain, and Mick De Vere, Shane Webcke, Shaun Berrigan and Brent Tate were also named.

AFTER FIVE weeks in a leg brace, I was happy when the Queensland selectors overlooked my lack of match fitness and brought me straight into the State of Origin team. The renowned trainer and conditioner Kelvin Giles whipped the Broncos into shape in the early days and now in 2004 we had a trainer and conditioner named Steve Nance as resident torturer at our Red Hill headquarters. Steve, who was dedicated to improving our performance and speeding up our recovery rate after injury, was ahead of the game and always trying new techniques with us.

I was living proof of his effectiveness when he had me back on the field in an unheard-of five weeks. Steve had worked me harder while I was in rehab than if I'd been playing. Under him I completed long sessions in the gym on the cardio equipment, physically replicating the cardio loads that the boys on the field were experiencing.

As soon as my knee injury healed I was ready to play for Queensland in Origin I and then backed up for a 60-minute stint against the Dragons two nights later.

In Origin I, we suffered a heartbreaking golden point loss. The score was 8–8, two tries apiece, at full-time, and after Blues halfback Craig Gower missed with three drop goal attempts, their centre Shaun Timmins nailed one from 37 metres out to win the match. Mark O'Meley played a blinder for the Blues.

We won Origin II at Suncorp 22–18, thanks to our forwards stepping up to fight O'Meley's fire with fire, and a classic try to Billy Slater. They still show Billy's four-pointer on Origin highlight reels and it never fails to take my breath away. On our 40-metre line, Locky grubber-kicked to the left. A lurking Slater, barely on-side, picked it up on the halfway line, veered right to bamboozle the defence, then changed direction to the left and kicked the ball for himself, over the head of Blues fullback Anthony Minichiello. The ball sat up on the New South Wales tryline. Billy pounced on it to score. The game was ours. Billy's try will always be remembered as one of Origin's greatest.

The decider was at Telstra Stadium, where they towelled us up 36–14, inspired by Brad Fittler, whom coach Phil

Gould had coaxed from representative retirement. To say that we were in despair afterwards does no justice to the way we felt.

Jason Ryles had been brought back into the New South Wales side for that deciding Origin game, and the papers tried to whip up a bit of aggro by harping on about how Ryles had been injured when tackling me the previous year. We both played along. 'I'm not intimidated by Petero,' said Jason. I shot back, right on cue, sounding a little like a pro wrestler: 'He's going to be after a square-up and I'm looking forward to the challenge. I'm not into talking tough . . . but I'll react to anything that happens on the field. I just go out there to hit blokes, and if they get hurt, well . . .'

Of course, as usually always happens in these media-orchestrated feuds, there was no blow-up. Jason and I played it hard and fair and after the game he was one of the first to offer his commiserations.


THERE'S NO place for filthy play on the rugby league field. It was in a second-round clash between the Melbourne Storm and Wests Tigers when Storm forward Danny Williams king-hit Mark O'Neill from behind. The judiciary rejected Williams' excuse that his post-traumatic amnesia contributed to him belting Mark and suspended him for 18 weeks, effectively ending his NRL career. I thought that was fair enough and, like some of my Bronco teammates, had no qualms about standing up and saying so. 'Williams deserved his suspension,' I declared, when once I would not even have been asked for my opinion. 'What he did was unacceptable.' Shane Webcke, who abhors vicious play, weighed in, 'Williams got what he deserved. Whether he had a brain explosion, or whatever it was, it was of a bygone era.' Even Gorden Tallis, who had been involved in his share on man-on-man, face-to-face on-field blues, drew a distinction to his kind of stoush and a sneaky king-hit. 'A one-on-one fight in rugby league is fair . . . but when someone's not looking and they get hit in the side of the head or the back of the head, everyone has a problem with that.'

As one who had been grapple-tackled many times when playing against the Storm, I spoke out against the practice that year. Against Melbourne, I had been grabbed around the throat so hard I couldn't breathe, my arms had been pinioned in so-called chicken-wing tackles, and Storm blokes had driven their knees hard and painfully into my calf muscles to stop me playing the ball at speed.

Sure, I'd had my own issues with high tackles, but I didn't feel I was being hypocritical by speaking out against tactics that I believed were not in the spirit of the game. With only one or two exceptions, when I was rattled or annoyed, my high tackles were usually the result of mistiming or the attacker ducking into the line of fire, whereas a grapple-tackle is a premeditated ploy, practised at training under the tutelage of a wrestling or ju-jitsu coach, to illegally slow down the play by tangling up the ball-carrier. Such tackles can cause serious spinal damage, break arms and legs and damn-near asphyxiate a victim.

I told the media that grapple-tackling should be outlawed and that if anyone ever grapple-tackled me, or any member of the Broncos' team, there would be retaliation. It was awkward making these threats, because the coach of the Storm, Craig Bellamy, had been performance director and assistant coach to Wayne Bennett at Brisbane and a mate. Some of the team's stars, such as Cameron Smith, were Queensland State of Origin teammates.

When I raised the issue with Cam during Origin, he

looked a bit sheepish, and it looked to me that the grapple-tacklers were acting under instructions. The Storm were, and are, such a good team that they have no need to resort to grapple-tackling. They are brilliantly and meticulously drilled by one of the best coaches of all time, and are jam-packed with champions capable of carrying out his instructions to the letter.

Before I climb down off my soap-box, let me tell you that another pet hate of mine is when a player takes a dive to win a penalty or have an opponent sin-binned or sent off. The great thing about the rugby codes is that it is a point of honour to play on when you are hurt and never give an opponent the benefit of knowing that he has damaged you. You get knocked down and somehow you drag your-self back to your feet and soldier on. Our game enshrines this kind of toughness. The whole idea of faking injury, of pretending to be unconscious or falling to earth in a spectacular swan dive like soccer players do makes me feel nauseous. Sadly, the practice has crept into rugby league in recent years. Diving is alien to the spirit of our game. Those who do it, and those who coach them to do it, should be rubbed out.

I CAPTAINED the Broncos for the first time in round 24 against the Wests Tigers at Suncorp Stadium, after Gorden was suspended and his deputy Locky was injured. It was my 141st game for Brisbane. When Wayne told me I'd be skipper, a big smile spread across my dial. Apart from it being the first time in my life that I had captained a team, *any* team, I was stepping into enormous boots because the Broncos had had some wonderful captains in Wally Lewis, Allan Langer, Gene Miles, Kevin Walters, Gorden

Tallis . . . Now I would be leading the team onto the field, even if only for a week or two. Bonnie was there with Tallulah and our families in the crowd of over 26,000 to see me take the Broncos' reins in our 24–20 win. I had a dig at Webby after the game because I had chalked up a win in my first go at being skipper while he was 0–5 in his captaincy outings.

In our final competition round match, a demoralising 46–20 loss to the Panthers, my hard head was at it again. Joel Clinton and I clashed noggins and he was knocked out. The Sydney *Daily Telegraph*'s Paul Kent had some fun when he wrote:

> Today's news flash is that they have finally acknowledged the one element harder than diamond. Monty Betham broke his arm on it earlier this season . . . Then came Joel Clinton taking it up last Friday and, next thing you know, big Joel fades to black. The element in question is Petero Civoniceva's head – the place where bones go to die, where consciousness takes a nap . . .
>
> The Broncos make toughness their trade and none comes tougher in their pack than Civoniceva. NRL rivals overwhelmingly vote him as the game's hardest hitter. He ranks towards the top when it comes to being the hardest player to tackle. And Civoniceva, with the cheerful malevolence of the born hitter, loves nothing better than creating the big hurt. 'There's a great feeling of satisfaction,' he says, 'especially when you rip in and come out the other end and you're OK and he's in a bit of trouble. It's the best feeling you can have, I suppose.'

I was satisfied with my form in 2004. It was definitely my strongest season since coming into grade. At the end of season awards night, I was astonished and happy to win the Paul Morgan Broncos Player of the Year award, the Players' Player award, and the Best Forward award. Being the Paul Morgan medal winner made me especially proud, and also sad because Paul, of course, had passed away. I knew him well at the club and also when his son was in the hospital bed next to me when I broke my arm and Paul came to visit. I was always struck by the way he, who was a founder of the Broncos and a successful businessman, and Cyril Connell, his former teacher and Bronco partner-in-crime, took the time to encourage us young blokes. They made us feel wanted and part of the outfit.

Such kindness and concern for our welfare left a lasting impression on me and I also try to make time for others, no matter who they are or what they do. I think that's very much part of who I am now. Rugby league gave me so much and by saying hello to a fan, shaking their hands, doing them a them a favour if I can, and listening to what's on their minds, apart from being enjoyable, is a way to put something back into the game. Some people only realise when they've retired what a blessing it is to play this code of football at a high level and actually be paid for doing so. I can say that, thanks to Paul Morgan and Cyril Connell, I understood that from the start. Paul's death in 2001 and Cyril's in 2009 have left a hole in the heart of the Broncos that will never be filled.

I was offered and signed a new three-year deal in 2004 that took me to the end of the 2007 season. My contract improved, although it was still not what I could have earned at any other club at that stage of my career. I consoled myself with the knowledge that Wayne had told me that my time would come.

•

I WAS picked in the Australian Tri-Nations squad for the end-of-season series against New Zealand and Great Britain, but before that I had a rendezvous with the Kumuls of Papua New Guinea in an Australian invitational side at Dairy Farmers Stadium in Townsville. Of our team, only Jason Ryles and I had played against the Kumuls before, in a Test in Boroko, near Port Moresby, in 2001, and so we felt qualified to warn our teammates to expect pain and bruises.

From front row to fullback, they are extremely physical and anyone playing against Papua New Guinea knows they are going to be sick and sore. The Kumuls bodies are as hard as steel, they have no fear, and like to hit, hit so very hard. I found it took me longer to recover from a game against the Kumuls than most other sides.

That 2001 match in Boroko was an experience I will never forget. They take their rugby league very seriously in Papua New Guinea. It's the country's No. 1 sport. When we got off the plane, we were mobbed like rock stars. We had heard they were fanatical fans, but experiencing their passion first-hand was unbelievable. There to greet us at Port Moresby was a sea of fans stretching as far as the eye could see. The cheering was deafening. Every time one of us waved back the crowd would erupt. Our bus was protected by a squad of security guards with lethal-looking automatic weapons. It felt like the entire country was there running beside our bus, yelling and cheering, those beautiful smiles, tapping on the windows. It blew us away to see how passionate and knowledgeable the people of PNG were about the game. They knew all about our careers. It seems we were very much heroes to many of them. In what must have been a world first, they even cheered the referee, Bill Harrigan. To get to the game, families had walked for days from the Highlands to Port Moresby; then at full-time they turned around and walked all the way home.

The Kumul players, too, were polite and friendly at the official reception . . . then they got us out on the field and bashed us up to a soundtrack of the screaming crowd, the barking of security dogs, the ka-boom of firecrackers and, I'm pretty certain, the crackle of gunfire. The field was wreathed in thick, acrid smoke from the fireworks and brush fires. We won the game 54–12, but at the end were very much the worse for wear. We lost kilos in the 40-degree heat and there wasn't one of us who didn't ache for a fortnight.

In the 2004 game in Townsville, we won 70–22, but, as usual, came off Dairy Farmers Stadium battered and busted.

At season's end, the Kangaroos went to England for the Tri-Nations Series. I was chosen in the starting line-up for the Tests. I had to pinch myself that I was now a regular in the run-on side. We were victorious in the series, winning the final 44–4 against Great Britain after they had beaten us 12–8 in a qualifying game. Darren Lockyer was stupendous in that match. Our hooker Danny Buderus said of him, 'He is one of those players you will tell your kids you played with.'

I was especially pleased to win that Tri-Nations Series because Wayne, who coached the team, had been under fire from some New South Wales-based pundits for playing five Broncos in the Test side – Darren Lockyer, Shane Webcke, Tonie Carroll, Shaun Berrigan and me – despite Brisbane's poor end to the season. Our emphatic victory in the final justified Wayne's faith in us. A proud man, Wayne was offended and angered by the accusations of favouritism.

My last footy act for the year was joining with Wendell

Sailor and Danny Buderus to call for a ceiling of 30 games a season to help avoid players being burned out by the arduous club and representative schedule. I played 32 official matches in 2004 and my body was feeling the strain as I took my two-month off-season break. Willie Mason notched 36 games that year, Andrew Ryan, Anthony Minichiello and Willie Tonga played 34, Nathan Hindmarsh, who, as we all know, exhausts himself each game with his high work rate, played 33. Nothing came of our plea, apart from a few critics saying, 'They're well paid. They should shut up and play.'

I HAD never looked forward so much to an off-season as at the end of 2004. Apart from it being a chance to have some running repairs to my 28-year-old body, I could finally spend time with Tallulah. For that precious hiatus it was Tallulah, Bonnie and me, with welcome appearances from our family and close friends. I changed nappies, and rose from bed in the wee hours to settle Tallulah while Bonnie got some much-needed and deserved rest. It was beaches, parks, barbecues, sleeping in. We could leave Tallulah with grateful grandparents for a couple of hours while we went to the movies. A baby can deplete a parent's energy and be the only focus of attention, and it was so important, Bonnie and I found, to do things together, maybe have a night out once a week, and talk about things other than Tallulah and footy, and keep the relationship strong. It was a joyous Christmas at the Civonicevas'. Training and playing was only a few weeks away, so we made every moment count.

Listening to music relaxes my mind and body, so the CD player was on a lot that off-season. I love all music, with no real preference of genre. Everything from rock, RnB, blues, reggae, heavy metal to rap and hip hop. They're all there on my iPod. I love going to live gigs and musical festivals. I've been lucky enough to see AC/DC, Red Hot Chilli Peppers, U2 and Ben Harper, to name a few. But one of the best was Bruce Springsteen and the E Street Band. He blew me away. He was on-stage, going full belt, for three hours. The Boss's incredible energy and the way he engaged with the crowd were phenomenal. As well as seeing live music, Bonnie and I go to musicals, when family commitments allow. I get a thrill experiencing talented people at their best, whether they're in the arts, sport or whatever. I'm envious of those talented musicians, though!

Which, to my embarrassment, brings me to my drum kit. I have a passion for music, but unfortunately that doesn't mean I can play it. I dreamed when I bought my drum kit that it would be a simple matter of sitting down and pounding away. I found that was not the case. I played for a bit, probably getting worse instead of improving. I couldn't get myself together enough to have lessons. Bonnie hated the racket I made. It gave her headaches and woke up Tallulah. I took the hint. Soon my drum kit was in the garage covered in dust. I counted my losses and sold it to a friend. Maybe I'll learn the guitar in years to come. I have visions of family get-togethers at picnics or over a few beers with my mates, me playing the blues – perhaps some great old Cold Chisel, Bob Marley or Springsteen songs – and singing and the family joining in. I think I'll be waiting a while.

IT WAS strange, and a little sad, to kick off season 2005 without Gorden Tallis, who had retired at the end of 2004. He was the guts and soul of our team with his aggression and refusal to ever give in, and would not easily be replaced.

Wayne made it clear to Shane and me that he expected us to lift our game even further to compensate for losing Gordie. Our job was made easier when Brad Thorn returned to the Broncos from rugby union and young Sam Thaiday, who we all were confident would be an Origin and Test player before too long, became a first-grade regular. Like Gordie, Sammy was hard, intimidating and played the game at a million miles an hour. Another thing Sam had in common with Gordie was he was a decent, funny and fiercely loyal guy who was terrific for team morale. As Gordie was finishing his career, Sam was just beginning to realise his great potential.

Darren Lockyer took over as captain. He was by then the best five-eighth in rugby league and an Origin and Test regular. He had gone from being an unknown to an elite player virtually overnight, and this is a testament to his temperament as much as his ability. He had steely determination, never panicked, never conceded defeat until the final whistle, and I have never known a player to pull a seemingly-lost game out of the fire in the dying moments as regularly as Darren. He did it for Brisbane, Queensland and Australia so many times. Out on the field, he was beautiful to watch. He didn't run so much as glide; his pass was the sweetest in the game; his kicks were pinpoint perfect. He was also tough. No player has been singled out for rough treatment as much as Darren, as rival teams figured the best way to stop the Broncos was to hammer our playmaker. Many times he got absolutely smashed, but bounced right back up to continue controlling the game. He could read a game so well, made the right decisions, and seemed to have so much time to work his magic. And, you know, he was the same modest, serious, self-effacing bloke as captain of Australia as he was when he played in the Broncos lower grades. He never changed, despite every award in rugby league being heaped upon him.

We had a talented side with Locky, Shane and Sammy, Brad Thorn, Tonie Carroll, Justin Hodges, Brent Tate, Karmichael Hunt and Dane Carlaw. Tom Learoyd-Lahrs and Neville Costigan were up-and-comers. But we under-performed, winning just 15 of our 26 competition games, and then being beaten by the Storm 24–18 in the qualifying final before Wests Tigers ended our season in the semi-final.

It was a treat to have Brad Thorn back in our colours. I'd missed his skill and toughness on the field and his mate-ship off it. Reporter Greg Davis wrote in Brisbane's *Sunday Mail* that, like ebony and ivory in the Paul McCartney–Stevie Wonder song, Brad and I were in 'perfect harmony': 'Enforcers on the field and quiet family men off the paddock, the longtime best mates will gladly shoulder a heavy workload' for Brisbane and Queensland. Davis quoted Brad:

> Along with Shane Webcke, Petero is the guy I've enjoyed playing with. You know he's always looking out for you. He's a mate as well as a teammate and we both perform similar roles for the Broncos and Queensland so it's great to know you are not alone out there. We used to hang out a lot when we were young and we are now raising families at the same time . . . we are laid back and share a laugh.

Brad then said to forget ebony and ivory, we were more like Crockett and Tubbs, the cops in the TV show *Miami Vice*. I think he was joking.

●

IN THE Anzac Test against New Zealand, there was a battle royal for the vacant starting front-row spot after Shane Webcke's crook knee saw him pull the pin on his representative career so he could give the Broncos his all. The contenders for the two run-on prop spots were Luke Bailey, Jason Ryles, Steve Price, Mark O'Meley and myself. It was a close thing, but Steve got one prop's position and I won the other. Mark and Jason were on the bench. Shane gave me his blessing to be Australia's forward leader in his stead:

> I don't think Petero's got any stepping up to do. He'll play the way he always does. He doesn't need to be putting pressure on himself. Over the last couple of seasons, he's really developed into a top player. Some players think they have to be world-beaters, but they don't. They just have to be consistent, and that's what he is.

Mark O'Meley, with whom I'd had many physical encounters in club footy, said he believed that Pricey and I, while neither of us were firebrands like him and Jason, were a good choice to take on the Kiwis' hard-nuts Ruben Wiki, David Kidwell, Paul Rauhihi, Roy Asotasi and Frank Pritchard in the early stages of the Test. He said:

> Obviously it will be physical in the middle, but these days you don't pick guys for their ability to fight. Petero and Steve are as hard as they come. Toughness is measured on being able to cart the ball over the advantage line again and again no matter how hard you get hit or how tired you are. Those two are warriors in that department. We don't need a designated enforcer. Petero and Tonie Carroll intimidate with their tackling.

Before we played the Kiwis, Steve Price and I had an issue of our own to resolve. We both wanted to wear the No. 10 jersey. One of us would have to relent and play in Shane's old No. 8 jumper. So, in the time-tested method of resolving disputes, we played scissors–paper–rock. I won.

### STEVE PRICE

Petero and I both grew as men and footballers in the shadow of Shane Webcke. Our friendship came out of our fierce rivalry to be picked in the rep games alongside him. We had some pretty willing club encounters. Then when Shane retired and Petero and I became regular front-rowers for Queensland and Australia, we stopped smashing each other and concentrated on demolishing the opposition.

Anyway, in the end it didn't matter. Maybe a little of Shane had rubbed off on the jersey, because Steve played a blinder in our 32–16 win at Suncorp. He had a bit to prove, having been knocked out in his debut Test against New Zealand back in 1998. This time it was him putting the monster hits on his opponents. That game was really the start of a long and successful representative front-row partnership between Pricey and me for Queensland and Australia.

SHANE'S BULL-LIKE running and stiff defence were missed in State of Origin that year. There was another changing of the old guard when Michael Hagan took over from Wayne Bennett as coach. Things began well enough when we were victorious in Origin I, though only after the game went into golden point time when the scores were locked at 20-all. Matt Bowen intercepted a pass from Blues halfback Brett

Kimmorley to Matt King and scored, to give us a 24–20 win.

That was pretty much as good as it got for the Maroons that year. Andrew Johns, 31 years of age then, returned in Origin II after seven weeks out with a broken jaw. He chewed us up and spat us out. New South Wales won that match 32–22 to square the series. In that game, I thought referee Steve Clark was playing a 13-metre rule, rather than 10 metres, which gave Mick Crocker, whose job it was to pressure Andrew Johns's kicking and passing game, no chance of getting up into Joey's face.

The Blues finished us off 32–10 at Suncorp. Mick Crocker and I were both under instructions from coach Hagan to move up fast and deprive Andrew Johns of space, and we tackled him hard. One shot I put on Joey in the 19th minute made him slump to the ground. This hit, and all the others we put on him, didn't prevent him having a hand in the first six New South Wales tries. That's what truly great players can do.

The record crowd of 52,496 left the ground under a collective black cloud. That cloud was also in evidence in the Maroons' dressing room, and not just because we'd lost the game and the series. That 2005 series loss was our third in a row. Mick Crocker, Carl Webb and Pricey, who was man of the match in game one and missed games two and three, were great, but defeat is not tolerated in Queensland, and everyone's job, we all realised, was on the line.

DESPERATE THAT the Broncos didn't succumb again to the dreaded post-Origin slump, Wayne demanded more aggression from the Bronco forwards. We responded by overpowering the Melbourne Storm's star-studded side

28–15 and, as *Rugby League Week* noted in its match report:

> The 'get-aggro' policy was evident against the Storm last Sunday as the Broncos' squeaky-clean engine room broke from their ultra-professional but robotic mould to inspire a comeback victory. Brad Thorn stood toe-to-toe with Matt King after a dust-up at the play-the-ball, Webcke was reported for a lifting tackle on Jake Webster, and Civoniceva lined up opponents like clay pigeon targets.

I had damaged my shoulder in Origin III and now was playing hurt. I missed a number of games in that disastrous back end of the season. In the matches I did get onto the field for, I was stand-in skipper because we had so many other guys out with shoulder and leg injuries. Gone from the team, just when they were needed most, were Darren Lockyer, Shane Webcke, Justin Hodges, our halfback Brett Seymour, Dane Carlaw, Corey Parker, Berrick Barnes and Casey McGuire. In the end, we were beaten by injuries as much as by the other sides. The Broncos who were healthy pulled their weight and others' too, and none more so than Brad Thorn and Sam Thaiday.

The Melbourne Storm's grapple-tackling tactic reared its ugly head in the days before our qualifying final match against Craig Bellamy's boys. We were on our guard because there'd been a number of blues in the Storm's match against the North Queensland Cowboys the week before, with Cowboy Carl Webb KO'ing Storm second-rower Ryan Hoffman after Ryan had grappled Carl around the neck.

I took the opportunity to apply a little pressure on Melbourne by appealing to the ref via the media to police the practice in our match. Once more, I warned that if anyone grapple-tackled me I would not take it lying down, but grapple them right back. I told reporters:

> As a player, it frustrates you. They go overboard. When a tackle blocks your airway, it is going a bit far. The best way to get them is to do it back to them. If the ref says they are playing within the rules with these tackles, then you have to. Melbourne can swear they don't do it all they want, but the evidence is there. Their last bloke in always has control of the head.

In the end, the game was fairly clean. We lost 24–18, and took solace that we had played better than we had for a while. We had a do-or-die date with Wests Tigers in the elimination semi the following weekend.

I was a little distracted that week because Bonnie and I became parents for the second time when our daughter Ruby entered the world. I didn't think I could ever feel as happy again as I did when Tallulah was born, but when Ruby arrived my joy was just as immense. The wonderful thing about parenthood is that every child you bring into the world is the greatest. I stayed at home until the last minute loving my new baby daughter and helping Bonnie where I could, then flew to Sydney for the semi at Aussie Stadium. Unfortunately, the Broncos had run out of gas and fit players, and we were unceremoniously dumped out of the comp, 34–6, by the eventual premiers, Wests Tigers, led by Scott Prince and Benji Marshall.

Despite our ordinary season, it was terrific to see Shane Webcke win the Paul Morgan Player of the Year award and the Players' Player gong at the presentation evening. I was voted Best Forward again and I also won Hit of the Year for a big tackle on Newcastle's Steve Simpson in round 13.

Sam Thaiday was Most Improved Player and Brad Thorn was Most Consistent.

FIVE DAYS later, on 7 October 2005, there was a Night of the Long Knives at our club. After another season when we didn't play up to our potential, losing our last seven games straight, Wayne reacted savagely by sacking three of the Broncos' favourite sons. Fired were two assistant coaches: our former skipper, the very popular Kevin Walters, and Broncos and Kangaroo champion Glenn Lazarus; and performance co-ordinator ex-Queensland and Kangaroo star Gary Belcher. He hired as assistant coaches Ivan Henjak, Allan Langer and Paul Green. Peter Ryan was defensive coach, the new performance director was Dean Benton, who had been mentored by Kelvin Giles, and Jeremy Hickman was rehabilitation co-ordinator.

As Darren Lockyer put it so well in his autobiography, 'Around the club, it was as if there had been a death in the family. No one was speaking. There were heads down everywhere.' Every player felt a little responsible for the demise of our mates. None of us saw the sackings coming, and they reinforced to us that modern rugby league could be just as brutal off the field as it was on it. Having to get rid of men he had liked and respected for many years, and with whom he had shared so many wonderful moments, because he had come to believe that it was in the interests of the Broncos to do so, tore Wayne up inside. At the time, he put on a typically stoic face.

It was only when I read his 2010 autobiography, *The Man in the Mirror*, that I realised how hard it was for Wayne to do what he did:

I have to say this was my most traumatic time at the club. It was very, very difficult and I nearly left myself. The reason I didn't go was that I knew we had to change and I didn't think there was anyone more capable than me of orchestrating that change. If I thought there was I would have stepped aside . . . It was just so sad. We have all got on with our lives but that will always be among the lowest days of my coaching career . . . As always, I did what I thought was in the best interests of the Broncos. It hurt some guys who were really close to me, I understand that, but I still had to do what I believed was right.

What happened between Wayne and me in 2007 was perhaps easier to understand in the light of the events of October 2005. For him, the welfare of the club that employed him as head coach came first. It would happen with me . . . just as it happened with Kevvy, Gary and Glenn, and had happened with the great Wally Lewis back in 1990, when Wayne found him surplus to requirements. It's professional sport. Clubs have to keep changing. Nothing lasts forever. That doesn't mean that hearts are not broken.

Back in those traumatic days at the end of 2005, as a senior player I was asked to front the media. I told the press pack that I felt for the guys who lost their jobs because we were a tight group. We were under no illusions that there was a simple mantra at the Broncos: perform or be moved on. We needed to change things because the last couple of years had been disappointing in the way we had finished. But we couldn't just rest on changes in the staff. [As players] we all had to have a good look at what was going on and hold ourselves accountable. We couldn't blame any one man. As a group we had to take ownership of our results. The new staff would change our focus but the buck stopped with us.

•

THE SACKINGS at the Broncos weren't my final trauma of the year. I still don't think I have totally got over our 24–0 thrashing at the hands of the Kiwis in the final of the 2005 Tri-Nations series at Elland Road in Leeds. Was Wayne, who coached the Kangaroos, still preoccupied over the Broncos' tribulations? It didn't seem as though it was playing on his mind through our Tri-Series campaign in England. Still, with Wayne, you never really know what's going on behind his poker face.

What I will say is that, in 2005, I felt the Kangaroos were complacent in our preparation. We did not respect the Kiwis as their form and results deserved. They had a fine team led by the formidable and inspirational Ruben Wiki. They were primed for battle, we were not, and we got our backsides kicked. They went into the game with a siege mentality, prepared to do whatever it took to win. We were lulled into a false sense of security due to the way we played and dominated in the lead-up to the final. We presumed that if we applied pressure in the early stage of the game then the opposition would fold. This presumption was our downfall against the Kiwis. This game was different to a lead-up match, it was a final. New Zealand had enforced an alcohol ban in the week before the Test as they prepared to try to smash the cocky Kangaroos. This was the first time I had ever been aware of looseness in a Kangaroo camp. An ambush is the best way I can describe that encounter. Underestimating the Kiwis manifested itself in a high error rate. You can't turn the ball over as often as we did against a top side like New Zealand and expect to win.

This Tri-Series win was the start, I believe, of New Zealand's emergence as a true contender for the title of best international rugby league side in the world. From then on they have always run onto the field against Australia believing that they had a good chance of winning, and often they have come out on top. Ruben Wiki is a true warrior. Along with the confidence the Kiwi boys get from competing in the NRL, serving it up to Aussies every week, Ruben has helped create a proud team culture and you can see that now in the way they carry themselves and perform the haka with pride and passion.

Wayne would recall that final with distaste:

Completely out-played and out-enthused. One of the most disappointing games of my career. We just did not want to be there. Tried to rally them at halftime but they just couldn't lift . . . I decided with about 20 minutes to go that I would not coach Australia again.

We expected to cop it from the media and fans for our poor performance in that final against New Zealand, but nothing prepared us for the media reception that we received when we landed at Brisbane airport. This mob at the airport wanted blood. Wayne did not duck the reporters and the TV cameras as he has been accused of doing . . . he was simply ushered out a side door when airport security became alarmed by the size of the media pack.

Because many of the boys had remained in Europe for a holiday and I had hurried home to be with Bonnie, Tallulah and baby Ruby, it was left to me and Luke O'Donnell, who had come home on the same plane as Wayne and me, to front the swarm of reporters, photographers and TV news cameramen who had turned up for Kangaroo blood.

I just told them what I thought, that we were all disappointed to let Australia down. I said that in the final we got it wrong and the New Zealanders were fantastic. It wasn't Wayne's fault. We players had to take the blame. I said we all enjoyed working under Wayne and that he had our full support. I felt empty and pathetic trying to explain the debacle. It was the start of a very long off-season. Seeing my girls was about the only positive of returning home.

# 6

# Fighting back

Throughout that off-season I couldn't switch off the highlight reel in my head that kept repeating images of our final loss to New Zealand. We deserved the criticism we received. We had embarrassed ourselves, our jersey and the people it represented. The empty feeling lingered throughout my time off. The criticism was the catalyst for serious reflection on what I needed to do to earn the right to wear the green and gold jersey again. I promised myself that if I survived the selectors' axe that the 2006 Anzac Test would be the Kangaroos' chance to make amends. In fact, I promised myself, we would win and win well.

At the Broncos, some die-hard fans bayed for our blood after our disappointing 2005, and the sacking of Kevvy Walters, Glenn Lazarus and Gary Belcher from Wayne's staff upped the ante. Nothing less than a premiership, we suspected, would satisfy our supporters.

Under the stern eye of a brilliant and demanding new strength and conditioning coach, Dean Benton, our pre-season training was vastly different from anything we had undertaken before. The Wests Tigers had won the 2005 premiership with a fast, lightweight forward pack, and while Wayne and Dean recognised that smaller wasn't necessarily better – size and strength will never go out of style in rugby league – we had to lose excess weight and become fitter, stronger and faster than we had ever been in our lives. My forward mates and I worked hard on the training paddock and in the gym.

After I had a heart-to-heart with Wayne and Dean about what I wanted to achieve in 2006 and the role the club wanted me to play, Dean mapped out a training regime focusing on position-specific fitness that suited me and my game. It was based on increasing my endurance – being able to keep going fast and hard while playing at higher intensity.

The game was getting faster, especially in the ruck, which was becoming the domain of fitter, faster, leaner forwards. I could no longer afford to carry 112-115 kilos. With the help of our club dietitian Holly Frail, I was able to strip six kilos to drop down to 106 kilos, the lightest I had been for quite a while.

Dean had the backs running longer distances interspersed with explosive sprint drills. We forwards concentrated on short explosive sprints to help us get up and back the 10 metres repeatedly in a game.

In the trial games and early rounds I was happily surprised to find that this lean version of myself was a better ball-carrier than the old me. The lost weight made no difference to the impact with which I crashed into defenders. In 2005 I had run an average 144 metres a game with the ball in my hands, and in the first matches of '06, despite oppressive heat, I was averaging 176 metres. With my improved agility and cardio I was able to get up off a tackled man and back into the defensive line more quickly. I felt incredibly fresh, even though I was turning 30.

The Broncos' increased fitness levels allowed us to play a more expansive brand of football. So long as we still performed our traditional platform-laying role, Wayne didn't mind the forwards displaying ball-playing skills, wide running and all-round flair.

The game had evolved, defences had grown more sophisticated and what worked once worked no more. We players had to adapt and evolve. Styles and standards change fast in modern rugby league. Our old one-out style of play that had served us well for some years was now easy for opponents to handle. Teams were able to gang-tackle us, slow down our play-the-balls, and have an extra second or two to come at us off the defensive line. But, we figured at the start of 2006, if we could string some passes together and get some second-phase play happening, opposition defences had to make adjustments.

We had a lot to prove in 2006; we all put in and we all pulled together. At training and in a game we were more vocal than ever before, exhorting each other to go harder. Said Ben Hannant of the Broncos circa 2006:

> The work ethic instilled in us by Shane and Petero is making a difference. They push me at training and in games, which is what I need. They don't let me take short-cuts or do anything half-hearted. I'm really happy with the way things are going . . . Since the off-season I've lost half my body fat in skin folds . . . I'm actually playing heavier than I was at the Roosters but I'm feeling much fitter and stronger.

And it wasn't just the way we played that was changing, the personnel was turning over too. Shane Webcke, our war-horse prop, a man who had taught me so much and whom I had played alongside in the front-row trenches for the Broncos, Queensland and Australia for years, announced that 2006 would be his final season. I knew that the onus was on me to prove myself the man to take over from Shane as the leader of the pack in '07. This was what Wayne expected.

One of many wonderful things about rugby league is the way it constantly regenerates. Just when you think a retiring star is irreplaceable, someone emerges from our code's production line of future champions to stake a claim for their turf. When we saw Ben Hannant, new from the Sydney Roosters, and a hulking giant of a 17-year-old from the Broncos' junior nursery named David Taylor, we knew we would be okay post-Webby.

Ben had enormous potential back in '06, and it's history that he soon realised that potential, for the Broncos, for Queensland and Australia, for the Bulldogs, and now he's back at the Broncos. The man they call the Polar Bear plays tough and runs hard. His great motor makes sure he gets a lot of minutes in a game. When our paths first crossed in '06, he was a snowy-haired surfie kid who really listened when, in my new role as mentor to the young blokes, I took him under my wing.

Wayne also expected me to help bring David Taylor along. The first time I laid eyes on Dave was when a few of us Broncos went to watch the Queensland under-17s team train before a match against New South Wales and one kid towered over not only his teammates but the trainers and coaches as well. Dave was enormous. He must have weighed 110 kilograms even then, with that huge chest and massive legs. He had a *beard*. In that team, it was as if he was a fully developed man among boys.

Anyone can be big, that's just genetics. What made Dave Taylor stand out along with his power and speed was his silky ball skills. He passed and chipped-kicked beautifully. He could beat a man with speed, a step, or trample right over the top of him. He trained a few times with the senior squad that season and in a year or two he was one of us. In time he joined the South Sydney Rabbitohs, then signed for the Gold Coast Titans. He became a regular State of Origin player and made his Test debut for Australia in 2012.

They say that you're only as good as your last match, so I couldn't wait to hit the ground running that year, because as soon as I had a game under my belt, the 2005 Tri-Series final would no longer be the last game I had played. I was desperate to move on and notch some wins. Unfortunately I would have to wait another week. As we trudged off the field after our first round 36–4 loss to the North Queensland Cowboys, I was wondering whether the trainers had pulled the right strings in the off-season. Nothing worked for us. Our attack was as stilted as our defence and the Cowboys ripped us apart. What made it even worse was that we put on this shoddy performance in front of 46,229 devoted fans at Suncorp Stadium.

Thank goodness things clicked the following week when we beat the Sharks. We won eight of our next 10 games. I scored a try in the round-seven match against Penrith that I'm convinced I could not have pulled off in pre-Dean Benton years. Shane Webcke popped a low ball to me which put me into open space. I passed to David Stagg, who tore upfield. I had backed him up for 25 metres, so that when Dave was tackled, he passed back to me, and I scored. Before 2006, I might not have been fit enough or fast enough to put myself in the position to accept Shane's popped pass, run into the clear, set up David and back him up to score the try.

The Broncos had assembled a mix of experienced play-ers and up-and-comers. Among the former were Webby, Locky, Brad Thorn, Casey McGuire, Justin Hodges (back from the Roosters), Brent Tate, Dane Carlaw, Shane Perry, Shaun Berrigan and yours truly; while on the rise were Darius Boyd, Karmichael Hunt, Sam Thaiday, Corey Parker and Ben Hannant. The alchemist turning all this talent into gold was Wayne Bennett.

Another factor contributing to our good form and intensity was the determination of everyone to send Shane Webcke out a winner. We all lifted for him. I made myself believe that if I had a poor game, or the Broncos lost a match, I was letting Shane down.

In the Anzac Test against New Zealand, the Kangaroos – Minichiello, King, Gasnier, Cooper, Tahu, Lockyer, Johns, Mason, Buderus, Civoniceva, O'Donnell, Hindmarsh and Kennedy with Thurston, O'Meley, Menzies and Simpson on the bench – ran onto the field determined to make amends for the thrashing of 2005. We demolished the Kiwis 50–12.

As a sidelight to that Test, I felt good about our chances when I saw Andrew Johns and Darren Lockyer training together a day or so before the match. They seemed to be competing with the other to throw the most pinpoint accu-rate 20-metre cut-out passes, hitting runners I hadn't even seen. Same when they kicked: they were putting that ball wherever they wanted it. I was in awe.

State of Origin 2006 was a rollercoaster of terrible lows and ecstatic highs. The focus of the camps that our new coach Mal Meninga conducted before the series began was to instil in each of us an enormous pride in being a Queenslander. This concept was not new to Queensland Origin players, but Mal took it to a higher level. He had a number of the former Maroons champions, such as Wally Lewis, Gene Miles, Greg Dowling and Chris 'Choppy' Close join us in camp for periods and there was total silence as they told us of their Origin exploits and what being a Queensland player meant to them. To be honest, we had lost that connection to our past. Mal made sure that we understood that Origin had to be played on another level to NRL. Physically, mentally and emotionally, we had to be better to beat the Blues.

Rammed into each of us by Mal was the injustice of pre-Origin days when Queensland-born and bred players who played in the elite New South Wales Rugby League comp actually represented New South Wales against the blokes who played in local competitions north of the border. The usual result was a big win to the Blues. Since Origin, of course, players who played their first football in Queensland, no matter what club team they represented, donned the maroon jersey. Origin's defining moment was when Arthur Beetson led Queensland onto the field in the first State of Origin match in 1980 and showed just how seriously he took the concept by belting his Parramatta teammate, and good friend, Mick Cronin. There is an element of every Queensland win that is payback for what happened in the bad bygone days, even though most modern players were not born then. Mal is old-school. He believes in state pride, loyalty, heritage, and never letting your teammate or state down. All that sat well with me.

Played in front of 76,773 at Sydney's Telstra Stadium, game one was a cracker, but ended badly for us. Moments from full-time the score was 16–all, after Greg Inglis (two),

Johnathan Thurston, and Steve Bell had scored tries for us and Thurston kicked two goals. For the Blues, new half-back Brett Finch, Willie Mason (who was the best forward on the field and in claiming that honour smashed my nose), Brett Hodgson and Matt King had notched four-pointers, and Hodgson booted two goals. Then, as the timekeeper reached for his siren, Finch booted a field goal to win the match for New South Wales.

We knew in our hearts that we had tried hard but came unstuck because we had not produced our best. Sure, we were one down in the series but we'd taken that first match to the wire and knew we could win the next two games. That confidence was all the motivation we needed. It was not all the motivation we received.

I soon realised that Steve Price and I, the Maroon front row, were being held responsible for the strong showing by the New South Wales forwards Willie Mason, Mark O'Meley, Nathan Hindmarsh, Brent Kite and Steve Simpson; and that Darren Lockyer was being blamed for our loss as well. Steve and I were accused of being 'too old and slow'. Former Blues and Kangaroo fullback Garry Jack called us 'cream puffs' and their former great Benny Elias said we needed a 'miracle' to win Origin II, the most likely result being New South Wales by 20. One other so-called expert even stated that Pricey and I were 'too nice' to match it with Mase and Shrek. All that was bad enough but not unexpected, coming as it did from the enemy camp. What really stung Pricey and me was the savage criticism from within our own ranks, from Greg Dowling and Paul 'Fatty' Vautin. Steve and I were shocked by what Dowling wrote in the press and Vautin told us to our faces in camp just before Origin II.

Fatty unloaded on Pricey and me at the official jersey

presentation in front of the team and the coach the night before Origin II. He told us that the New South Wales people were laughing at us for not standing up to Mason, O'Meley and Kite and that he agreed with them. He told us we were past it. His tone was sneering and derogatory. He said that we were lucky to be in the team for Origin II and if the same thing happened in that match it would be the end of our representative careers.

He humiliated us in front of the younger blokes, who looked up to us, and I was afraid his words would have a negative effect on them. I could see from their expressions and body language that they resented Vautin's tirade as much as I did. I only wish that Paul had said what he had to say to me in private. If he had I would have told him that we had taken a lot of confidence out of the one point loss in Origin I and that we had what it took to beat New South Wales. We had had a top preparation for Origin II and Locky, Pricey and I were ready to prove the doubters wrong. I don't know if Mal put Fatty Vautin up to his attack, but whatever, it left a foul taste in my mouth.

I told Steve, 'Let's make sure that as long as we play this game we remember what Paul Vautin said to us and keep on proving blokes like him wrong.'

### STEVE PRICE

A defining period in Petero's and my careers came in the days before game two in 2006. Queensland had been beaten by New South Wales in Origin I and Petero, Darren Lockyer and I were held responsible by the media and even people within our own camp. If we lost the second game, and the series, the Blues would have beaten us in four series in a row. Losing Origin II was not an option. Mal

Meninga and Paul Vautin told all three of us that if we were defeated in Origin II our Origin careers were over. The pressure from outside and within was enormous. To say we took that criticism to heart is an understatement. Pet and I were roomies. We were both grimly focused on victory, and told each other we would do anything to achieve it. I looked across the hotel room at Petero and knew he meant it. We went out there in that match and dominated. We won Origin III too, and today as I write this, six years later, the Blues haven't beaten us in a series since. To me, toughness is coping with pressure.

Just before we ran onto Suncorp Stadium I went to each of our forwards and my message was the same: be aggressive, never give up, and we'll win. I have never been so fired up before a game.

We won 30–6. Our forwards dominated theirs and Darren Lockyer was man of the match, with Johnathan Thurston and me in contention. Andrew Stevenson in the *Sydney Morning Herald* rated me nine out of 10, saying: 'His best Origin in years. Charged the line like a mad elephant. Stung with his shoulder.' Adam Mogg from the Canberra Raiders, an old Redcliffe boy, had been brought into the Queensland team and scored two of our five tries.

The pressure, self-imposed and from outside forces, to win Origin III was the most intense I ever experienced in football.

The series decider was to be played in neutral territory, at Melbourne's Telstra Dome. Before the match, Willie Mason, Nathan Hindmarsh and Mark O'Meley said they didn't think we could replicate our efforts in the second match and, besides, they were annoyed that Queenslanders seemed to think that they were more proud of their state than New South Welshmen were of theirs. I disagreed with the former, and agreed with the latter.

In the lead-up to Origin III, a number of Queensland players, including Nate Myles, Sam Thaiday and me, were laid low by a stomach bug. For a while, we were in serious doubt, but we came good by game day.

Before the match, Locky and I and a couple of the other senior players who had experienced the highs and lows of Origin over a number of years spoke to the players about what was expected of them that night. Again, I reminded the boys that we had to be aggressive and intensely focused for the entire 80 minutes. New South Wales would be hurting and desperate to avenge their heavy loss in Origin II. I told the boys to put that victory out of their thoughts and that redemption would only come with a series victory tonight. I also encouraged the boys to cast their minds back to what our critics had said about us after Origin I.

More than 54,000 people witnessed an Origin classic. Ten minutes from full-time, the Blues led 14–4 and the game and the series were in their grasp. Then, as we had done before and would do again, we refused to panic, worked methodically for position, and scored two late tries for a 16–14 victory. Again, we forwards provided the platform for Locky, man of the match Brent Tate and new fullback Clinton Schifcoske to cut loose.

In the final 10 minutes of that match, I looked at the faces of my teammates and everyone was calm. We had the unshakeable self-belief to know not that we *could* but that we *would* claw our way back and win this game. Our cool confidence must have unsettled the Blues boys. In that late second half they were camped in our territory, knowing they had enough points on the board to win and all they had to do was contain us in our half till the siren. They forced a dozen line drop-outs on us and each time when they charged the ball back at us we defended our tryline with our hearts and guts. We kept them out set after set. Our lungs were on fire and our bodies in agony, but nobody was going to shirk his duty. Adam Mogg scored for us, then Clinton Schifcoske threw a great wide ball to put Brent Tate into space and Tatey ran the length of the field to score. With five minutes till the final siren, New South Wales led 14-10. They seemed to be coasting to victory. Then, 20 metres out from his line, Blues fullback Brett Hodgson threw a loose pass from dummy half, Locky swooped on it and scored between the posts. Clinton Schifcoske converted and the match and the series was ours. How sweet that was. We all embraced, ecstatic, exhausted and so proud of what we had achieved.

Afterwards, I hugged Bonnie, whose eyes were brimming with proud tears. Nothing ever changes with Bonnie. She has always been there for me. I was uncharacteristically grumpy and preoccupied during that series. She put up with me because she knew I was feeling the strain. She is very wise and always drummed into me that I should cut negativity out of my mind and concentrate on the positive. If you think negatively you will act negatively, and the opposite applies.

That 2006 series win began a Maroon dynasty. In 2003, 2004 and 2005 we had lost three straight series to the Blues, and it meant the world to us to break that losing streak. Queensland has now beaten New South Wales in seven straight Origin series.

### MAL MENINGA

There is such a player as a prototypical State of Origin player. Petero was a perfect example. He could cope emotionally and physically with the incredible demands of Origin. He did not score many tries or make the crowd gasp at his brilliance. What he did was roll up his sleeves and work his guts out. He made large numbers of effective tackles, he hit the ball up long after he was exhausted, he supported the ball-carrier, and his positional play in defence was astute. He was calm in a crisis. He gave 100 per cent every time he ran onto the field.

Pet had a competitive spirit that belied his gentle nature. He understood his body and emotions, and he never wanted to let anyone down . . . that's what drove him. He was a wonderful prop, hard as they come. He was unselfish and he made the right decisions under pressure. He was loved and respected by his teammates, and by me. We listened to what he had to say. On the field, he was 100 per cent reliable in any situation. He also understood the Queensland legacy. He respected the men who wore the jumper before him and wanted to make them proud of him.

A great Origin player, like Petero was, plays with his heart as much as his head and body. The thing about State of Origin is that it is physically so hard, but the key to winning is emotional intelligence, something innate that has just got to happen, that allows you to play harder and faster for longer and to play to your potential under immense pressure. It's about passion. It's about who you are and where you come from and how that place has made you the man you are. It's about not giving up. Origin is much more than a game, it's an event. It's about how if you're physically and emotionally exhausted at the end of the game, the result usually takes care of itself.

Petero was a fine Origin player because he is very smart. The people who succeed at this level tend to be intelligent. They understand life. They are humble despite all that they have achieved. What I loved about Pet and Locky was their humility and the respect they showed to others. That is the mark of a man.

What I expected of Petero every year was to lead from the front, and he did this really well. I relied on Darren Lockyer and Cameron Smith and Petero enormously to take their preparation seriously and if they saw any chink in our armour to speak up about it so it could be repaired. I relied on them to drive the week in camp.

On the Friday after Origin II, the Broncos played St George and I felt great despite Wednesday's torrid match.

To try to introduce a different mindset at the club in 2006, Wayne and his crew had us participating in some extracurricular activities. There was an Amazing Race through the streets of the Brisbane CBD. We were divided into groups and with just $30 in our kick had to try to get from Suncorp Stadium to six designated destinations around the city before the other groups. Skulduggery was not only allowed, it was encouraged. Bicycle tyres were let down, misleading maps distributed, money nicked and, for some reason, Tunza Carroll ran through the City Mall shirtless.

Another time, Brad Thorn and I read to children in a big tent at the Out of the Box Festival at QPAC on Brisbane's South Bank. Both of us being doting dads of young kids, that was no huge feat, and it was fun watching the little ones' faces as we did our best to bring the stories to life.

My dad, Petero Senior, and me
at home in Fiji in 1977, shortly
before he brought Mum and me
to Australia to make a new life.

Bonnie Chisholm, my future
wife, and I met at school. We
were joint school captains at
Frawley College in Scarborough.
We had just started dating.

Where it all started – Redcliffe Dolphins as a 15 year old.

A premiership with our U/19 Colts team, 1994.

A memorable day for the club with our reserve and first grades winning on the day.

I came off the bench in the Broncos' 1998 grand final win against the Bulldogs. An unbelievable debut season – and a premiership ring to top it all off.

The irrepressible Alfie Langer – brilliant on the field, hilarious off it.

Dreams come true –
2001 State of Origin debut.

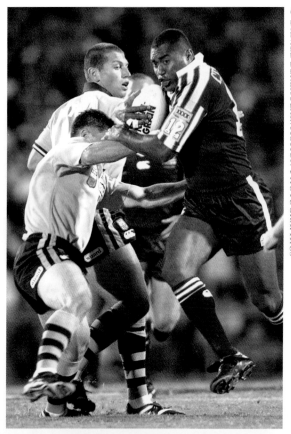

The return of Alfie Langer saw
us claim the 2001 Origin series.

The ferocious and inspiring Gorden Tallis. A man you'd rather play with than against.

Bonnie and me on our wedding day, 2002. A wonderful day celebrated with our friends and family on the beach in Fiji.

Legends, mates and mentors: I was in the best of company at the Broncos' 20-year anniversary luncheon. At rear, from left: Gene Miles, Michael Hancock, Chris Johns, Steve Renouf, Glenn Lazarus, Andrew Gee and Gorden Tallis. Front: Kerrod Walters, Michael De Vere, me, Tonie Carroll, Shaun Berrigan, Allan Langer, Shane Webcke, Darren Lockyer, Kevin Walters and Brad Thorn.

Press conference time as Wayne Bennett, coach and mentor, looks on.

Celebrating the 2006 grand final win with my great mate, Brad Thorn.

A sad farewell for me and my daughter Ruby after my final match for the club in 2007. A few weeks later, we had made a new home in Penrith.

My mate Steve Price and I were long-time front row partners for Queensland. I was as happy as Pricey when he scored a try in Origin I in 2007.

Everyone loves a winner: NRL CEO David Gallop and Prime Minister and staunch Maroons fan Kevin Rudd wanted the lowdown on the game after Queensland wrapped up the series in Origin III, 2008.

I took on the captaincy when I joined the Penrith Panthers in 2008.

My four years at the Panthers were challenging and rewarding. Good times, great mates.

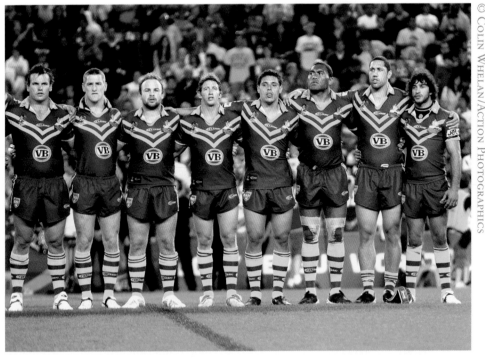

Brothers in arms – lining up for the national anthem before a pool match against the Kiwis in the 2008 World Cup.

Taking on the French in the
2009 Four Nations tour.

The spoils of victory. Luke
Lewis and I after winning the
2009 Four Nations in Leeds.

In 2011, the inspirational Darren Lockyer (front, centre) bowed out of State of Origin football in a fitting way, as a winner in front of his adoring hometown fans.

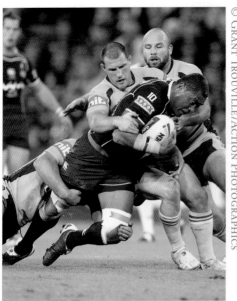

Taking on the Blue Wall – charging through in Origin III, 2011.

A wave to the family. Bonnie took this photo of me at fulltime in Origin III, 2011.

I turned 36 midway through the 2012 season. I was happy to play my part as a member of a great Broncos team, but by now my body was telling me it was time to call it a day and make this year my last.

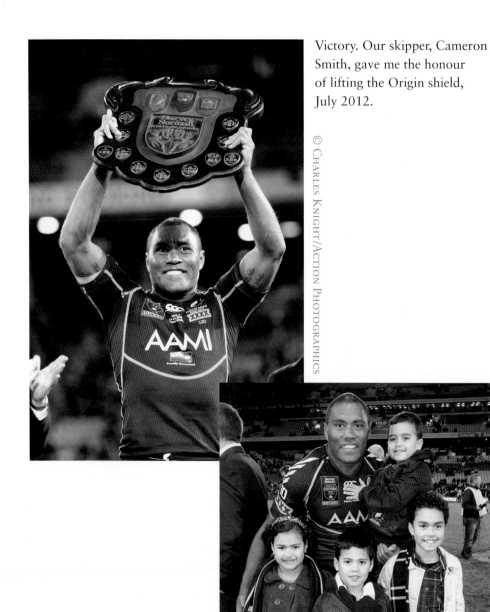

Victory. Our skipper, Cameron Smith, gave me the honour of lifting the Origin shield, July 2012.

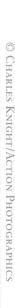

A memory to last a lifetime: Tallulah, Ruby, Kaden and Jacobi after my last ever Origin game.

Being chaired off the field by Greg Inglis and David Shillington.

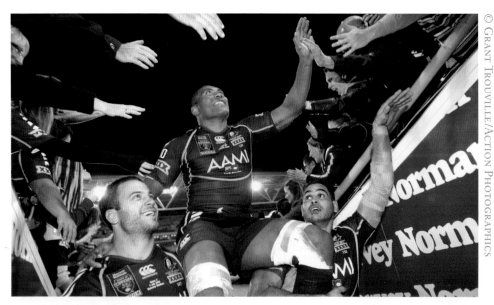

Saying goodbye to the fans.

A proud moment for the family. My 300th game, presented with the game ball by NRL Commission Head John Grant and great mate Darren Lockyer.

Bonnie brought Tallulah and Ruby along. It must have been quite a sight: these two huge footballers reading to tiny children. Mind you, the book we were given to read was appropriate: Nick Bland's *A Monster Wrote Me a Letter*.

When we heard that a devoted Broncos' fan, a father of two named Scott Lillicrap, had been badly bashed and stomped by six cowardly thugs because they took exception to the Broncos' jersey he was wearing home from a match, Darius Boyd (after whom Scott had named his seven-week-old son) and I went to Princess Alexandra Hospital where Scott was recovering after having been placed in an induced coma while his head injuries were treated. We were inspired by Scott's bravery and determination to regain his health and follow his team again, but we were also sickened by the savagery of the attack on this nice young bloke. We thanked him for being a supporter and gave him a new jersey to replace the one that had been ruined in the assault. I told him we were there for him if there was anything we could do to help him and his family through this tough time. I understand Scott recovered. I hope life is going well for him again, and that he and young Darius, even though his namesake is now at the Knights with Wayne Bennett, are Bronco fans.

After Origin, we suffered what had become our usual slump, losing five straight games to the Storm, the Cowboys, the Tigers, the Raiders and the Storm again. We were fit enough, our trainers had seen to that. It was simply, as ever, the mental burden of so many of our guys carrying on after that emotionally draining Origin series. We knew we would be vulnerable to the perennial form slump and worked to overcome it . . . we just couldn't. We kept turning up and hoped our fortunes would improve.

The string of losses really brought me down – in just over

a month we had plummeted from first position on the ladder to fifth and were in danger of missing the semi-finals. So before our next game, against the high-flying Bulldogs, I took it upon myself as a senior player to address the team. I demanded of the boys how much they wanted to win this comp, how much they were prepared to sacrifice to hold up that trophy on grand final day.

It was a sign of my new self-confidence that I would even dare to address the team and of my standing in the squad that my teammates listened. I ranted and raved a bit, and this was so out of character that the room was dead silent. I said it was time to step up, and that if we played to our potential no team in the comp could beat us. Our fate was in nobody's hands but our own.

We all vowed to give our campaign everything we had and as proof of our serious intent we agreed to limit any activity or line of thought that could have a negative impact. Everyone had to make a personal sacrifice to achieve our goal of winning the premiership. We imposed an alcohol ban on ourselves until after the grand final. Even Wayne Bennett gave up his beloved chocolate. Two days later, we beat the Bulldogs 30–0 and a week after that we thrashed the Parramatta Eels 23–0. We were back on track.

In the semis, we lost our qualifying final, going down to St George 20–4. That was a hell of a speed bump and a shock to our new confidence. If we wanted this premiership, we were going to have to pick ourselves up and return to our best form. We came out against Newcastle in another sudden-death match, the semi-final, and beat them 50–6.

Against our old nemesis, the Bulldogs, in the preliminary final to determine who would play the Melbourne Storm in the grand final, things were looking hopeless when we found ourselves down 20–6 at half-time. The momentum was definitely with the Dogs and when we trudged off the field we were out on our feet, even though we knew our season was on the line and that, while being 14 points down wasn't great it was not a death sentence, and we were determined to fight back hard in the second half . . .

Then help came from a very unexpected quarter. Bulldogs' prop Willie Mason, who is a mate and one of rugby league's great larrikins, started mouthing off in the tunnel as we left the field at half-time. 'We're home! They've got nothing! We're on our way to the grand final, boys!' he was crowing, whooping and hollering, clapping his hands and slapping his teammates on the back, as if it was full-time and the game was won.

In our dressing room, Shane Webcke was furious at Willie's performance. He said to us, 'Did you hear what Mase was saying? He has no respect for us.' To a man, we had our backs up and wanted to ruin Willie's night. Wayne's contribution at half-time was to stay calm and tell us that this game wasn't over unless we wanted it to be. We had to score first.

And he moved Justin Hodges to fullback and Karmichael Hunt to the wing. When we returned to the field – instant dividend. Hodgo ran 60 metres and sent Shaun Berrigan over for a try after two minutes. In that 120 seconds the momentum that was theirs became all ours. We went on to score five more tries with just one, at the very end of the game after a loose pass from me, lodged against us. We outscored the Bulldogs by 31 points to six in the second half to win 37–20. We were on our way to the grand final against the Melbourne Storm.

I wish I could say I enjoyed the lead-up week to the grand final. The fact was that I was a worried mess, because I had been cited for clipping the Bulldogs' Sonny Bill Williams in the 57th minute of the semi. In tackling him – same old story – my arm had hit his shoulder and bounced up onto his chin and down he went. I was at risk of being suspended and rubbed out of the grand final. I hoped that my relatively clean record over many years would compel the judiciary to let me off, but I was truly at their mercy. I felt helpless. I told reporters:

> It's been such a battle this year I'd be heartbroken if something came of this and I missed the grand final and the chance to have one last match with Webby. I was surprised the ref even called me back. I just sort of lunged at Sonny Bill, I certainly didn't go in there with any intent. If you ask him, it wouldn't have hurt him.

Sonny Bill came out and said there was nothing in what I'd done to him: 'I wasn't knocked out, so I don't think Petero should miss the grand final . . . He's a good bloke on and off the field. He came up to me straight away and said, "Sorry". I wasn't expecting that and I think that just shows the character of the bloke.'

Even Storm coach Craig Bellamy agreed that it would be a huge shame if I couldn't play in the premiership decider. While awaiting my fate, I didn't sleep much that week. I was preoccupied and miserable – Bonnie, as usual, was a saint and put up with me – when I should have been lapping up the atmosphere, and enjoying an experience that not many rugby league players get to know. Brisbane, in fact all Queensland, was going crazy. Maroon and gold euphoria was in the air. It was an enormous task to put my looming date with the judiciary on the back burner and try to focus on training. I had no idea whether all my effort would be for nothing. To have come so far and be eliminated from the big one would have been a tragedy. Who knew if the chance of playing in a grand final would ever come again?

Thank God, word came from the judiciary that I was only being charged with a bottom-of-the-range grade one careless high tackle charge, which freed me to play.

In grand final week, Wayne didn't make a big deal of this being Shane's last match. He didn't have to. Each of us players would thank Webby for all his sweat and inspiration over all the years by giving him the victory he deserved.

The Storm was a terrific side – coached by Craig Bellamy, with Billy Slater, Cameron Smith and Greg Inglis showing the promise of being the superstars they would become – yet so were we. We believed that if we played as well as we could we would beat them.

Wayne Bennett took a little time out of preparing us for the grand final to give an interview to *The Australian*'s Wayne Smith. He used the opportunity to say that the three blokes who'd be packing down in the front row on Sunday, Webcke, Thorn and me, were as good a front row as he had ever seen. 'If you want to put them in the grand final of the best front-row units, I can live with that.' He said the key was that we were mates:

Forwards play better when they are mates. Forwards have that psyche. They know they rely on each other. Backs are different, they're more individual. Forwards rely on each other more and are more team-orientated. Shane, Brad and Petero are great friends and would die for each other on the field. In terms of their efforts every week, the respect they enjoy in the game and the representative honours they've achieved playing for Queensland and Australia – and don't forget Thorny also played Test rugby for the All Blacks – they'd stand up against any competition.

In that grand final at Telstra Stadium on 1 October 2006, I took the hardest hit of my life. I'd been belted by the best, but I will never forget the bell ringer I copped from a rampaging David Kidwell. He well and truly switched my lights off. It happened midway through the second half. We were pinned deep in our territory, although gradually getting the upper hand after a torrid and tight first half, and were well on the way to our eventual 15–8 victory. I hit the ball up. Dave raced out of the line at me. I didn't see him coming. Usually your peripheral vision can pick up a defender shooting up off their line and you can evade the tackler or brace for the collision. Unfortunately I did neither. I may not have seen him, but I felt him, all right. He hit me flush on the chin with a combination shoulder charge and stiff-arm and wiped me out. I saw stars, then white, then black. I felt as if I'd been run over by a Mack truck.

Kidwell stood over me as I lay prone and screamed at the top of his lungs. Even as I lay prone on the ground, struggling to get up but with my arms and legs not working, I knew I was concussed. I kept repeating, 'Where am I? What game is this?' I think I knew it was a big game. I didn't know the score or who we were playing. When the cobwebs cleared as much as they were going to, I climbed to my feet and took my position in the defensive line. I owe a huge debt to Casey McGuire, who stayed beside me, talking to me, focusing me. 'Bulla, don't run with the ball. Save yourself for defence,' he was calling out. Somehow I completed the match.

David Kidwell didn't get sent off. He was penalised for a high tackle and that was all. I was fine with that. Dave played rugby league in a hard and uncompromising way, as it should be played.

There were many stars that day, apart from the ones I

was seeing. Darren Lockyer was a master the way he guided us around the park, making all the right decisions. We forwards had a ferocious encounter with the formidable Storm pack and we won . . . narrowly. Cameron Smith tested us all day, with his incisive dummy-half work, kicking in general play and punishing defence. He has always lifted against the Broncos. He was a Brisbane local junior but the Broncos, unusually for them, could not see his greatness and ignored him, so he ended up in Melbourne. Every time he plays against the Broncos, every time he stars for Queensland and Australia, I reckon he is saying, 'See what you missed out on!'

My concussion may or may not have had a hand in an embarrassing incident at the end of the match as we got up onto the stage in the middle of the field to be awarded our medals. Whatever, I was celebrating, and didn't see a television cord stretched across the front of the stage. I tripped and went flying head-first off the platform into a pile of confetti. I picked myself up, thinking, 'I hope not too many people saw that!' Of course, millions watching on national TV did and no doubt replayed it many times. My mates were texting me, not to say 'Great game!' but 'Great tumble!'.

What a night. We partied very, very hard because we believed we deserved that premiership. There was no fluke about it. We had played tough all year and beaten the best in the semis. We had also been able to give Shane the gift of a premiership in his last game of rugby league.


I WAS selected again for Australia in the Tri-Nation Series, and at the end-of-season awards night, I won the Paul Morgan Player of the Year award, beating Locky and Webby by eight points and Justin Hodges by 10. That was a gala night, for as well as the awards being presented, it was a farewell to Webby.

Playing in Australia and New Zealand that year, it was a turbulent Tri-Nations Series. This was the series when in a match won by the Englishmen 23–12, Willie Mason and Great Britain's Stuart Fielding, after sledging each other from the kick-off, shaped up and Willie got in first and knocked Fielding cold. Willie then was sat on his pants by British prop Jamie Peacock. My grand final tormentor, the Kiwis' David Kidwell, also smashed Willie in the New Zealand–Australia game and cracked his eye socket.

In Great Britain's match against New Zealand, Adrian Morley flattened his idol Ruben Wiki with a high shot and, for good measure, punched Brent Webb in the head. Everyone got off. I feared that things would explode as the series wore on, but happily the boys cooled down.

We played the Kiwis in the final in Sydney and, after the score was 12–all at full-time, we won 16–12 thanks to a typically cliffhanger Darren Lockyer try in the seventh minute of extra time.

At the end of the series, I was humbled to win the Harry Sunderland Medal for Australia's Test Player of the Year. Wayne Bennett commented:

There was just something about Petero this year. I think the criticism was an issue for him. He wanted to show everyone he still had plenty to offer. The media and some other coaches said he was too old and too slow. But he worked hard and got himself fitter, and he has proved them all wrong. He has that quiet aura about him that champion players have. He has this pleasant, unassuming manner that brings enormous confidence to a team.

•

SHANE WEBCKE received many well-deserved plaudits when he retired. It was very gratifying to me that he took time out from saying goodbye to rugby league to speak glowingly about our friendship and partnership on the field:

Petero and I played 180 games together for the Broncos and represented Queensland and Australia in the front row many times. He is undoubtedly the most gentlemanly footballer I have ever come across. He is a genuine family man and a great bloke to count as a mate. For all his kindness, though, I have seen him get angry on the football field and it's a sight to behold. Big Petero hits them as hard as anyone and it's a good idea to keep him onside.

Off the field, I have only ever seen him angry if he feels someone is being done an injustice. I don't know a lot about how he grew up, but I get the feeling that there are events that formed his deep-seated sense of fairness and morality. It has been my great pleasure to play alongside him and, more importantly, witness how a man can blend uncompromising toughness with gentleness extended to all.

I was able to publicly repay Shane's kind words when *The Big League* asked me to sum up Shane:

When I was learning the front-row trade, I was the apprentice learning everything from the master tradesman. Webby helped me so much. I owe him everything. It was so wonderful that he was able to go out the way he did, with a grand final win.

How good was all this! At age 30, I had found a deeply satisfying balance in my life. I was at the peak of my playing powers. I was fitter and stronger than at any time in my career. I was injury-free. The Maroons had won the 2006 State of Origin, the Broncos the comp, Australia the Tri-Series, and I had received best player awards for club, state and country. Football had never been kinder to me. Away from the paddock, Bonnie and I were the parents of two little girls, and now she was pregnant again.

Next year, 2007, my contract with the Broncos was up for renewal and Wayne Bennett had promised I would be paid fairly for my contributions. I felt I had proved myself the man to step into Shane's and Gorden's boots and lead our forwards. I couldn't wait for the new season to begin.

But as they say, be careful what you wish for . . .

# 7

# Unsaddled

I have kept the diary page where I noted down the meeting I set up for 23 January 2007 with Bronco CEO Bruno Cullen to discuss my new contract that would keep me at the Broncos for the rest of my playing days. My manager David Phillips and I had come up with what we believed was a good and fair case for a salary increase to $400,000 a year, which is what Origin and Test players routinely received then. The contract would extend to the end of 2009 with an option in my favour for a further year if I was still playing well. We were sure I would be offered what I was seeking, based on Wayne's promise that when Shane Webcke and Gorden Tallis retired he expected me to take over as forward leader and that I would be paid what they were being paid, which was considerably more than the $240,000 a season I was on.

I had paid my dues with the Broncos over many years and, although paying me more would put pressure on our salary cap, I believed I was worth it. I had played my heart out for the Broncos, captaining the side when called on, and proved myself at the highest level of the game, in State of Origin and with the Kangaroos.

For the Broncos, over 10 years I had played when injured, done my job well enough to have twice won the Paul Morgan Player of the Year award and Forward of the Year. I had kept myself fit and testimony to this was that in the previous three years I had played 107 games, the heaviest workload of any NRL player. I had been a proud ambassador for the club off the field. I was a mentor to many of the young players. I had never been involved in scandal, drunken behaviour or violent incidents, nor in any other way dragged the name of the club in the mud. None of this is to paint myself as a saint, just to make the point that I was on sure ground seeking my contract upgrade.

On the 23rd, I arrived at Bruno's office at the appointed time but he was unable to see me. I was a bit taken aback, but relaxed about it. I'd simply make another appointment. I hoped my seniority would ensure I was one of the first guys spoken to, even though Bruno was a busy man and other blokes' contracts had to be attended to as well. I wasn't the only fish in the sea. Then, over the next weeks and months, further meetings I'd organised with Bruno were postponed. I began to get the impression that management was avoiding me and that I might have a problem.

When I went to England in early February to play for the Broncos against the English Super League premiers, St Helens, in the World Club Challenge, I did some media interviews and used the opportunity to put pressure on the Broncos by mentioning the nibbles I'd received from some other clubs.

My fears were justified. When I returned to Brisbane, I was informed by Bruno that the salary cap was making it hard for the club to pay me any more than I was currently earning, but that there was a chance that the sum could be sweetened with some third-party agreements that could possibly be arranged.

The club was crying poor, so I was shattered when I learned that the Broncos were planning to sign props Ashton Sims from St George and Joel Clinton from Penrith for 2008, as well as Penrith halfback Peter Wallace. Bringing in the new front-rowers was a real kick in the pants. How come my club had no time or money for me but had completed negotiations with three other players? Sims and Clinton were good players, but why would the Broncos want them with me, Ben Hannant, Dane Carlaw, Brad Thorn, Greg Eastwood and the promising young props Nick Kenny and Dave Taylor already on the books. I was definitely unwanted. If only my club had informed me of their intentions and the direction in which they wanted to go earlier in the year.

Making matters even worse was that I had turned down the North Queensland Cowboys' offer in 2002 that would have secured my family's financial future. I had also declined $500,000 offers from Hull and St Helens in England, not to mention feelers from the Australian Rugby Union. I said no to them all because I had been led to believe that I would be looked after by the Broncos, the team I followed as a boy, had bled for as a player for a decade, and wanted to represent until I retired. Besides, Bonnie and the kids wanted to remain in Brisbane. We were well settled in Redcliffe, surrounded by family and friends.

I told David Phillips, who as well as being my manager is a friend, that I still wanted to play for the Broncos, but now, and especially in light of the way I was being treated, there was a big principle at stake and he should make them honour their promise to me. I was prepared to leave the

club if they wouldn't treat me with respect. I wasn't bluff-
ing. I didn't want to play for a club that would dud me. And
I wanted the matter settled one way or the other ASAP so
I could make any plans I had to and wouldn't have to play
Origin and the finals series with this mess hanging over my
head.

David had a series of meetings with Broncos' management. The administration reiterated to him that there was
no money in the kitty to pay me anything remotely like
what Shane and Gorden had been paid. Their best offer
was pretty much what I had been receiving. David replied
that because his job was to look after my best interests he
had no choice but to invite offers from other clubs.

The trouble was that, this now having dragged on until
near the middle of the year, many clubs had already spent
their salary cap recruiting their sides for 2008 and beyond.
There was nothing in their coffers for me. If the Broncos
had let me know earlier that they could not afford what I
was seeking, I could have negotiated with other clubs before
they locked in their playing roster.

I also know that a number of NRL clubs, such as the
Gold Coast Titans, were interested in talking to me but
did not even contact me because they assumed that Bruno
Cullen would do what was necessary to keep me at the
Broncos.

I sat down with Wayne Bennett and asked him what was
going on. I said that I had fulfilled my part of the bargain as
a player and leader, and surely he and the club had to keep
their promise to me. He was steely and gave me the bad
news straight and without apology. He said that the situation had changed from when we initially spoke and the club
could not afford to pay me what Shane and Gorden had
been getting, and that was that. The Broncos' top spending

priority was to lock up such younger off-contract players as Kiwi international Greg Eastwood, Steve Michaels, Darius Boyd and Joel Moon. Wayne implied that they were the future and I, 31 years of age now, was yesterday's man. I was being thrown onto the scrap heap. That meeting with Wayne Bennett was one of the low points of my football career, and my life. I felt that I had earned the right to be negotiated with first, not last.

It's an understatement to say that it was a traumatic time at home. Bonnie had recently given birth to our third child, Kaden, and now, more than ever, my family's future was my priority. Like any young couple, we had hopes and dreams and they all revolved around a secure income from the Broncos and raising our children in Redcliffe, and now these dreams could be dashed because of a broken promise. Bonnie and I had many tense discussions long into the night. I was angry that people I'd trusted had reneged on their word.

In spite of all this, I tried to put it out of my head and not be distracted from playing my best footy, not even when the club finally confirmed that they had indeed signed Sims and Clinton. In spite of all the contract turmoil I continued to give the Broncos my best.

It eased the pain just a little when so many of my fellow players, and not just from the Broncos, came out and said they were disappointed that this had happened to me. Luke Bailey of the Gold Coast Titans, one of my greatest State of Origin rivals, even offered to take a pay cut if his club could try to fit me into their plans. I thanked Bull, but of course I would never dream of taking a man's hard-earned pay.

Then, ironically, right in the middle of this nightmare, the Broncos celebrated their 20th year by naming their greatest-ever team and I was in it. My head was spinning. What on earth was happening?

Another trial for a private guy like me was having the contract negotiations plastered day by day all over the newspapers. David Phillips and I were portrayed by people at the Broncos as greedy and not doing the right thing by the club. I did not dignify those accusations with a rebuttal, just hoped the fans knew me well enough to realise this was not the case.

The time had come to play hardball. In May, David Phillips told management that he had received excellent offers from other clubs and, although my preference was to remain a Bronco, unless they paid me what I had been promised, I would leave the club at the end of the season. Just before Origin II, in June, David received an email – *an email!* – from Bruno Cullen saying that since I obviously had plenty of options, the Broncos were ceasing negotiations immediately.

Their best offer remained $240,000 with a $50,000 marquee player loading a season, a two-year extension with an option in *their* favour for a third year, and the offer of an unspecified job on my retirement. I could take that or I could leave it.

The issue was no longer the value of the contract. It was more about the way the negotiations had been handled by my club. That for me was the most disappointing aspect of it all.

I left it.

Bruno Cullen fronted the media to say:

If Petero goes, then obviously we're very disappointed because he's given us great service over a long period of time. But like with the other fellows who are leaving

[Brent Tate, Brad Thorn, Shaun Berrigan, Dane Carlaw and Tame Tupou] these are all salary cap issues and this is what the salary cap does to a successful side. If we were able to spend the money on Petero to keep him, we'd gladly do so, but we can't. We wish him all the best and hope he finishes his career with us on a high note this season and finds the contract he's looking for to finish his career off. It makes me sick to the stomach to tell you this, because he has been a wonderful servant.

Wayne Bennett maintained that the Broncos had a 'clear conscience' over the issue, that 'it has all been a huge distraction, but decisions have been made and we have all moved on'. That hurt.

I made a press statement:

As much as I love the club, I think what has happened in the past few weeks would make it very hard for me to play here next year. I have had some great years in Brisbane and I love the Broncos. But I am really disappointed how this has all played out. I am a quiet sort of a guy and I never wanted this to be a public issue.

Being portrayed as 'money-hungry' by the club has been hurtful, because people who know me know that this is not what I'm about. If that was me, I would have taken up offers of far bigger money to leave in the past. I am a loyal person and I went into this deal with an open mind. But before I knew it, the deal they made was off the table. When they signed other players [Clinton and Sims], I knew that was it. The saddest thing was it came in the form of an email via my manager. No one was brave enough to come and tell me man to man.

Then, out of the blue, in mid-June, the Penrith Panthers threw me a lifeline. Their chief executive officer, Mick Leary, contacted me to say that Panther captain Craig Gower was quitting the club to play rugby union in Italy and, along with the departures of Peter Wallace and Joel Clinton (ironically to the Broncos), the Panther now had room under their salary cap to pay me $370,000 a year for two years with the option for a third year; and there was the possibility of third-party deals.

The decision was mine: do the best for my family and myself by taking the Penrith offer, or back down from my principles and stay at my beloved Broncos for less money, less security and in the knowledge that I wasn't valued. On 27 June, I announced my decision to become a Penrith Panther.

Naturally, before I severed my ties with the Broncos, I spent time with key people at the Panthers. I had encouraging conversations with the coach, Matt Elliott, a man I liked. He said the side had under-performed in recent years – the Panthers would be wooden-spooners in '07 – and he wanted me to be captain because I came from a successful culture and I could show the team what it took to win. He saw me heading up a tight senior group with seasoned stars Luke Lewis, Trent Waterhouse, Rhys Wesser and Luke Priddis. He told me there were some bright young talents at the Panthers such as Tim Grant, Sam McKendry, Lachlan Coote, Michael Jennings, Michael Gordon, Nathan Smith and Frank Pritchard, who would benefit by being associated with me.

I also spoke at great length to my old friend and former Bronco teammate Luke Priddis before I made my decision. I respected Luke as a man and regarded him as one of the best I'd played with. He encouraged me to join him at the

Panthers because he thought they were lacking a strong and focused leader who could end the losing culture at the club. The challenge appealed.

I would have my work cut out for me. The Panthers were anything but a premiership contender these days and their grand final win in 2003 was ancient history. I had qualms about being made captain immediately. I well knew that, despite the assurances of some at Penrith, I would not simply be able to waltz into the joint and lay down the law (not that this is my way of doing things, anyway). As an outsider, I would have to prove myself and win the boys' trust before they accepted me as their leader. Plus my experience as skipper was limited to only a handful of games at the Broncos when the regular captain was out injured or suspended. It would all be a steep learning curve.

After all this due diligence, I sat down with Bonnie and told her my impressions of the Panthers and she said, 'Let's make this work.' We would see out the season at the Broncos, pack up our home, and head to Penrith, in enemy territory, New South Wales, at the foot of the aptly-named Blue Mountains. Instead of making my end of career farewell lap at Brisbane's Suncorp, it seemed that I'd be running it at Centrebet Stadium.

I was sad that my time as a Bronco was winding down. I bottled up all my hurt and disappointment, kept playing hard, and did not confide in my teammates about my disillusion, with the exception of Brad Thorn. He is a very close mate and supported me all the way in my stand. Brad is a positive, driven guy. He, too, was leaving the club at the end of the season to return to New Zealand to play rugby union, and he told me that no matter what was happening off the paddock our job until the end of the year was to hold our heads up on the playing field and training paddock and to look after our young teammates and put our misgivings on the back-burner.

I tried once to approach Darren Lockyer to give him my side of the story and tell him why I had to leave, but as I approached him I realised I could not go through with it and I turned on my heel and walked away. Locky is a man who bottles things up, too, and it wasn't till I read his eloquent words about my departure in his 2011 autobiography that I had an inkling how he felt:

> The lack of professionalism and respect for all big Bulla had done for the Brisbane Broncos organisation and the NRL was staggering. The whole thing was a tragedy . . . The club's abysmal handling of its negotiations with Petero in 2007 left the most significant scar . . . Petero's status was such that all players were left to question the idea of loyalty in the modern game . . . During the negotiations, clearly the parties lost sight of the objective, which was to ensure Petero remained at the Broncos, where he belonged. With a guy like Petero, you just find a way . . . Petero should have been a Bronco for life. Personally, it was gut-wrenching to watch Bulla go through all that. We had been friends since meeting as teammates in the Broncos Colts side way back in 1995. The Broncos was in his blood. It was home to him and he was an irreplaceable part of not just the playing group but the entire club.
>
> Petero is a rock of a man. He didn't ever give too much away through what was a really tough time for him and his family. He didn't want the boys to know it was affecting him, but I know Bulla well enough to know how much it hurt him . . .
>
> What happened with Petero has ramifications for the whole of the NRL . . . We often hear in the modern game

that loyalty is dead and that the NRL is a big business. I like to be a little old-fashioned and feel that in some instances loyalty is alive and well. Sadly, for both Petero and the Broncos, this old-fashioned thought just did not prevail.

My own unhappy experience and watching the same thing happen to other players made me an advocate of the establishment of a system that gives salary cap dispensation to players who have been with a club for, say, 10 years. It's unjust that a long-time player such as Steve Menzies was forced out of Manly-Warringah. Matthew Johns at Newcastle, Craig Fitzgibbon at the Roosters and Bryce Gibbs at the Wests Tigers were in the same boat, and should have been allowed to play out their days at the club where they had given great service for so long. Similarly, salary cap leeway should be granted to a club that identifies a talented youngster and develops him into an elite player. That the club has to say goodbye to that player and watch him do well at another club just because their talent scouts and coaches did their work well is ridiculous. It's in the best interest of the club, its supporters and rugby league in general to allow men who have given good service to the club to be one-club players.

SEASON 2007 was far from the Broncos' most successful on the field, yet it was a season that fills me with pride. The big honours eluded us – mainly, once more, because of our injury toll – but, boy, we gave it our best. Even while my contract negotiations were deteriorating, I was expected to step up and be a team leader and I hope I let nobody down. The decisions of management did not make me love any less the club which had given me so much. I could have coasted to get even with head office, but that was never an option. I will always remember that season as a test of my character.

Our year began badly on 23 February when we were defeated 18–14 by St Helens in the World Club Challenge. These games, the vast majority of which have been held in England, are always hard for Australian sides to win. You only have a week to acclimatise to the cold and slippery north of England conditions and handle the jet lag. Then you're pitched in against a good team in front of a rabid home crowd. But what a thrill running out in front of those English crowds. Yes, you cop plenty of stick but what a tremendous atmosphere they create with their singing and chanting in time to marching bass drums and trumpets. Usually it is the first match the Australian champions have played since winning the grand final, while the season in England starts a little earlier than ours and they will have had a couple of matches to find form and combination. As I write this, in the 20 World Club Challenge games that have been played, the Brits have won 12. No excuses, though – St Helens beat us fair and square that night, giving Locky a dose of his own medicine by winning with a last-ditch try.

Back home in the NRL competition, we got off to a miserable start, winning just two of our first seven games. After we were widely tipped to be wooden-spooners on our current form, and the newspapers were claiming that Wayne's job was in jeopardy, we lifted to beat an under-strength Newcastle by 71–6 at Suncorp, our highest-ever winning score. For a change, we had no post-Origin slump, but we lost five of our last seven games and only made it into the final eight by the skin of our teeth. In the semis, we were eliminated 40–0 in the first week by the Melbourne Storm, who went on to win the grand final.

That brief summary of the season does not, however, do us justice. Our players fell to injury like ninepins, and sometimes I was hard-pressed to recognise some of the boys who ran onto the field in a Broncos' jersey. Darren Lockyer, our captain and most valuable player, did his anterior cruciate ligament in the match against the Cowboys in July and didn't play again that year. I took over the captaincy of the team. Also missing with injury for large chunks of the season were Justin Hodges, Shaun Berrigan, Tonie Carroll, Karmichael Hunt, David Stagg and Brent Tate.

A highlight of the season was our 48–18 win against Wests Tigers at Suncorp in round 15. There were around 30,000 fans there that day, and the great majority stood and cheered me after I was sent to the sin bin – for the first time in my career – for shoving Tigers hard man Bryce Gibbs after he had dived on a fallen Corey Parker. My emotions were raw all year, and getting rawer, maybe that's why I squared up to Bryce, which was most uncharacteristic of me. Our final home game at Suncorp was a win against the Canberra Raiders in the second-last competition round. This was the last chance for Brisbane fans to say goodbye to me – and Brent Tate, Shaun Berrigan, Brad Thorn and Dane Carlaw – and 31,199 turned up. Many had signs bidding me farewell. One read: 'We'll miss you, Petero.' Well, I would miss the fans too. I blubbered through most of the game. At the end of the match, Bonnie and the kids joined me on the field and we did a slow walk, waving farewell.

The following week, we fielded a badly depleted team and Parramatta took us apart 68–22 at Parramatta Stadium.

That left one match, a qualifying final against the Storm at Melbourne's Olympic Park. This was a game I'll always remember, and not in a good way. If I had dreamed of leading us to a fairytale victory, and I did, I was sorely disappointed. During the lead-up week I once again drew the media's, and therefore the referees', attention to the Storm's grapple-tackling. In our second-round match, Nick Emmett, Greg Eastwood and I had all been grappled. These tackles can maim. After that match, I told reporters:

We talk about this every year and nothing gets done. Grapple-tackles should be banned ... [Many of the Storm's tackles] were suspect ... The game is tough enough. I would hate to see a neck injury because the League has been too lenient on grapples. Are we waiting for someone to end up in a wheelchair, or worse?

In the days before the qualifying final against the Storm, I was accused by the Melbourne papers, and by some of the Storm players including my Queensland State of Origin mates, of being a whinger. Consequently, Melbourne's fans turned up loaded for bear. Because of our great rivalry, we Bronco players were used to being booed by Storm fans, but the reaction when we ran onto the field in this match was venomous. Every time I touched the ball or made a tackle I was hooted. To the delight of this baying mob, Cameron Smith, Greg Inglis, Cooper Cronk, Billy Slater and co. were too good for us. This was no dream ending to my Broncos career, it was a nightmare. As I left the field, I shook hands with the Storm boys and hugged my teammates, so sad that I would never play with them in a Broncos' jersey again. Next day the Brisbane *Courier-Mail* ran a photo of a Melbourne fan, his face contorted with rage, giving me the finger.

As the skipper, I had to front up with Wayne at the

post-match press conference, and in the tunnel before the conference I broke down in front of my teammates, Wayne and Bruno Cullen. The emotion of playing my last match for the Broncos and the terrible 40–0 beating we'd taken simply overwhelmed me and my tears flowed. I pulled myself together and took my place, red-eyed, at the desk as the press boys demanded that I tell them what had gone wrong. After the match, I flew back to Brisbane and cleaned out my locker.

Driving to the end-of-season awards night later that week, I kept saying to Bonnie, 'This is the last time we'll do this . . . This is the last time we'll do that . . .' As it happened, I won the Paul Morgan award for Player of the Year, the Players' Player award, Best Forward; and shared Clubman of the Year with Brad Thorn. That was all wonderful, but the kudos did not ease my sadness and, perhaps, bitterness as I made my way around the room saying goodbye to my teammates and their partners. And, yes, to the administrators who had discarded me. To tell the truth, I wasn't surprised when I learned that club management had successfully lobbied to host the Penrith Panthers at Suncorp Stadium in the opening match of the 2008 season. They knew my first match against my old club would draw the fans and they wanted to cash in.

Season 2007 will always leave a bitter taste because of the drawn-out contract negotiations and the prospect of leaving a club that Bonnie and I loved so much. None of what happened that year affected the respect and gratitude I have always felt for Wayne. No doubt it took me a while to move on. It is a reality of the modern game that decisions will be made that will test the strongest of loyalties. Reflecting as I write this, I realise that I was pulling free from the safety net of home and stepping into new and unfamiliar territory that would see me grow and be challenged like never before. I owe my career to Wayne as much as I owe it to anyone and as far as I am concerned we have never stopped being mates.

THE 2007 Anzac Test against New Zealand at Suncorp Stadium was my 29th for Australia, just four behind the record-holder, the great John Raper. Before the match, New Zealand and Penrith second-rower Frank Pritchard, who had knocked out Karmichael Hunt the last time the two teams met as punishment for Kiwi-born Karmichael wearing the green and gold, tried to rev up his fellow forwards by publicly threatening to tear the Aussies apart. I came back at my future teammate Frankie in the press: 'He can talk it up as much as he wants but at the end of the day it's what you actually do on the field that matters. Guys who mouth off often go out there and fizzle.'

Frankie didn't fizzle, he had a good game. Nevertheless, we overwhelmed the Kiwis, who had the in-form stars Benji Marshall and Sonny Bill Williams in their side, 30–6. The Broncos in the team, Karmichael, Darren Lockyer, Brent Tate, Justin Hodges, Shaun Berrigan and myself, made the most of our home ground advantage and Locky was the man of the match. With eight rookies on board, we beat the Kiwis again in a Test in Wellington in October.

The 2007 Queensland State of Origin team contained blokes who would dominate Origin for years to come. Coming together in our side that series were Darren Lockyer, Greg Inglis, Justin Hodges, Johnathan Thurston, Cameron Smith, Steve Price, Tonie Carroll, Nate Myles, Dallas Johnson and Brent Tate. Billy Slater was still a year away from being a regular in the maroon.

The bonding ritual for State of Origin that year included a visit to Enoggera Army Barracks for a little shooting competition. Some of the boys were pig-hunters and they hit the target. Former Origin star Steve Walters, who joined us for the big shoot-off, was a regular Jesse James. I had never fired a rifle, and it showed. I won the booby prize of a bag of rice. My future is definitely not in the armed forces. Another ex-Queensland champion, Bob Lindner, quipped that if my countrymen shot like me nobody was ever going to get hurt in a Fijian coup. We also played a friendly footy match against Australian Defence Force personnel who were just back from Iraq and East Timor.

We knew that the Blues would be fired up after last year's series loss, and just in case they were not, their former players Ben Elias and Mark Geyer said their best hope of success was to wind back the clock 15 years and bash us. We were ready for whatever New South Wales brought to the party.

As I always did when I played Origin, or for Australia, I waited until the last moment before the match before I put my jersey on. It is such a special ritual for me, the only superstition I have. That maroon jersey brings back all the best memories of being a kid growing up in Queensland, especially on Origin night when my family crammed around the TV as we yelled and cheered our heroes on. To know that I had been given the honour of wearing the Queensland jersey and that there would be families all over the state riding on my every run and tackle made me feel I could never let my state or the fans down.

I renewed hostilities in Origin I with the Melbourne Storm, New South Wales and Australian front-rower Brett White. I had been having run-ins with him for a couple of seasons. In our first-round clash with the Storm, Brett raised his elbow as I made to tackle him and caught me flush in the face. I retaliated. I have to say that I took out a lot of my frustrations that year on Whitey.

Brett is a confrontational player who can handle himself when tempers flare. Pack down opposite him and it's always personal, as it should be. After our round-seven game against the Storm, which they won, he came out and accused the Brisbane forwards of being easy to dominate now that Shane Webcke had retired and Tonie Carroll was out injured. He said he no longer felt sore after playing the Broncos. His intention, of course, was to provoke us so when the two fierce rival teams met again we would forget our game plan and spend the match trying to get square with him.

What Brett said did rile us, and we decided we would repay him in kind if we got the chance in the game. I entered the spirit of things by telling a reporter, knowing it would get back to him: 'That stuff doesn't worry me when it comes from Brett White, because I don't really rate him. I don't fear him. You go and have a look at the lines he runs out there and tell me why he mightn't be sore after a game.'

There was no doubt I was in a prickly and sensitive mood all year for obvious reasons, and White's taunts had really got under my skin. I told another journo, 'If [the attack] had come from a Mark O'Meley or a Nathan Hindmarsh – a guy who's been around and done it all in the game – that would be different.' White should expect 'something extra' from the Broncos' forwards in future.

(Just for the record, I *did* rate Brett.)

During Origin I, Brett and I got stuck into each other again. Our clashes became inevitable when in the lead-up to the game I warned him that if he came into my sights I wouldn't miss him. In the end, it was Tonie Carroll who didn't miss White, breaking his nose the first time Brett hit the ball up. Whitey went down, and got straight back up again.

At the end of the match, Brett approached me, shook my hand and said he didn't mean any disrespect when he said what he did about the Broncos' forwards. I said I didn't mean it either when I said he ran soft lines. He was okay, he'd had a real go out there. A few years later, we were teammates on a Kangaroo tour and got on well, then after a particularly nasty Origin incident which I'll go into later, we fell out again. We're friendly today. There'll be plenty of time in retirement to sit down over a beer and remember our battles. That's rugby league.

In Origin I, we won 25–18, after coming back from an 18–6 deficit at half-time. There was no panic during the break, just a firm resolve that we could overhaul the Blues and nullify their best attacking weapons, rookies Jarrod Mullen and Jarryd Hayne. We did exactly that. Steve Price was the best player on the field, closely followed by Johnathan Thurston and Greg Inglis, who scored two tries. Pricey made 14 hit-ups for a fabulous 221 metres gained, pulled off 22 tackles and a vital charge-down and regather when the Blues looked a chance of snatching a last-gasp win . . . Oh, and he also scored a try. Not bad for a 33-year-old. He certainly inspired me. I supported him with 31 tackles and 189 metres notched in 21 hit-ups. As Origin II at Telstra Stadium loomed, Willie Mason came out and declared that he was making it his personal mission to hammer Pricey and me. It was a back-handed compliment. 'They made a ridiculous amount of metres in Origin I, and that can't happen again,' said Mase.

There was drama before the game when we went into camp at Terrigal, on the coast north of Sydney, and were battered by a monsoon. At our hotel there was no electricity or hot water. We had to prowl around the corridors with only candles to light our way.

It was potentially one of our worst Origin preparations ever, but getting through the big blackout together drew us closer. We trained in driving rain on a field that was under water . . . and we had a ball. We could have made any number of excuses, but we turned up for the match in high spirits and won a tight match 10–6. The score was 6–6 after 20 minutes and stayed that way until near the end, when our centre Steve Bell picked up a Thurston grubber and scored in the corner.

For Origin III, we were back at Suncorp. New South Wales were desperate not to be whitewashed and came at us hard, led by the 'Bash Brothers', Paul Gallen and Greg Bird. Dallas Johnson was KO'd when making a tackle in the opening minutes and we lost Inglis and Tate to injury. They beat us well, 18–4. Yes, the series was ours, although I have to say we felt hollow carrying the shield around Suncorp Stadium after a gut-wrenching loss.

It was in this series that Steve Price and I really clicked, on and off the field. We had risen to the occasion and proved our detractors wrong in 2006, and now in '07 we were established as the first-choice Queensland front-rowers. As long as we packed down together for the Maroons, each of us vied to make more tackles and hit-ups than the other. We drove each other on.

### STEVE PRICE

Pet and I had a lot in common. We were both motivated by not letting our teammates or ourselves down by handing in a sub-standard performance, and we both played rugby league the same way, running and tackling hard, and as hard in the 80th minute as we did in the first. We both copped it because of our longevity in the game. It seemed that every year around Origin time, the pundits from south of the border said we were too old . . . and every year we made them look stupid. Pet and I loved to prove 'em wrong.

# 8

# Relocation and racism

Moving from Brisbane to Penrith was a journey from my comfort zone into the great unknown, for my footy and my family. At the Broncos, I had been part of the furniture for a decade. I knew the players, the coach, the coaching staff, the fans. I knew the officials (well, perhaps not quite as well as I thought I did). I was virtually familiar with every blade of grass at the Broncos' home ground, Suncorp Stadium, and our training field at Red Hill. I reckon I was on first name terms with the weights and treadmills. At Penrith I knew hooker Luke Priddis, I'd had some positive phone conversations with coach Matt Elliott and I'd shaken hands and said hello to some of their players after games or on Kangaroo duty. That was it.

If anything, Bonnie, mother of three little children (and now with a fourth on the way), faced an even greater challenge than me. At home in Redcliffe she was surrounded by a support network of loving family (hers and mine) and our friends. This was a blessing when you were married to a footballer who is interstate for days every second week and during Origin, and often away for much longer in New Zealand or England on tour with the Kangaroos. In Penrith, Bonnie would know hardly a soul, and would have to raise the kids largely alone and create a home for us all from scratch.

This was an emotional time for us. Once we'd decided to leave the Broncos and Redcliffe, Bonnie, who is a positive thinker, reinforced to me that we'd made the right move. Starting over in Penrith, she said, would be good for me; and inevitably we'd make great new friends. And, at the end of my contract with the Panthers, Redcliffe would still be there for us. As usual, Bonnie was correct on all counts.

In late 2007, Bonnie and I left the kids with my mother and sisters and spent a weekend in Penrith to formally meet the Panther players and officials and scout out accommodation. We found a good house in a nice part of town, signed the rental papers, then returned to Redcliffe to pack up.

I called Steve Price, who had relocated from the Canterbury Bulldogs to the Warriors in New Zealand. I took heart when he told me that his relocation had been good for his wife and young children and they were all enjoying Auckland. (They are still living happily there today.) Plus, his footy had taken on a new lease of life in a new environment where he faced the challenge of proving himself all over again. Steve saw no reason why I couldn't have a positive experience at Penrith. I hung up the phone feeling that all was going to be okay.

**STEVE PRICE**
When Petero was forced out of the Broncos and joined Penrith in 2008, he gave me a call. He was understandably worried about leaving the club

he loved and had played for over so many years, worried about leaving Redcliffe where he and Bonnie had grown up and where their families lived. He was also troubled by the prospect of not fitting in to a new culture. There are many stories of top players whose careers have not survived a change of club. I told him what I had learned after I left Canterbury Bulldogs for the Warriors. If you embraced the new culture and didn't live in the past, if you continued to do the things on and off the field that you did at your old club, the very things why you had been signed in the first place, and tackled the footy and domestic changes with an adventurous spirit, you stood a good chance of regenerating your career and your life. As I had done.

Luke Priddis was every bit the ally I knew he would be. Luke is special. With his wife Holly, he established the Luke Priddis Foundation, raising money for kids with Autism Spectrum Disorder, after their son Cooper was diagnosed with ASD in 2006. When I hear the detractors of our game, I feel like putting them in touch with Luke. For that matter, I could direct them as well to many other good men who grace both our game and community.

Luke and I had enjoyed a lot of success at the Broncos when he was there from 1999 to 2001. He had represented Australia and been the man of the match when the Panthers won the comp in 2003. Needless to say, I respected Luke's opinion. When I called him to get his impressions of playing at Penrith, he said the players were a great bunch of boys, and he thought well of coach Elliott.

He said the team had recently had some very difficult times and that there was a divide between the players and coaching staff and some club officials. Okay, I figured, this isn't going to be easy, so it will make it all the sweeter when we start winning games and establishing ourselves as a premiership force.

Not long into the season, Luke, who was 31, learned that because of Penrith's salary cap issues, his contract would not be renewed at the end of the year. That rocked the players, not least me, especially with what I had just gone through still weighing on my mind. Men of vast experience like Luke, who are a pillar of the side and set a good example, are vital to a team that is blooding a lot of youngsters, as Penrith was then.

Typically, Luke played on, giving his best until the full-time siren in his final game, because he knew no other way.

My misgivings about not fitting in at Penrith proved unfounded and I was welcomed into the Panthers' lair. Bonnie and I are a self-reliant couple, but it would have been so much harder for us to settle in at Penrith had not the players and their partners accepted us.

Yet I have to be honest. The Panthers were not the Broncos. In Brisbane we had a culture of success, which bred happiness and harmony. Most of my Bronco teammates were Queensland and Kangaroo players who were devoted to the club. They worshipped Wayne and, by and large, enjoyed a good relationship with the officials, who mingled with them at any opportunity. My problem with head office was an aberration.

The Panthers, on the other hand, had come last in 2007 and, as is usually the case, on-field failure breeds off-field discontent. The players fretted about the club's money woes and had little confidence in an administration which they considered aloof and uninterested. There were some in the team who grizzled about Matt Elliott, believing that his game plans were too complex and his demanding pre-season training regimes burned them out. It was obvious to me, too, that some of the boys lacked confidence in themselves.

Matt made me captain, replacing the departed Craig Gower, in spite of my objections. I worried how I was going to exert my authority and that my appointment might not go down well with guys like Trent Waterhouse, Tony Puletua and Luke Lewis, who had been Panthers when Penrith were premiers five years before and who were very capable of leading the team. Although I had achieved a fair bit in the game and was the oldest bloke there, I was a new boy. I wouldn't have blamed the others if they'd got their backs up and made life hard for me. I worried needlessly, for once my appointment was official and my teammates knew that I had Penrith's interests at heart and wasn't just a mercenary come to loaf and pick up big bucks, Trent, Luke and the rest of the boys supported me all the way.

It didn't take Einstein to know what my role had to be at Penrith. I had to instil confidence in the side and parlay that confidence into wins. I had to inspire improved performance on the field and harmony off it by leading by example, playing hard and setting the pace at training. I would be upbeat, approachable and always positive. I would mentor the promising young props Sam McKendry and Tim Grant. Without muscling in where I wasn't wanted nor needed, I let my teammates know that I was there for them if they wanted a chat about footy or life.

When I arrived at the club, the players didn't socialise together much. I tried to change that by organising nights out with the boys and their partners. I had learned at the Broncos and in Origin camp that if you were mates with your fellow players you were unlikely to let them down on the field. I stayed back after training to help stow away the gear. I wanted to help bring along the fine young players who made the Penrith junior league one of the best rugby league nurseries in Australia. I would also go all-out to mend bridges between the players, the coaching staff and the administration.

I was always on call to the media and immersed myself in community activities.

Mixing with the community comes easy to me. I really enjoy that part of the game. It's a good feeling to get out there and strike a blow for rugby league, and it is gratifying when you see the work you do in schools, shopping centres and hospitals pay off when the fans flock to games whether you've been winning or losing dressed to the nines in club colours.

I don't mind standing around signing autographs for fans. When I was a kid, I was a determined autograph hunter and a quick chat with a hero would make my day. Recently a father asked me for an autograph for his boy and he remarked, 'Gee, Petero, you must hate doing this all the time', and I replied, 'No, I love it. It's an honour to be asked', and I meant it.

MATT ELLIOTT was a good and committed coach. Being coached by him was a refreshing experience. Matt pays attention to the details that can win or lose a game and genuinely cares for his players. He thinks deeply about rugby league and life. I found him to be intelligent and innovative, always prepared to try new ways. Some examples? There was the pre-game stare down when we partnered up and stared deep into each other's eyes. Whoever blinked lost. Unfortunately blokes couldn't help laughing and pulling faces to make his partner break. Matt told us off and ordered to keep staring and not laugh. 'Laughing is a sign of weakness,' he roared. 'Show your teammate you're prepared to do whatever it takes to win.' We all got very serious very quickly. That first season, the pre-game stare down was our thing. Matt also mentored top surfers on the pro surfing tour who were sponsored by Billabong. One was the world No. 1 and Panthers tragic Mick Fanning. Matt invited Mick to address our squad at a pre-season camp and attend some of our games. Mick told us how he would become calm before his surfing competition heats. He would sit quiet and still and ignore external noise such as loudspeakers, the crowd, the crashing surf, so he could concentrate solely on winning. He would slow his breathing, visualise himself attacking the wave. Matt encouraged us to do the same before a match. He said it would de-complicate our thinking and help us focus our mind on our individual role within the team structure. Matt is his own man, and a bit of a rebel. He thinks outside the box and has ideas that no other coach in rugby league has. That's what I loved about Matt. It was refreshing to be pushed into new directions. He could be hard to figure out at times, but I valued his advice, and his thoughts on footy and on life.

I did believe that some of his game plans were complex, but rugby league is an increasingly sophisticated game with the best of the coaches, such as Wayne Bennett and Craig Bellamy, endlessly devising new tactics to catch rivals napping and provide a winning edge. As for pre-season training . . . it was not as gruelling, or potentially fatal, as, say, boot camp at Canungra . . . but it was *very* tough.

The quality of the players belied the Panthers' lowly position on the premiership ladder. In the senior playing group were Luke Priddis, Luke Lewis, Trent Waterhouse, Rhys Wesser and the Puletua brothers, Tony and Frank.

Complementing the veterans, there were stars of the future in Michael Jennings, Sam McKendry, Tim Grant, Michael Gordon, Wade Graham, Nathan Smith, Lachlan Coote, Jarrod Sammut and Brad Tighe.

No, talent wasn't lacking. Attitude was.

Thanks to Matt and the players, once I moved to Penrith I put my love for the Broncos right out of my head. I was a Panther and proud of it.

I WAS a nervous wreck in the lead-up to our first competition match . . . against the Brisbane Broncos at Suncorp Stadium. I didn't feel conflicted about mixing it with my old teammates and with the props Joel Clinton and Ashton Sims, who had replaced me. I was looking forward to that, just as I knew they were looking forward to getting stuck into me. I was uncomfortable because I believed the game had been wangled by Brisbane as a money-spinner: the old-stager taking on his former teammates and the new men who'd replaced him. It's all business, I guess.

When I ran onto the field, the 31,000-plus crowd booed me, an incredible contrast to the cheers I got in my last game at Suncorp. We were flogged that day, 48–12. The Broncos beat us all over the park. My former teammates sledged me in a good-natured way and I gave some back, though my words rang a bit hollow as the Broncos piled on the tries. All was forgiven at the final siren, when the crowd's boos turned to cheers and the boys shook my hand, arranged to meet for a beer later, and asked me how things were panning out for me and the family at Penrith. I said hi to Wayne, and wished him well, for by then he had announced that he was leaving the Broncos at the end of 2008.

In the away team dressing room at Suncorp (which, by

the way, is much smaller than the home side's), I felt flat. It had been a stinking hot March day and we'd worn the heat-retaining black Panther jerseys, but what was deflating me even more than that was being beaten so badly by the Broncos. I felt embarrassed, too, for Bonnie and our families, who were all at the game. I wondered as I sat cooling down, the sweat pouring from me, if I had made a terrible mistake and should have swallowed my pride and stayed at the Broncos. That doubt lasted only a short time, as the Panthers regrouped on the flight back to Sydney and we all started talking excitedly about next week's game. 'That was only round one,' I told them. 'There are 25 to go.'

The Broncos disaster was a tough start. Going into the match, our hopes were high that we would be able to put last year's dismal form behind us and make a serious bid for the premiership. Then came the Brisbane defeat. I thought we would be able to get back on track and so did the players. I was deeply impressed by the enthusiasm and positivity of the younger guys, who were hell-bent on making their mark in first grade.

After a narrow defeat by Canberra the following week, our ship steadied, and in the following games we beat the Rabbitohs, the Tigers, the Sharks, the Bulldogs, the Warriors and the Cowboys. Halfway through the season we had won 50 per cent of our games, a big improvement on 2007, and we were on course for a semi-final spot. Frank Pritchard, Luke Lewis (who showed his incredible versatility by playing halfback when required, and playing the position very well), and the young guns Lachlan Coote, Michael Jennings and Michael Gordon were in top form. In the matches when we blew away the Warriors 46–22, the Gold Coast 36–22 and the Bulldogs 52–16, I saw the wonderful potential of that side.

A word about Frank Pritchard . . . On his day, he is one of the most devastating players I've played with or against. He and Sonny Bill Williams have that ability and mix of talents in their game. His athleticism and raw power can turn the fortunes of a game in a blink. He is big and fast, has a beautiful offload, and as a tackler he can be a destroyer. When he hit you, you stayed hit. Whether he wore the black of Penrith and New Zealand or the blue and white of the Bulldogs, his latest club, when he is in the mood to play he'll have a hand in a try or two that may win the match.

I definitely believed that if we stuck together and supported each other, established ourselves as a solid, hard-to-beat side and became regarded by the league public in general and by our fans in particular as triers and winners, then the Panthers would acquit themselves well in 2008 and be a major force in the competition next year or the one after, and I let the blokes know that.


I HAD never known a club to generate so many rumours as Penrith. The place leaked like a sieve, and it was so counter-productive . . . Apart from the fact that most of the rumours turned out to be rubbish, they did plenty of damage when they were in circulation. One whisper being aired mid-2008 concerned me. I was apparently an unhappy Panther and keen to get out of my contract and join another club; the scuttlebutt was that the club was Wigan in the English Super League. This was simply baseless garbage and I said so.

Then there were rumours that spread through the club, and were printed in the newspaper sports gossip columns, that a group of Penrith players had fronted Panthers' management and complained about the coaching of Matt Elliott and as a result he was facing the axe. If this was so, I knew nothing about it. I reckoned I had a pretty good idea of what constituted a good coach, and Matt was one. Consequently I supported him strongly. I did my best to stamp out any griping among the players, convince them to forget the distractions and concentrate on winning games.

The trouble that year was that we were inconsistent, and never more so than late in the season when we were coming sixth and were a real chance of making the semi-finals. Against the Raiders in Canberra we were annihilated 74–12, then the very next week we walloped the Bulldogs 52–16, with Luke Rooney scoring four tries and Michael Jennings running riot.

In the Canberra match, we scored the first 12 points. Suddenly, with Terry Campese playing a blinder, the Raiders went up five gears and piled on 74 points to our zero. There was nothing we could do to switch off the horror movie playing out before our eyes. Matt was appalled: 'We got our pants pulled down, our bums spanked. There's not a lot to say about that game, but there's a lot to feel.'

So how to explain the turnaround in our form when we whipped the Bulldogs just seven days later? During the week, all the players met behind closed doors with Matt and together we honestly assessed our strengths and weaknesses. It was a brutal meeting where we tried to exorcise the demons that were bringing us undone. We also put our hands up for having let down our supporters badly. That week seemed to last an eternity. All we wanted to do was atone for our terrible performance against the Raiders, which we did.

Unfortunately, we could not sustain our intensity and bowed out of the comp with successive big losses to the Storm, the Warriors and Manly. That year we were incapable of stringing wins together. We would have a victory, then relax and be easy pickings the following week. Maintaining intensity for long periods of time, it was clear to me, was the key to success at Penrith.

While I was disappointed when our season ended prematurely, for me, personally, there were positives. I averaged 142.6 metres a game, the most ground gained by any prop in the NRL. I was named the Dally M Prop of the Year and shared the Rugby League Players Association's Players' Player of the Year award with Braith Anasta. And it meant a lot to me that at the Panthers' end-of-year awards night, I was voted Player of the Year and Clubman of the Year.

I WILL never forget this year either for a disappointing incident. It occurred in the 72nd minute of the Panthers' match against Parramatta on Sunday, 6 July 2008, at Parramatta Stadium. We were on our way to a solid 22–16 win in the local derby. I was feeling the effects of Origin III four days before, but had played strongly against the Eels. I was on the sideline, about to re-enter the game after a spell on the interchange bench, when I heard a blast of foul language. The culprits were four men sitting right on the fence, in row A of bay 49, just near me. At first I didn't think their abuse was being directed at me. Then I realised that it was. 'You fuckin' black monkey, Civoniceva!' one of them was screaming right at me, his face distorted with rage. 'Hey Civoniceva, you nigger . . . get back up your tree!' They were relentless with their abuse as I limbered up.

I was shocked, stunned. I'd been racially sledged about my Islander origins, about being black, by opposition players and supporters since I was a boy. It always rankled, even though I thought it was becoming a rare occurrence. But I had never been subjected to abuse as vicious as these blokes were spewing at me.

Our trainer Carl Jennings was by my side and Carl was gobsmacked. I looked at Carl and he looked at me. We simply couldn't believe that this was happening. Carl had some words with the ringleader and his mates and they took no notice of him, just continued yelling at me.

I lost it. The red mist fell. I went straight to where they were sitting and challenged them to repeat what they said. They did so. They were very drunk. On the edge of the fence where the four were sitting they had lined up a number of plastic cups of beer. What enraged me even further was that they didn't care that their behaviour was ruining the day for all those supporters who were sitting in their vicinity. I was tempted to throttle the main man, then reined in my anger and instead lashed out with my hand and knocked their beers flying. The men scampered away. Unfortunately the upturned beers splashed a young family and other supporters sitting in the row behind. I'll never forget the look of terror on those people's faces. My anger had got the better of me and I had made a bad situation worse.

I pulled myself away from the ugly scene and ran back into the game.

At full-time I had mixed feelings. I was happy we'd won, and that I'd backed up well after Origin, yet I was deeply upset that some fans' day had been ruined by a few angry people and my retaliation. I discussed the incident with the boys in the dressing room afterwards, and a trainer overheard and soon the media knew.

After the match, I contacted Parramatta secretary Denis Fitzgerald and told him what had happened, how I had lost control after being racially abused, and sprayed the culprits and, by mistake, a family with beer. I told Denis I would publicly apologise to everyone who was splashed or offended, apart from my abusers. The last thing I would want is for genuine fans to stop coming to games because of an incident caused by an ignorant minority.

Here, in part, is the statement I put out:

Unfortunately I may have sprayed spectators behind the front row where these guys were sitting. I'm pretty sure there were some young families around and I want to apologise to them for my actions, hopefully it won't turn them off coming to the football. I have great memories of going to the football as a kid with my parents and what a great day it was. Parramatta Stadium has always been a great venue for me to play at, not just with the Panthers but with my former club the Broncos and the response from the fans has always been positive. It's unfortunate that a few fans spoiled the day for myself and the other spectators in that area.

Soon after, I received a letter from the father of the family I'd splashed. He said he had no issue with me but what *had* destroyed his family's day at the footy was having to sit behind the louts and put up with their appalling drunkenness, and unacceptable racial abuse.

Our trainer and former player Matt Adamson later told me that fans had earlier complained to security guards about the men's behaviour. The guards had approached the blokes and asked them if they were misbehaving and when the men assured them that they were not, the guards, though they knew they were lying, took the soft option and walked away, abandoning the good supporters to the unpleasantness.

The media learned of the incident and it was all over

Monday's papers. I chose not to fuel the fire by giving interviews about what had happened. I just wanted the furore to go away so I could concentrate on football, however the controversy had taken on a momentum of its own and soon became a national news event.

Reporters canvassed other players and they backed me to the hilt. Joe Galuvao – the Samoa and New Zealand front-rower – said my action was a line in the sand, a statement that racial abuse would no longer be tolerated: 'Petero's refusal to accept the racist abuse will in future years be seen as a landmark moment for players of Pacific Island and Polynesian lineage. He has my full support for what he did and I know a lot of the boys feel the same. He didn't take it, and from now on nobody else should either.'

Frank Pritchard said that the men's behaviour was 'shameful'.

Gorden Tallis praised my 'remarkable restraint . . . I know what it's like to have those taunts thrown at you and sometimes it reaches the point when you can't keep turning the other cheek. Hopefully Parramatta will track down the idiots involved'.

Willie Mason weighed in, saying: 'All players cop their fair share from fans and they have the right to say things, but no one deserves to be racially abused . . . It shows the sort of person Petero is that he felt bad because some kids might have seen what happened. He shouldn't be the one apologising, because he's done nothing wrong.'

'It's surprising and upsetting. Petero had every right to get upset with those comments,' said the Eels' champion Jarryd Hayne.

Shane Webcke tore into my tormentors: 'Those blokes who are sitting up there drunk and saying that shit are idiots and they will be idiots their entire life . . . I know Petero.

He wouldn't react like that unless he had been pushed well and truly beyond the boundaries of what most of us think is acceptable.'

NRL chief operating officer Graham Annesley called the abuse 'outrageous, disgraceful' and said, 'the person responsible should be hanging his head in shame and if we can identify the person we will take action against him. We have the ability to ban people from rugby league matches . . .'

The Parramatta club began an investigation to find the ring leader. Denis Fitzgerald distributed this media release:

> We are disgusted with the behaviour of one of our patrons in making derogatory comments towards Petero Civoniceva. We are doing everything possible to identify the person and I would like to appeal to him to come forward voluntarily so he can apologise directly to Petero. The Parramatta Eels are a proudly multi-cultural club and it is unacceptable that our standing has been tarnished in this manner.

Not surprisingly, no one came forward.

Executives at Channel 9, which had televised the match, pored through the footage and found images of the men abusing me and me knocking their drinks for six. Fans and some Eels' lower-grade players who were in the vicinity offered to make enquiries to identify the men. With their photos being circulated, it was only a matter of time before they were flushed out, and they were banned from attending NRL games for five years. The person who had done most of the abusing was ordered to apologise to me.

Here is his apology. Some who have read it call it half-hearted and slippery and lacking in logic. See what you think.

To whom this may concern, I would like to offer my apologies for the manner in which my comment was taken last Sunday afternoon regarding Petero Civoniceva. My comment regarding the word 'Monkey' was not meant as a racial slur regarding the colour of his skin, but a general comment. I do not see myself as a racist. I understand that what I said was taken in the wrong context, as I was only repeating other slurs that were being yelled around me. I can understand how Petero may have taken the comment the wrong way but I would just like to let him and his family knows [*sic*] I am deeply apologetic for the way in which this slur was taken. It was not meant to upset or anger anybody or anyone in this, to this extent. Once more I would like to offer my genuine sincerity to Petro [*sic*] and his Family, Penrith Panthers, Parramatta Eels and the NRL. Thank you for your time. Yours sincerely, Sper Vega.

If I had been expecting a *genuine* apology, expecting this bloke to own up to his actions and words, I would have been disappointed.

I told reporters that the affair was now over and done with and hopefully it would send a message to people about the standards we wanted in our game, and that racial abuse was unacceptable. I said that I knew Parramatta, Penrith and the NRL would sort it out and I was happy with the outcome and relieved to put it all behind me. The last thing I wanted to see in the papers was that kind of stuff, I wanted to talk about football. I also conveyed my appreciation of the support shown to me and my family by rugby league fans over the previous week.

I said that it was not the first time I'd been racially abused, and unfortunately it would not be the last. That was the society we lived in today. I said:

With the number of guys from different ethnic backgrounds in the game, we need to start setting the tone for what we want, the standards we need. The last thing we want to be like is European soccer, where racism is a real issue. Most of the abuse I've received has been from fans. Certain grounds – you can ask any player in the competition, especially if they are Polynesian or Lebanese – there are always idiots in the crowd who talk about those kinds of things.

For all my calming words, my head was still a mess after the incident, and the Panthers gave me four days off to spend with Bonnie and the children to try to pull myself together. It goes without saying that Bonnie was as upset as me. I was thankful the children were too young to know what had happened to their dad.

I hope the families I accidentally sprayed understood why I did what I did and that they are still fans, cheering on their Parramatta Eels. I hope the men who abused me learned a lesson and when they are permitted to attend games again in a year or so they will have changed their ways. I hope other supporters who have hurled racist jibes took note and felt ashamed. As for Joe Galuvao's comment that by not putting up with it I made a stand, I can live with that if what happened that day deters other cases of racism.

### GORDEN TALLIS

Petero had every right to attack them. Just like when those idiots had the sign abusing my mother, there are some things a man just doesn't stand for. Here is Petero, a man who has never said a bad word about anybody. I've seen him being racially taunted before and he's ignored it. What those bastards said must have been really bad for him to even react, let alone lash out. I've never asked Pet what they called out to him, that's none of my business. There wouldn't be a soul who knows Petero who wouldn't back him up over this. I, for one, would go to war for Pet, and I'd be the millionth person in line.

Racism is not acceptable in life, and life includes sport. Boo a bloke if he drops a ball or misses a tackle or quits your club for another outfit, that's a paying spectator's right. Barracking is great, and a colourful part of the game, so long as it does not cross lines of common decency.

AT SEASON's end, the consensus among the Panthers was that with 10 wins, one draw and 13 losses we'd been better than we were in 2007, finishing 12th instead of last. But no one was kidding himself. Twelfth spot was unacceptable and we would need to improve in 2009. I fronted the media to sum up the season and go in to bat for coach Elliott: 'It has been a disappointing year. With a month to go, we were well inside the top eight and we blew our chance. It is a bit soft to blame the coach or staff for that. Individually, our attitude wasn't up to scratch . . .'

I said that we players needed to take responsibility for our attitude. It hadn't been Matt Elliott who had missed all those tackles when Canberra ran riot against us. I said: 'As for me and Matt, we have a great line of communication. He's always been open to listen whenever I needed to speak to him this season, but certainly our club has some issues they need to deal with in this off-season.'

Matt was summoned to appear before the board and together they talked through the problems, including his training methods and game plans and the low morale of certain players, and at the conclusion of the meeting Penrith chairman Barry Walsh said that while he acknowledged that there were disappointing aspects of the season, the directors saw a positive future and the board had unanimously reaffirmed that Matt Elliott would remain as coach for 2009.

After the meeting, Matt gave a typically upfront and honest interview to journalist James Phelps of Sydney's *Daily Telegraph*. He admitted that when he had to front the board to explain where the season had gone wrong he considered resigning from his post before enduring the ordeal. 'I asked myself if I wanted to continue,' he said.

Then he addressed the rumours that Frank Pritchard and I wanted out of the club. He confirmed that I had no thoughts of leaving, adding:

> . . . but one thing I would say is we have to look after Petero better than we did this year, because we probably squeezed the orange dry. I need to be a bit smarter with the way I use him next year, because he was a bit burnt out. But he didn't complain and there is no release clause in his contract. He doesn't want out.

Matt admitted there were issues with Frank: 'There is some element of truth . . . We aren't going to get rid of him, you can't do that unless you have someone who can fill that role. To be honest, I think he has some personal things going on and he wants to maximise his income, which is understandable.'

Matt now addressed the rumours that had festered all year that he was going to be sacked, and how they came to a head when the Panthers missed the semis, leading him to pretend to hang himself with his tie. He said: 'I was unaware of it all [the sacking talk] until my daughter told me. It was the Friday night and I got a call. A lot of people around me panicked but I didn't. The next night at the press conference everyone was staring at me. No one would ask a question. I always feel humour is the best fix in those situations. I just pulled my tie up very quickly and it was caught on camera.'

The coach was candid about there being some discontent at the club. He said that he wasn't expecting Christmas cards from some players, who resented him for carrying out his instructions from the board in 2007 and 2008 to clean out ageing and under-performing players. 'I made a lot of hard decisions and, to be honest, I may have made them too early.'

He denied that his game plans were too complex but agreed his critics had a point when they accused him of flogging the players too hard in the pre-season. He said: 'We don't play with a lot of complexity. That was rubbish. If anything we are too predictable because we *don't* play with complexity. But I did make a mistake in the pre-season. With the new interchange rules coming in, I made a miscalculation. I was guilty of training them too hard.'

He said he was looking forward to the new season, with success assured so long as the players and coaching staff made good their promise of becoming a tighter group.

Some good men moved on at the end of '08. Luke Priddis left the club, of course, and so did his 2003 grand final-winning teammates Shane Rodney, Rhys Wesser, Tony Puletua and Luke Rooney. It is true that some of them had fallen out with Matt Elliott.

I enjoyed my first year as a captain. Make no mistake, it was a tough gig because I had to keep taking the boys' minds off all the off-field distractions and get them to concentrate on being the best rugby league players they could be. Although there were huge challenges now and ahead, I was enjoying my time at the club. I was proud that Matt Elliott thought highly enough of me to confide in me and, as he admitted, load me up with responsibilities.

IT WAS weird being an enemy Queenslander in a New South Wales-based team at Origin time. No Panthers were picked for the Blues that year, yet I was left in no doubt where my teammates' sympathies lay. For those few weeks when Origin was being contested, I confess that I felt a bit of an alien.

It was yet another memorable series. The fuse was lit, as usual, by motor-mouth former New South Wales players. Tommy Raudonikis, in an attempt to get the Blues' dander up and niggle us, claimed to be outraged because six Queensland players had been born outside the state. He named Israel Folau, Michael Crocker, Greg Inglis, Karmichael Hunt, Sam Thaiday and me and demanded that we be made ineligible to wear the maroon jersey. 'Queensland is cheating, and it makes my blood boil,' he raged. Chipped in Garry Jack, 'If Queensland can rort the system they will . . . It isn't Queensland, it's a Rest of the World side!' Ben Elias bleated, 'If these blokes are Queenslanders, I'm Scandinavian.' Of course, what Raudonikis, Jack and Elias were saying was nonsense, because the stipulation is that you qualify to play for either Queensland or New South Wales if you played your first footy in the state. Izzy, Crock, GI, Karmichael, Sammy and I had all kicked off our senior rugby league careers, as the eligibility rules stipulate, in Queensland.

The Cockroaches were coached for the first time by the super-intense Melbourne Storm coach, Craig Bellamy. Craig is a winner and his take-no-prisoners attitude rubbed off on a terrific Blues team including Brett Stewart, Jarryd Hayne, Matt Cooper, Mark Gasnier, Greg Bird, new Bronco half-back Peter Wallace, Paul Gallen, Danny Buderus, my old sparring partner Brett White and Willie Mason. They beat us 18–10 in the first match at ANZ Stadium before 67,620 fans, most of whom were wearing blue and screaming for Queenslanders' heads. In defence, the Blues forwards, led by Gallen and Bird, raced off their line fast (I believed they were allowed by the refs to jump the gun) and belted us.

Nevertheless, there wasn't a member of our team who was not convinced we couldn't reverse the result in Origin II at Suncorp. Definitely helping our chances was the return of Steve Price, who had missed Origin I. At 34 (Steve) and 32 (me), we would be the oldest front-row pairing in State of Origin history. Wayne Bennett was glad to see us reunited. 'They bring a calmness to the team and a winning attitude. Other players just know they'll get the job done. I haven't seen signs that either of them is slowing up. Their age is irrelevant.'

Beware the wounded Cane Toads. We won Origin II 30–0. Our side was Karmichael Hunt, Darius Boyd, Greg Inglis, Brent Tate, Israel Folau, Johnathan Thurston, Scott Prince, Dallas Johnson, Mick Crocker, and Ashley Harrison, with Steve Price and me in the front row, and Cameron Smith was skipper, taking over the captaincy from the injured Locky. Our bench was a beauty: Billy Slater, Sam Thaiday, Ben Hannant and Nate Myles.

As well as the 52,476 fans in the Suncorp stands, a record 2.76 million TV viewers saw Greg Inglis return serve to Gasnier, who had bested him in Origin I. Greg made many long runs, gliding down the field in his inimitable way, and set up two tries for Darius Boyd. Thurston played a masterly game and kicked seven goals. Steve Price, Ben Hannant and I did our bit up front, subduing Willie Mason (who had angered the Queensland crowd by calling them rednecks and nutbags), Brett White and Craig Fitzgibbon (who had been shifted up into the front row), and laid the platform for a blistering display by the backs. This was only the second time that New South Wales had been held scoreless in an Origin match.

I knew that Craig Bellamy would have ignited a fire under the Blues in a bid to snatch the series in the decider in Sydney, so I decided to retaliate first. In the first minute, their prop Ben Cross hit the ball up, and I steamed in to put a big shot on him. I caught Ben high on the chest, he went down, and, with many Blues players assuming I'd hit him in the head, it was on for young and old. Many punches were thrown; as in most brawls, one or two connected. When the dust cleared, no one was hurt and I was penalised.

That match was close-fought and brutal. Every player was bloodied and battered by the ferocious tackling. Mick Crocker found a novel way to be knocked rotten when he charged down a Mitchell Pearce clearing kick and the ball slammed into the back of his noggin. Crock staggered around the paddock like a drunk and it would have been hilarious if it wasn't so serious.

With 13 minutes to go, the score was 10–all. Then, when we were trapped in our half and struggling to make progress against the fierce Blues' defence, Johnathan Thurston pulled out one of his trademark show-and-go moves and scythed through. As he was about to be hauled down, he passed to Billy Slater who'd raced up in support, and Billy the Kid scored the match- and series-winning try under the posts. Said Willie Mason, 'You just can't coach against shit like that!'

Even when the score was level, we had been calm and confident that we could pull the game out of the fire. Queensland has always specialised in miracle escapes. It just happened to be Johnathan and Billy who came up with the big play that night. Johnathan won the Player of the Series award, and rightly so. He is one of those guys I love playing with and dislike playing against. He is a fierce competitor and throws his wiry frame into the game, and he has sublime skills. Whether it's his trademark dummy, the show-and-go move, a chip kick for himself or someone else, or his sheer pace . . . His first instinct, like that of Darren Lockyer and Billy Slater, is always to attack, and he comes up with the right plays at the right time.

Paul Gallen, who came of age for the Blues in 2008, is another player I admire. When we play against each other it's always tough going. Off the field, we're good mates. We bonded while we were roomies in the camp for the 2008 Centenary Test against the Kiwis in early May, which Australia won 28–12. On a Kangaroo tour to England I discovered that Gal is a good drinking buddy, as was my Panther teammate Trent Waterhouse (which I had already confirmed at various Penrith watering holes). We were guilty of breaking a few curfews to have one or two last beers after a Test win. It was always a dream come true going away on tour and coming up against the best of England. There were many great memories on and off the field. All interstate hostilities are quickly put to rest when you are united representing your country and wearing that beautiful green and gold jersey.

There are a lot of things that have changed within our game. But one thing I'm glad that hasn't is enjoying a well-earned beer after a game. The modern-day player is under greater scrutiny and has to understand their obligations to their coach, team and club. But I like catching up with teammates and opponents over a beer or two, especially on the back of a good game. And I hope that's a tradition that doesn't change.

IT WAS around 2008 that I took a keen intrest in the welfare of Islander players in our game. Coming here as a baby, I've had no trouble assimilating into modern Australian society, but Island boys arriving in their teens can have trouble fitting in and, because they have enriched our game with their toughness and skill, I figure that anything I can do to help them, no matter which club they play for, is worth doing. My Fijian heritage is important to me. So with Nigel Vagana we discussed the pathways and programs for Islander players.

It was a good start in April that year when the Australian Fijian Rugby League organisation, whose aim is to foster pathways for Australian-raised Fijians to play for the Fijian national team – the Fiji Bati – as well as nurture their development into NRL stars, instituted a Best Fijian in the NRL award (a medal named in my honour) and Jarryd Hayne was the inaugural winner. They also asked me to be patron of the association and I was honoured to accept.

The AFRL is the brainchild of ex-Rabbitoh player and current trainer at the Roosters, Steve Driscoll, and the former Fijian players James Pickering and Manoa Thompson, who is Jarryd Hayne's father. When I was a kid I followed the careers of James, a tough and hard-hitting and -running forward who was a Bulldog and a Rooster, and speedy and elusive outside back Manoa, who played with Souths, Wests, the Warriors, Warrington and Carcassonne in France, and also Canberra's try-scoring freak winger Noa Nadruku. Their success inspired me to play rugby league. I also knew of the exploits of the giant Fijian brothers Apisai and Inosi Toga, who played for St George back in the late '60s and '70s. I remember as a kid being with Fijian friends at family get-togethers and they talked about the Toga brothers as legends who came over in those early days and made a go of rugby league. Apisai, a man whose heart, say those who knew him, was as huge as his body, died after stepping on poisonous coral on a return home to Fiji. I am passionate about the welfare of the Polynesian and Melanesian Island boys, and determined to make rugby league a major sport in Fiji, Samoa, Tonga and Papua New Guinea.

I WAS selected in the Kangaroo team to contest the World Cup that was played in late October and I felt fresher than I ever had for a post-season rep campaign because of Penrith's early exit from the competition. Instead of playing in semis and grand finals, I was able to let the bumps and bruises and strains of the season mend while I watched the semis on TV and by World Cup kick-off I felt fit and strong.

The Kangaroos' coach was Ricky Stuart. I admire Ricky. I found him to be tactically astute and he instilled in all of us a fierce pride in our country.

As A player, Ricky Stuart was a passionate and ruthless competitor and he transferred this commitment to his coaching. When he was coaching the Kangaroos, he was flogging us so hard at training that Locky and I had to tell him that the load was taking a toll on the squad, and he listened and backed off a little. Ricky was a winner: with

Canberra, New South Wales and Australia and then when coaching the Roosters to a premiership in 2002.

Some things never change. In the lead-up to the World Cup, former New Zealand and Manly coach Graham Lowe, who said that Steve Price and I 'looked old and out of gas'. Pricey and I had been hearing this refrain for years. You'd think by now we'd have been able to laugh at such taunts and see them for the misguided cheap shots they were, but Lowe's words got up our noses. Once more, in that World Cup, Steve and I ran onto the field with a point to prove.

All went according to plan in the preliminary and semi-final rounds. It became clear to us that New Zealand, coached by Steve Kearney with Wayne Bennett signing on to help him out, was our main threat. We'd beaten them comfortably, 30–6, in the Group A play-offs then both Australia and New Zealand beat England. It would be another Kangaroos–Kiwis showdown in the final.

In hindsight, our preparation wasn't ideal for the World Cup final. We had soft wins over Fiji and Papua New Guinea, so in spite of Ricky's best efforts we were not as match-hardened as we might have been. Then came the injuries. Steve Price and Josh Perry pulled out, leaving only Brent Kite and me as the team's starting props to pack down against Adam Blair and Nathan Cayless, with Sam Rapira coming off the bench. Anthony Watmough and Craig Fitzgibbon, both back-rowers, had to do fill-in front-row duty. Brent Tate was also ruled out.

That said, I offer no excuses for what happened in the final. Our team was star-studded and included Billy Slater, Greg Inglis, Israel Folau, Darren Lockyer, Johnathan Thurston, Cameron Smith, Glenn Stewart and Paul Gallen – no slouches there. The jury is still out on whether our decision to get in the faces of the Kiwis as they performed the haka before the match helped or hindered our cause. I've come to believe that what we did disrespected New Zealand and fired them up against us.

We led 16–12 at half-time after Darren Lockyer scored two slashing tries and Billy Slater had carved up the Kiwis off Thurston's and Lockyer's inside balls. Then, in the second 40 minutes, the game changed as we could not match the New Zealanders' enthusiasm and they powered home to win 34–20 on the back of uncharacteristic Australian mistakes. (As he was being pushed into touch, Billy Slater threw the ball back over his head to try to keep it in play and the loose ball was snapped up by Benji Marshall, who scored.) The Kiwis produced a powerful forward display and Benji Marshall gave a master-class. A turning point of the match was when video referee Steve Ganson of England awarded New Zealand a penalty try after our winger Joel Monaghan took out Lance Hohaia when he was chasing a Nathan Fien grubber bobbling towards our line. Our lack of patience and failure to continue to do in the second half what we had done in the first cost us the match. The Kiwis' spirit and ability to hang tough saw the momentum shift after half time. They smelled our blood in the water.

We were all bitterly disappointed at losing this game, which was in our grasp. After the match we slumped in our dressing shed and listened to the Kiwis celebrate outside. Ricky was specifically angry at the scheduling of the tournament that saw us go into the final under-done, and the performance in the final of referee Ashley Klein. Next morning, he bumped into Klein and the Rugby Football League's director of match officials, Stuart Cummings, and he abused both men, calling Klein a cheat. Ricky later apologised, and resigned as Australian coach. Australia's loss is New South Wales' gain, as Ricky today is pumping up Blues sides with his unquestionable pride and passion.

THE DISAPPOINTMENT of losing the end-of-season World Cup final to the Kiwis was banished by the birth of our fourth child, and second boy, Jacobi. Bonnie was always adamant that all of our kids be born in Queensland, despite us now living south of the border, and I agreed with her. The other three kids had been, and we couldn't let the new little fella down. Imagine him copping it from his brother and sisters at Origin time because he was a Cockroach! Jacobi arrived into the world safely at Brisbane's Mater Hospital. He completed our family. But Jacobi's birth also made us miss our families up in Queensland all the more. A new arrival in the family should be shared with loved ones. And, after the new football season started, they were not around to help Bonnie when I was away, as I often was.

# 9

# No place for the faint-hearted

Season 2008 was bloody hard and seemed to last forever. It began for me with two trial games for the Panthers in February and finished 10 months later in November when I played in the World Cup final. Amazingly, as the Panthers started training for season 2009, I felt terrific. Entering my second year with the club, I hoped that we'd cleared the air in 2008, got rid of the negativity from our wooden spoon year in '07, and that now we were ready to live up to our potential.

I also hoped that after he had been given a vote of confidence from the board, Matt Elliott would be left to coach us without the distracting dramas and politicking that led him to pretend to hang himself with his tie at that press conference. As the season got under way, I organised a meeting between Matt and the players and once more everyone honestly said what was on their minds and we seemed to bond after that.

As ever, I was passionate about playing again for Queensland and Australia. This year the Maroons had an opportunity to create history by beating the Blues four series in a row and although the World Cup had ended disappointingly for Australia, I was dying to pull that green and gold jersey on again. There would be the Anzac Test against New Zealand (we would avenge their World Cup final win by beating them 38–10) and at season's end there was scheduled a Four Nations Series in the northern hemisphere. People kept asking me how long I'd continue playing representative football before, at my grand old age, 33 in '09, it started adversely affecting my club form. I told them I was taking it year by year and as long as I kept being selected I'd keep playing.

The brand new system of having two referees on the field didn't do any favours for bigger, older blokes like me. Now, with that extra pair of eyes policing the ruck, there was no chance of jumping out of the defensive line early, nor of getting away with lying on a tackled bloke a second or two longer than necessary to give your defence a chance to regroup. Having two refs definitely made it essential for forwards to be fitter and more athletic than we had ever been to tear up the 10 metres, bring our man down, release him quickly and get back 10 metres in time to do it all again. There is a good reason why most teams' interchange bench is prop-heavy. Of course, in already lightning-fast Origin, which is played at a much faster bat than club football, the two referees saw the speed of the game go up another gear.

PENRITH STARTED the season with two losses, to the Sharks and the Bulldogs. At the end of that frustrating match against Canterbury – we blew a half-time lead of 20–12 to be beaten 28–26, despite me offloading to set up two tries – I saw red when the Bulldogs' feisty hooker Michael

Ennis pushed our back-rower Gavin Cooper into the fence and Mick and I, who packed down together at the Broncos in 2006 and 2007, clashed. No big deal – and there were handshakes all round in the sheds afterwards. No doubt about it, Mick is a great competitor. He hates to lose and will do anything within his power to win. He has the knack of upsetting the opposition. On this occasion he upset me.

We beat defending premiers Manly 12–10, and then thrashed Wests Tigers 42–22. I was pleased with my game against the Tigers. I gained 139 metres with the ball and topped the tackle count with 30. We lost our next two games, against the Storm and the Broncos, and then won four on the trot, against the Titans, the Raiders, the Sharks and the Roosters. We all knew the match against Canberra was a watershed game for us. Last time we'd met them, they had put 74 points on us. We needed to beat them, and at their home ground where they'd beaten us, to prove that the Panthers of 2009 were a different proposition to 2008 and bury that humiliating loss. We won 18–10.

There were good signs that we had turned the corner. And although the whispers persisted that Matt Elliott's job was still on the line, there was generally a good feeling among the boys. Tim Grant told a reporter, 'The club is like a family now and you can see that with all the wives and girlfriends in the sheds after games. Things have changed here. Everyone is enjoying each other's company.'

Around this time, the Broncos asked me to consider returning to the club in 2010. They were in touch again later in the year when they were in the midst of a form slump. I could have walked out on the Panthers, because there was a clause in my contract stipulating that Penrith must release me after the second of my three years if things were not working out for me. It's a measure of how determined I was to make the best of things at Penrith that I turned the Broncos down.

Maddeningly, the Penrith rumour mill continued at full-throttle. I was told that Matt Elliott had the first half of the season to get results or he was gone. Trying to nip this unrest in the bud, I released a statement to the club and fans:

I'd like to see Matt stay . . . It was tough last year, but he has the support of the boys. It would be great for us as a club if we could move forward and he was part of that. Obviously there's been a lot said about where we are supposed to finish at the end of the season and the troubles we're supposedly having and the in-fighting that is supposed to be going on. But I tell you, we've got a really strong group of guys here in the playing ranks who are sticking together . . .

Whether it was my age or the stress of captaincy I don't know, but just before State of Origin kicked off again, I noticed that I had sprouted a few grey hairs on the top of my head. A reporter put it to me: Age? Stress? Neither, I said. Being the father of four kids was making me look like an old man! He suggested I put a black rinse through my hair. I laughed and said I wasn't that vain. My dad has a head of grey hair and it suits him. As he has done, my plan is to grow old gracefully. As I write this, those first grey hairs have been joined by many more.

I was enjoying being an elder statesman, for club, state and country. It seemed only yesterday that I was the kid, hanging back, too scared to be seen or heard in the company of Wayne, Alf, Shane, Andrew Gee and those other legends. It took me ages before I dared to approach them for advice. Now in a blink, it seemed, I was a senior guy myself and the younger players were coming to me. Where had the time gone?

I wanted to play a role in the development of young props Sam McKendry and Tim Grant, who were both 20 in 2009. It was obvious to me each had the talent and quality to represent his country. Sam, in fact, has been representing New Zealand since 2010. I take no credit for that. He did it all on his own.

Sam and Tim are very different. Mongrel comes naturally to Sam. It wasn't always like that. In the beginning, he wasn't as focused and had to make some decisions about his life and football and where he wanted both to lead. He needed to decide how badly he wanted success. If I helped him understand that he would be wasting his time and talent if he didn't get his act together and be the best he could be, then good.

With Tim, on the other hand, I never had to say too much because he was always in the right headspace and understood what it takes to go to the next level. Tim knew what he wanted and that was to hit the heights of rugby league, and he trained and made sacrifices accordingly. He was prepared to do whatever it took to get there. He is a fine leader in the making. A future Penrith captain, no doubt.

DÉJÀ VU all over again. The next Origin series it was former Blues great Laurie Daley's turn to say that Steve Price and I were over the hill. 'Petero has had his time,' declared Daley. 'He has been an outstanding player but if New South Wales play correctly, he and Steve Price can be exposed.' (Daley also suggested that Darren Lockyer was suspect under pressure.) Once more, Steve and I found ourselves approaching the series with a grim determination to prove to our critics that we were anything but past it.

After the dust of that series settled, I approached Laurie about his criticism and he insisted that the way he had been quoted didn't reflect what he truly thought. What he meant to say was that I had had my time in the elite league of props over many years and now it was the chance of the young Blue forwards to take their turn and experience the highs that I had. He had meant to pay tribute to me for having played at the top level for a long time and caution the Blues not to go easy on me because of what I had achieved. I was content to take him at his word. Whether he meant it or not, Steve Price and I used Laurie's criticism as motivation.

Then, as that controversy died down, former Blues' coach Graham Murray suggested that the quick New South Wales hooker Robbie Farah would make fools of Queensland's lumbering old front-row relics. 'They are great players, but they are getting older,' he said.

Our coach Mal Meninga, Daley's teammate from Canberra's glory days, stuck up for Steve and me. 'I envisage they will be playing [for Queensland] next year. It's up to how they're thinking, of course, and how they're playing.' So far that year in club matches, Steve had hit the ball up for an average 145.6 metres per match, and I had averaged 145.1. We were the number one and two ground-gainers in the NRL.

My Penrith teammate Luke Lewis, who had been picked for the Blues, also backed me up: 'It will be tough playing against him. I will just have to get my body in front of him and get him down. He'll keep coming all day and if the pace picks up he'll handle it. If it slows down he just plays at the same speed. He is a workhorse . . .'

Just when you think State of Origin could hardly get more dramatic and exciting, along comes Origin '09. New South Wales came in dead-set determined not to lose and therefore record an unprecedented fourth consecutive series loss. The selectors and coach Bellamy had sacked some regulars and the new-look Blues contained Jarryd Hayne, Terry Campese, Michael Jennings, Ben Creagh, Peter Wallace and Robbie Farah. Our team for the opener was Billy Slater, Darius Boyd, Greg Inglis, Justin Hodges, Israel Folau, Darren Lockyer, Johnathan Thurston, Dallas Johnson, Sam Thaiday, Ashley Harrison, Steve Price, Cameron Smith and me, playing my 23rd Origin match; and our bench was Karmichael Hunt, Ben Hannant, Nate Myles and Michael Crocker. Injuries would see Willie Tonga, Dave Shillington, Cooper Cronk, Matt Scott and Nev Costigan come into the side later in the series.

In Origin I in Melbourne, the Blues started confidently, only to be shaken in the eighth minute. Jarryd Hayne crossed for what looked to many like a fair try only to have it disallowed when the video ref ruled that he'd put a foot out on his long and spectacular run to the line. We took advantage of New South Wales' disappointment and Slater, Inglis and then Thurston scored to put us comfortably ahead 18–6 at half-time. Right after the break, GI seemed to put the result beyond doubt when he scorched down the field for a try to make it 24–6 to us. Then the Blues battled back and scored twice. Pricey and I rolled up our sleeves and kept hitting it up in those closing minutes. We got belted, picked ourselves up and charged into the desperate Blues defence again. We shut them down and we held them out. Darius Boyd scored at the death and we won 28–18.

The experienced rugby league journalist and former coach Roy Masters seemed to take pleasure in Steve and I showing up our detractors. He noted in the *Sydney Morning Herald* that while the packaging and the payment of State of Origin football had changed, the technology had become advanced and the coaching better researched, the essence of our code, the grunt and the struggle, was timeless:

Origin I was won via the relentless go-forward of Queensland's veteran props when only six points separated the teams in the dying stages of the match. With the Maroons leading 24–18 and some of their young players showing signs of panic, front-rowers Petero Civoniceva and Steve Price carried the ball from the Queensland quarter, sapping the energy of the New South Wales pack and extinguishing the Blues' hopes of retrieving the ball in an attacking position. [They] sucked the last breath from the Blues.

They are a reminder that footballers don't play State of Origin games for glory, or even money . . . These men play because it is still their time and place in the 30-year history of a series that continues to confound and confuse, never following a script . . .

Last rites for Petero and Price turned to last laughs.

Two days after Origin I, I pulled on the black Panther jersey and led the boys to a 26–10 win over Wests Tigers. Before the game I was still stiff and sore. I ran that out and pulled up well. Before the match, Matt Elliott proved what a caring guy he is when he took me aside and asked me if the constant chat about my age was upsetting me. I told him the truth. Sure, I'd grown tired of people calling me too old, but I had learned to transform criticism into motivation. I told Matt I wanted to keep playing for Penrith, Queensland

and Australia as long as I let nobody down. I, not my critics, would know when it was time to retire, and I wouldn't hang around a moment later because I was terrified of not playing well and nor did I want to keep out a more deserving younger player.

WE KNEW the Blues would come at us hard in Origin II in front of their home crowd at Sydney's ANZ Stadium. Telegraphing the physical approach we knew that New South Wales would take to knock us off our stride, hard-heads Paul Gallen, Michael Weyman, Anthony Watmough and Trent Barrett joined Luke O'Donnell in the team.

We were fired up to meet the challenge by the death on 9 June of the great Bronco talent scout and mentor Cyril Connell. I attended Cyril's funeral, and by his casket was a framed Bronco jersey signed by all the internationals he had discovered. There were a whole lot of names on that jersey. Cyril stories were told, such as how he always knew where to find the best pies while on scouting trips to the bush. I owed Cyril, for having faith in me as a young bloke and sticking up for me when Wayne was unconvinced about me. For me, for so many of the other Queensland boys who worshipped him, Origin II was for Cyril.

After 22 minutes, Trent Barrett belted our strike weapon Greg Inglis with a high and late cheap shot which put GI out of the game with a suspected broken jaw (Greg was later cleared of the injury). We led just 18–14 with one minute to go and the Blues hurling everything at us. With them pressing our line, it was still anyone's game. Then Cameron Smith scored a try to get us home 24–14 and clinch our fourth consecutive series win.

I played through that cliff-hanger finish in terrible pain.

Twenty minutes into the game we'd been barely hanging on, defending on our line, when I pushed forward to accelerate up in defence and felt something go in my foot. I feared I'd broken my ankle. When I realised I could still run on it, there was no way I was coming off despite the pain in my foot.

After the match I pulled off my boot and my foot was badly swollen, the pain centred on my big toe. A few pokes and prods confirmed that the toe was not broken. What had happened was worse. As I pushed off the line, I had torn two tendons in my big toe. I would need an operation to reattach the tendons and there would be a lengthy spell on the sideline while it healed.

I was on crutches for a month after surgeons pinned the tendon back onto my toe bone, then for the next eight weeks my foot was immobilised in a protective moon boot. Apart from missing Origin III – the first Origin I had missed in 21 games – I wouldn't play for the Panthers again in 2009, although the doctors said there was an outside chance I would recover in time to represent Australia in the Four Nations Series in October.

The toe injury broke up my partnership with Pricey, who had packed down with me in eight of the last Origin matches. I texted Steve to tell him that I had been ruled out of Origin III and he sent me three text messages in return: 'Oh no', 'I can't believe it', and, 'Are you sure this is happening?'. Steve wore my No. 10 jersey in Origin III, with my replacement Matt Scott wearing Steve's usual No. 8.

So I was sitting on the sideline with my foot encased in a moon boot unable to stick up for Steve Price when he was knocked unconscious in the dead rubber Origin game at Suncorp. Nearing the final siren, with the Blues leading 28–16, Steve and Blues prop Brett White traded heavy blows at the play-the-ball. Just as Brett caught Steve with a right, my Penrith teammate Trent Waterhouse leapt on Steve from behind and Steve went down. His head hit the ground and he was out cold. Now Justin Poore, their other prop, bullocked in and tried to drag the unconscious and limp Steve up to his feet by his jersey front.

The Maroons went ballistic at this insult to a champion. There was shoving, grabbing and plenty of threats. Justin Hodges went for Trent Barrett, whom he later claimed to have seen laughing at Pricey and then he challenged White to a fight right there on the field. White licked blood from his lips and snarled at Justin. Order was momentarily restored. Steve, suffering severe concussion, was carted off the field in a medi-cab while his wife Jo and brother-in-law Brent Tate stood grim-faced and anxious on the sideline. Trent Waterhouse was sent off for being the third man in.

With 55 seconds to go and the game out of our grasp, the Queenslanders decided to take revenge. Cam Smith hoisted the ball high. Blues fullback Kurt Gidley got under it. He bravely stood his ground and caught the high spiralling kick, and a moment later he was smashed by five Maroons. Another blue broke out. There were more shoves and punches and grappling on the ground. Justin this time went after Ben Creagh. The full-time siren sounded. The teams shook hands – reluctantly.

It was an uneasy feeling sitting there on the sidelines, watching this unfold. We were a tight-knit group. You could see that in the way the boys reacted after their most senior player was knocked out and man-handled.

Yet more than anything Brett White did that night – after all, he and Pricey went at it man-to-man, one-on-one – I was furious at Trent Waterhouse's involvement and Justin

Poore's manhandling of Steve when he was unconscious and defenceless. I blazed away to the media, saying that there would be scores to settle next year and hammering Trent – 'I don't think you can get any worse [than smash a man] when he's not looking.' When I'd calmed down, I rang Trent and we buried the hatchet.

Justin Poore's, I still believe, was a low act. I said at the time that it was one of the worst things I had seen on a football field. I called Poore 'gutless' and 'stupid'. His excuse was that he thought Steve was faking injury to get White and Waterhouse sent off, but anyone who knows Steve knows that he is too proud ever to take a dive.

In the days after that torrid match, my anger turned into disappointment at losing Origin III. We were the better side and so should have won it. Too often a team that has won a series loses the dead rubber. There is an inevitable mental and physical relaxation when the series has been decided, yet if your mindset is right complacency should never creep in. Besides, you can always count on the opposition's determination not to be humiliatingly whitewashed.

I thought that our preparation had not been as good for Origin III as it had been for the earlier games – for some in our team, the celebration party started when we won Origin II. That was reflected in our performance. We seemed distracted and not as incisive as we had been, and should have been. The fight re-focused us, but by then the game was over. When the Maroons came together the following year, we spoke about the importance of faultless preparation for every match, alive or dead, and never again letting our guard down. If we had the chance to hammer the final nail into New South Wales's coffin with a three–zero win, we would.

•

BACK AT Penrith, while my teammates were training and playing I was on the rowing machine, keeping my cardio up while my toe healed.

Still unable to play, I was frustrated out of my mind as a semi-final spot loomed, then was snatched away by injuries to some of our key players. I very much wanted to be out there, rallying the boys. We won just one of our last five competition games and some of those losses were huge: 25–6 to the Dragons, 58–24 to the Broncos, 48–6 to the Eels. If we'd beaten Newcastle in round 26, the last competition round, we would have made eighth spot. We lost 35–0. We finished 11th on the ladder, one spot better than 2008.

Our centre Michael Jennings broke out that season. He was picked for the Blues and Australia. From the first time I laid eyes on him when I joined Penrith, I knew he was special. He has blinding speed and wonderful balance. Like Justin Hodges, Greg Inglis, Brett Stewart, Jamie Lyon, Mark Gasnier and, although they were before my time, Brett Mullins and Reg Gasnier, Michael makes running fast look effortless. He *glides*.


I WAS named captain of the Prime Minister's XIII to play the Kumuls in Papua New Guinea while the semis were in progress, but although my toe had just about mended thanks to conditioner Carl Jennings' rehab regime, I pulled out after doctors warned that the hard grounds up there might cause further damage to the re-attached tendons. I did however recover in time to be selected for the Kangaroos to go to England for the Four Nations, despite not having played since June. Matt Elliott generously encouraged me to make myself available for Australia, even though doing so might not be the best preparation for Penrith's season 2010. Joining me on that Four Nations campaign were Panther teammates Michael Jennings, Luke Lewis and Trent Waterhouse, all of whom had played State of Origin. Our selection was a tribute to our coach and our club.

I had been playing for Australia since 2001 and every time I ran onto the field in my country's colours it was a thrill. I grew up idolising the Kangaroos and would set my alarm for the wee hours and creep out to our lounge-room so as not to wake Mum or Dad, and sit there with the sound down low on the old Rank Arena TV set with its rabbit ears antennae watching Australia play Great Britain or those romantically-named club sides Wigan, St Helens, Leeds and Warrington on misty fields where the packed grandstands crowded down onto the very sideline.

I was always intrigued by how just a few weeks or months before the Australian players such as Wally Lewis, Greg Dowling, Bob Lindner, Mal Meninga, Gene Miles and Ben Elias, Peter Sterling, Paul Sironen, Brett Kenny and Steve Roach had been bashing the hell out of each other for club or state, but became a united force prepared to die for each other when they wore the green and gold. This, to me, was pretty special and a bit mystifying. I would come to understand.

The 2009 Kangaroos comprised some of the participants in that violent and bitter third State of Origin match. There was Brett White, Justin Hodges and Trent Waterhouse, and Greg Inglis, Cameron Smith, Sam Tháiday and Kurt Gidley, who were also throwing punches and sledges that night at Suncorp. Of course, everyone got on famously. We were all a little worried when we went into camp that the Origin hostility would rear. There was nothing to worry about. We had a job to do for Australia and any scores to be settled could wait till Origin next year. I found that Brett White, Queensland's Public Enemy Number One in Origin III, is a good bloke, as I deep down had always suspected.

Now, once again, in 2009 I ran out of those same dressing sheds at Wigan and Leeds from which my Kangaroo heroes once emerged, into the boos of the fans and the icy blast of a northern England autumn.

It took just one game, against New Zealand, to snap me out of my reverie. The bloke mainly responsible was a young firebrand named Jared Waerea-Hargreaves, who played for Manly then and was making his Test debut. From the moment he came off the interchange bench, Jared roughed me up in tackles and called me an old-timer. It seemed like it was only yesterday that I was the young bloke trying my best to stamp my authority against older, more experienced opponents. How time flies when you're having fun!

I survived the Test against the Kiwis, my first game in many months. My fitness held up and I recovered quickly from the pounding Jared and his teammates Adam Blair and Fuifui Moimoi inflicted on me.

In our match against France at Paris's Stade Sébastien Charléty on 7 November, I played my 39th Test and equalled Johnny Raper's record for the greatest number of Tests by an Australian forward. We won 42–4, the 14th consecutive Australian Test win over France. Afterwards, there was a ceremony in the dressing-room and the boys and staff were kind.

For the Four Nations final against England our side was Slater, Brett Morris, Inglis, Hodges, Hayne, Lockyer, Thurston, Luke Lewis, Hindmarsh, Gallen, Hannant, Cam Smith and me, with Gidley, White, Watmough and Thaiday on the bench. The English side was a mixture of champion veterans in Adrian Morley, Jamie Peacock and Gareth Ellis, and youthful up-and-comers James Graham, Sam Tompkins, Ryan Hall and a huge 20-year-old forward named Sam Burgess who, much like Jared Waerea-Hargreaves had done with me, had taken on the powerhouse Fuifui Moimoi in a previous match and sat Fui on his bum.

The English gave us a real shock in the early section of that match, especially when Sam scored two tries, including a beauty from 40 metres out in which he stood me up and dummied past Billy Slater and showed the pace, footwork and determination that makes him a star of the NRL today. As usual, though, the steadying influence of our 6, 7, 9 and 1, and our ability to sustain pressure for long periods took us to an easy 46–16 win.

In this match, I became the most-capped Australian forward. Afterwards I sat and quietly reflected on the milestone. Who would have thought? I don't rate myself in the same class as a player as Chook Raper, whose attacking genius and peerless cover defence in the 1950s and '60s for St George, New South Wales and Australia made him a rugby league Immortal. In many ways I feel a bit embarrassed to have played more Tests than Johnny. I attribute my continued selection over so many years to knowing my role as a prop and staying mentally and physically strong enough to keep carrying it out. Perhaps it has helped that I have my dad's footy longevity genes.

Bonnie and the children called me after the final to send their big hugs and love down the phone from Redcliffe. Tallulah asked the same question she always did, 'Daddy, did you score a try?' and I gave my usual answer, 'No.'

# 10

# A job to do

The new season, 2010, was the third and final year of my contract with the Panthers. In the off-season, Brisbane again made it crystal clear to me that they wanted me back in 2011. Their new coach, my friend and former 1997 Broncos' reserve grade coach Ivan Henjak, as well as Bruno Cullen, football manager Peter Nolan and my former teammates were keen to see me get back on the maroon and gold horse that had thrown me.

I said no to the Broncos because in spite of one part of me wanting to take my family home, the fact was that I had unfinished business with Penrith and would take up the extension to my contract that they were offering me. Although we only came 12th in 2008 and 11th in 2009, in both years injuries had beaten us as much as any other team. I knew that if we could stay healthy in 2010 we would achieve something special. We had the cattle. Luke Lewis, Michael Jennings, Lachlan Coote, Frank Pritchard, Trent Waterhouse, Tim Grant, Sam McKendry and Michael 'Flash' Gordon were genuine stars of the NRL. That year we signed Luke Walsh, a skilful halfback with an ace kicking game, as well as Kevin Kingston, Travis Burns and Nigel Plum, all noted hard men and top-line defenders; and speedy back Adrian Purtell. As we began our campaign, we all believed that a semi-final spot was ours for the taking.

Captaining the Panthers had become a crusade for me. I was determined that those boys reached their potential. I wanted to repay with on-field success our devoted fans, the league-mad people of Penrith with their Panther gear and licence plates and bumper stickers who rocked up to our matches. The time was not right for me to turn my back on Penrith. I called Ivan Henjak and told him I was staying put. Good man that he is, he said he understood my position. I signed on as a Panther for two more years: 2011 and 2012, when I would be 36 years of age.

Matt Elliott, making good on his promise not to flog me as hard in 2010 as the year before, offered to give me strategic rest games during the season. I said thanks, Matt, but no thanks.

We lost our first two games. I made my 250th first grade appearance in round two, a 28–20 defeat by the Cowboys, then after beating the Storm we played Newcastle at Energy Australia Stadium and found ourselves down by 18 points at half-time. I'm not a guy who gets angry. Bonnie, in fact, says she has never seen me in a rage, but during that break Matt let me have my say and I ripped into the boys and demanded that they extricate themselves from the hole they had dug themselves into. I demanded that they show pride and toughness under pressure and never give up. They could see how much it meant to me to turn that game around. We went back out and won 34–30. Before, we tended to hang our heads when we fell behind in a game and struggled to find a way out of a dire situation. That was the game when it sunk in that, like the best teams, we could fight back, we could come from behind and win.

In succession we beat the Roosters, Warriors and Tigers, lost to the Gold Coast then downed the Sharks (with Michael Jennings scoring three blistering tries) and the Bulldogs, were beaten by the Rabbitohs, then strung together wins over the Knights, the Broncos, the Sea Eagles and the Dragons.

As well as our never-say-die attitude, what brought us many a win that year was our newfound respect for the ball – we had reduced our error rate and were completing our sets of six tackles more often than in past seasons. And new recruit Luke Walsh's heady halfback play and pinpoint accurate kicking in general play was giving our attack an extra dimension.

In 2010 Penrith scored 42 per cent of our 111 tries from kicks, many of those from Luke's boot. Luke was a master at grubber kicks and of putting up a ball on the fifth tackle that hung in the air over our opponents' line and, right on cue, Coote, Jennings or Gordon would pluck it out of the air or fall on it for the try. Our kick-chase improved, and we always had numbers on the ball when Luke kicked it to the corners.

That year we copped plenty of criticism for our reliance on scoring from kicks, yet nowhere in the rule book does it say you can't win games from kicking to the corners and players catching the ball and scoring. We would have been stupid not to keep at the tactic because it was scoring us points and winning us games. (The following year we didn't score nearly as many tries off kicks simply because we lost Michael Gordon and Lachlan Coote for long periods with injury.)

•

I'D NOT always seen eye to eye with the Melbourne Storm, even though I had some good mates there in Craig Bellamy, Billy Slater, Cameron Smith and Greg Inglis. I felt for them when the NRL came down hard on the club in April for breaches of the salary cap over five years totalling $3.17 million. The Storm was stripped of their 2007 and 2009 premierships, the minor premierships they won in 2006, 2007 and 2008, banned from receiving premiership points in 2010, and fined $1.689 million.

In a sense, the club deserved what it got. I was just sorry for the Storm boys. I have no way of knowing for sure, but I would be surprised if the players knew the extent of the rorting by a few members of their management and, having won a few grand finals myself, I understood how much sacrifice and steel and physical and emotional effort it takes to be crowned premiers, how *hard* it is to win a grand final, and how terribly it would have hurt when their premierships were snatched away. The players suffered the stigma of being thought cheats, and I thought that wasn't fair.

It was about then that I was invited to represent the players of all clubs in talks with David Garnsey, the CEO of the Rugby League Players' Association, a body looking after the welfare of the blokes who put their bodies on the line each week. Until then, I had had minimal contact with the association. I soon discovered how necessary the RLPA is and how vital it is for the players to have a say in the running of the game. David heard me out as I raised the issues close to my heart and the hearts of my fellow players. Having been in so many rep teams in Australia and overseas, I had a good idea what was on my peers' minds.

David and I talked about the need to ease player burnout. The players should not be ground into the dirt by having to play an excessive number of matches a year and fans have a right to see them fresh and at their best. We discussed the need for changes to the salary cap so that clubs which developed a player were not forced to relinquish him when he became a star and his pay increased, and that there be a dispensation on the cap for clubs' long-term players so they were not forced to leave 'home'.

There had to be a better collective bargaining agreement, a fairer distribution of TV rights and sponsorship funds to the players, including a better deal for guys on the minimum wage, and academic, trade and life education had to be made available to young players. The special challenges facing players of other cultures, such as indigenous and Islander boys, had to be addressed. Also on my agenda was better pay for representative players, the duty of care of player managers, and what must be done to rejuvenate rugby league in the bush. David Garnsey listened to what I had to say and we began working on solutions.

I had never been a vocal advocate of players' rights, in fact early on I was the guy at the back of the room in any meeting, never daring to say boo to a goose. Yet now, the more I knew about the work of the RLPA I realised how important it was for players to take ownership of the issues surrounding our employment. For too long, too many players had been happy just to pay their annual RLPA fees with a grumble and sit around waiting for the association to make their decisions for them . . . then grizzle when things were not going the way they thought they should. I concluded that if change was going to happen, we players needed to present a strong, united voice through our players' association and I gathered support from my fellow senior players from all clubs to recognise the importance of a strong players' association.

Later that year, in the Queensland State of Origin camp,

Darren Lockyer and I were invited to meet with NRL CEO David Gallop and, on behalf of the players, go head-to-head with him about the issues that concerned us. David saw our point of view and promised to deal with our concerns.

With the game floundering in the wake of the Melbourne Storm scandal and the recent defection of stars Karmichael Hunt and Israel Folau to AFL and Mark Gasnier, Sonny Bill Williams, Craig Wing and Craig Gower to rugby union, confidence in the current administrative set-up was waning.

I was also adamant, along with such good thinkers on our game as Locky, Brett Kimmorley, Johnathan Thurston and Benji Marshall, that there was a need for an independent commission comprised of top-line people in rugby league and business to run our game. (That Australian Rugby League Commission – the ARLC – with John Grant at the helm, would be established two years later, early in 2012.)

I couldn't bear to see rugby league going backwards while other codes powered ahead. I told reporters who asked me about my involvement in the RLPA:

> It just feels that as a game we are nowhere near reaching our potential. There are too many meetings where the only decision made is to hold another meeting. As players, we're not told what money is made in State of Origin – that could give guys second thoughts about wanting to leave. We need real honesty. At the moment the game has its hands tied. It's not growing. We're being left behind. Other sports are leap-frogging us because they have decision-makers making smart decisions in terms of the growth of the game.

Shortly after the State of Origin meeting with David Gallop, I organised Darren Lockyer, Johnathan Thurston, Shane Shackleton, Ben Hornby, Andrew Ryan and Keith

Galloway to talk with David Garnsey of the RLPA about issues relevant to their clubs. It was the first time we had various senior members in one room discussing our issues. I was later voted in as General President in 2011/12.

### DAVID GARNSEY

Petero brought special qualities to his role. He was respected by everybody in the game: his fellow players, his employers, the media, which was critical because we had to get our message out. It's easy to attack me and people do that with great regularity and joy but they thought twice before attacking Petero because he was so loved and respected because of his natural aura and his achievements in club, state and international football. In turn he brought respect to the association and to the cause of the players. People listened to him. He didn't get his point across by shouting or saying outrageous things. He simply quietly and calmly spoke his mind. Those who may have disagreed with him didn't try to talk over the top of him. He had an innate knowledge of what the players needed and what they deserved and, because he was a realist, what they could achieve. Since he first came to see me with some matters on his mind he became the spokesman for rugby league players from the elite level down to the young guys just breaking in.

THE MAROONS entered Origin camp in 2010 determined to atone for losing the match and the fight in Origin III the year before. There was no talk of getting square. Our best revenge would be victory in all three games.

The bleats of former Blue players were heard as usual before Origin I. Mark Carroll and David Gillespie called on New South Wales to again 'turn on the biff'. Such talk is good only for selling newspapers. At our level, by and large, a hard clean tackle does more damage than a cheap shot punch. Fighting does not win Origin games – elite players these days are too mentally strong to be put off stride by someone turning on a blue. Speed, power and heart do. We went in confident, and welcomed Cooper Cronk and Dave 'Coal Train' Taylor, my old Broncos teammate who is as skilful as he is big (123 kilos) and powerful, to our squad.

Origin I was a frantic affair, played at breakneck pace despite the rain at ANZ Stadium. It's fair to say the forwards cancelled each other out, and the match was largely decided by the flair of the backs. Johnathan Thurston, Locky, Darius Boyd and Greg Inglis starred for us, while Jamie Lyon and Jarryd Hayne had blinders for the Blues. We got in front early and stayed there, leading 28–14 with 13 minutes to go. Jamal Idris and Ben Creagh scored for New South Wales in the dying moments but it was too little too late and we hung on to win 28–24.

Just before half-time someone, I don't know who, trampled on my hand. State of Origin adrenalin made the discomfort bearable and I played on, sure it was just a bad bruise or a sprain. As with my damaged toe of the year before, the injury was way worse than I thought. It hurt like hell when I cooled down after the game and scans next day confirmed it was a broken bone that would keep me on the sidelines for around a month. I could not believe my bad luck. I would miss Origin II and key club games for the then second-placed Panthers. My hand was put in a splint and encased in plaster. At least this time, unlike when I hurt my toe, I was able to run to keep up my cardiovascular fitness.

It was a bitter disappointment when racism reared up again in the lead-up to State of Origin II. New South Wales centre Timana Tahu accused Andrew Johns, who was on Craig Bellamy's coaching staff, of racially vilifying Greg Inglis over drinks at the Blues camp on the Gold Coast. Timana was so incensed that he walked out of the camp. Joey also departed as the scandal broke in the media.

The furore brought the Maroons no joy, even though it must have badly disrupted the Blues' preparation. Speaking for myself, and I know this is also the case with other Queensland players, I consider Timana Tahu and Andrew Johns to be top blokes. Joey Johns is not a racist and God knows what he was thinking when he made his comments. Their bust-up, and the hits our code took because of it, was a tragedy. We Maroons talked about it, of course we did, then put it out of our minds to concentrate on the matches ahead.

Because I had been involved in a racism issue myself in 2008, the press came to me for a comment. I said:

> I think awareness has improved among the younger players that racism has no place in our game. We already have the Indigenous All Stars game, which is fantastic . . . but we also need a 'Stamp Out Racism' round to highlight the issue. There are so many cultures in our game and we really need to send a strong message. The stars of the game need to take a stand. Timana has taken a stand, he obviously feels strongly about racism, and other players will support him. I believe what he has done is brave.
>
> [On Joey Johns' words]: It will affect Greg [Inglis], for sure. It's Andrew Johns saying it, not some Joe Blow off the street. Joey has a huge standing in our game in terms of what he has achieved, and when comments come from

someone like that it will hurt. As a Queenslander, hope-fully Greg will use the incident as motivation to play the game of his life on Wednesday.

The timing in June of the Body Pacifica festival, an NRL initiative to celebrate the Islanders playing rugby league and promote tolerance and cultural awareness, was perfect. There was an event with speeches and an Island feast and kava tasting and an exhibition of paintings by Penrith stal-wart Frank Puletua at the Casula Powerhouse Arts Centre in Sydney's west. The highlight – or low-light depending on your opinion about a bunch of beefy blokes wearing next to nothing – was a calendar in which Jarryd Hayne, Jared Waerea-Hargreaves, Roy Asotasi, Fuifui Moimoi, Michael Jennings and I were photographed wearing tradi-tional Island warrior dress. At the event, organiser Nigel Vagana quoted Nelson Mandela: 'Education is the best tool, the most powerful tool, for change, and it can change this world.'

I missed the Maroons' 34–6 walloping of the Blues – seven tries to one, with Israel Folau scoring two – in Origin II, which saw us win the series. There was a fair amount of niggle in that game, lots of sledging and cheap shots, with Sammy Thaiday's trademark curly locks being targeted by Blues trying to goad him to lash out and incur a penalty.

I was back for Origin III, the match we had promised ourselves we would win to erase memories of our loss in the corresponding game in 2009.

There was no way we were going to lose the third match. We were on top early after tries to Darius Boyd and Nate Myles. The Blues roared back and with 10 minutes to go they led 18–13. Then Mick Ennis punched Nate and Billy Slater scored a try on the back of the penalty kick for touch.

We led 19–18 with four and a half minutes remaining. That gallant New South Wales side, desperate to avoid a 3–0 series loss, refused to lie down and came at us in wave after wave of attack. Many times they seemed certain to score and win the game. With one minute left on the clock, Israel Folau intercepted and linked with Willie Tonga, who touched down.

Those last 15 minutes of Origin III were epic. Blokes were busted, blokes were out on their feet. We yelled to each other, 'Don't give up! . . . Don't give up!' I don't know where we found our reserves of energy to keep repelling the Blues and save that game, but I suspect all the bonding we had done in the Origin camps had plenty to do with it. In camp we made a pact. None of us would be the one who let his teammates down, the one who missed the vital tackle or dropped the ball with the line wide open, the one who didn't push himself to repeatedly hit the ball up into the teeth of the brutal Blues' defence even though his muscles were aching and his lungs were collapsing, the one who shirked getting up and back in the defensive line, or succumbed to exhaustion and failed to back up a break. The one who didn't put his body on the line to take a high ball as the Blues stampeded down the paddock, their boots pounding on the turf.

As the minutes ticked on, Locky kept screaming at us, 'Hold your composure . . . Hold your composure!' We won 23–18 and recorded our first clean sweep of the Blues since 1995. Billy Slater, now well on the way to establishing himself as the finest fullback ever to play the game, was a deserving Player of the Series.

Shortly before Origin III, my great mate and fellow Maroon prop Steve Price had retired from rugby league because of an ongoing foot injury. He shed tears when he called it quits. I love Pricey for his passion. He had played his first Origin way back in the dark ages, in 1988, and we had teamed up in the Maroons' front row 14 times since. We dedicated the series win to our friend Pricey.

Another great loss was that of Israel Folau to AFL. He had been selected for Queensland when the news broke that he had abandoned our code and there was debate over whether he should be allowed the honour of playing Origin. Proud Arthur Beetson said Izzy had 'no right to play in our feature game'. At first I sided with Artie, then I softened a bit. As far as I was concerned, Israel's AFL career was in the future; he had played well enough for the Broncos to be picked for Origin and so he deserved to keep his spot for as long as he was a registered rugby league player. This wonderful young player had come to believe that he could prosper financially and challenge himself by playing a new game. That's his right and we wished him well. I hope he returns to rugby league one day.

RIGHT AFTER Origin, the Panthers were still second on the competition ladder, just two points behind the Dragons. The run-in to the semis that year mixed great highs with disappointing lows. Among the former was our thrashing of the Sea Eagles by 40–22 when Mick Jennings scored his second hat-trick of the season. (Having been mystifyingly overlooked for Origin, he was showing the New South Wales selectors exactly what they were missing.) We had a narrow win over pace-setters St George–Illawarra.

Tim Grant, Sam McKendry, Michael Jennings, Luke Lewis and Michael Gordon were all involved in contract talks with Penrith and I recommended to management that they should all be re-signed because they were our future.

We then lost three games in a row, to the Warriors, the Eels and the Storm, beat the Cowboys, then were downed by the Raiders and the Tigers. Suddenly we were in fourth spot and, if we couldn't stop the rot, in danger of free-falling out of semi-final contention. Our slump, after all had been going so smoothly, was due to a re-emergence of the silly errors that had cost us dearly in recent seasons and which we thought we'd eliminated from our game.

Then in rounds 24, 25 and 26, everything fell into place. We retained possession, our passes stuck, our defence was strong. Luke Walsh had the ball on a string and Jennings, Gordon and Coote ran riot. The forwards were an indomitable unit. We were playing as Matt Elliott had coached us to play. For this brief period, when we beat the Rabbitohs 54–18, the Bulldogs 24–18 and the Sharks, in the final competition round, 50–12 (departing Frank Pritchard scored a hat-trick of tries), we were as good as we knew we could be. We finished the comp in second place, with 15 wins and nine losses.

That was the good news. The bad was that in making the play-offs, many of our best men had been injured, and I was in hot water with the judiciary. At the 70-minute mark in the game against the Bulldogs in round 25, the second-last competition round, I was sent off for a high tackle on Gary Warburton. He fell into my tackle which, I admit, featured a pretty lazy swinging arm. When I was ordered from the field, I protested to referee Steve Lyons that I shouldn't be dismissed because Warburton had simply slipped into what was a legitimate chest-high tackle. 'I'm six feet four, mate!' I pleaded. Lyons was having none of it. 'It's a swinging arm. You hit him on the chin. You're off!' There was talk that there was a crackdown on high tackles that weekend after Manly's Glenn Stewart went unpunished after hitting the

Roosters' Braith Anasta high and hard. I was charged with a grade three reckless high tackle.

I hoped my good record – never sent off before, suspended for just five weeks in a 266-game career, and no charges at all since 2006 – would favour me. Facing a three-match suspension if I contested the charge and lost, I pleaded guilty and was banned for two weeks. I would miss our final match against Cronulla and our first game in the semis, which turned out to be a qualifying final against the Canberra Raiders. Because we had finished second, we were guaranteed a second bite of the cherry if beaten in that qualifying final, so I figured that missing the two matches would give my bruises a chance to heal, and I could go for broke in the semi-final the following week.

So with me gone for those crucial games and Frank Pritchard, Trent Waterhouse, and Michael Jennings all out injured and Luke Walsh, Lachlan Coote and Luke Lewis playing hurt, our year that began with such promise ended again in disappointment.

We were beaten 24–22 by Canberra in the qualifying final – I know if I'd been there I could have steadied the ship – and had to face the Sydney Roosters in a sudden-death semi at Sydney Football Stadium. The Roosters were playing some amazing football then and we had run out of troops. They beat us 34–12. We were done for another year.

Though we all felt empty, we took solace in our second-place finish and every one of us felt that if we'd been able to field our top side we'd have given the premiership a shake. Michael Jennings, Michael Gordon, Luke Lewis and I had all been selected for State of Origin, and Luke and I were named in the Kangaroos for the upcoming Four Nations tournament in Australia and New Zealand. Michael

Gordon was the season's highest point scorer, with 252. Luke Lewis was also the Dally M Lock of the Year. He is a quality player and a quality human being. I had two years to run on my contract but had no doubt that when I retired Luke was a tailor-made captain for the Panthers.

Personally, I'll remember that season as one of great success (the Maroons' Origin clean sweep), near success (the Panthers' second placing), hard slog and high emotion. At the Panthers, there had been enormous pressure to win matches and there was constant pressure, both financial and from club officials, over Matt's and the players' performance.

It was the first time I felt the pressure and uneasiness of the football club. Typically, too, being a bloke who has trouble saying no, I attended many Panther functions and took on too many speaking engagements, when I would have been better off having a quiet night. Consequently, as all my commitments snowballed and engulfed me, I slept little and, maybe for the first time in my life, felt extremely stressed.

PERHAPS STRESS, and the accumulated physical and mental effect of a dozen seasons of top-line rugby league, is why when I joined the Kangaroos for the Four Nations Series, I felt emotionally flat and lacking energy, despite being as proud as ever at being selected. Early on, I broke camp when coach Tim Sheens granted me leave to attend my sister Lily's wedding in Fiji. I flew to the wedding and raced back the following day. I was below form and off the pace in our games against England, Papua New Guinea and New Zealand.

Tim Sheens had dropped me from the run-on side to the

interchange bench for the Kiwis match. This was the first time I hadn't started a game for Australia for some years. Being a realist about my form, I knew my relegation was warranted. Tim said I should see my demotion as a challenge. Against New Zealand at Eden Park, a game we won 34–20, hostile and drunken Kiwi fans among the 44,324 crowd who had become convinced that their boys only had to run onto the field to beat us, bombarded us with rubbish and beer cans. One full bottle hit me fair in the back.

There was talk that I would be on the bench, or even dropped completely, for the final against New Zealand at Suncorp. Sure enough, mid-week Tim Sheens named me on a seven-man bench. I fronted Tim and told him my body needed a rest and that I wanted to withdraw from the final on the grounds that I had no confidence, even if I did make the four-man bench, that I could do justice to the green and gold jersey. I told him that I realised that I was not playing the football I needed to be to lead our pack forward and that Dave Shillington, Nate Myles, Tom Learoyd-Lahrs and Matt Scott all were, and would be better propositions for the game. They deserved their spots (especially Nate, who had come through some tough times off the field to redeem himself with Queensland and Australia and in the eyes of the fans), while I had been playing on reputation. Tim knew that I had to be really feeling under par to pull out of a match for Australia and he agreed to my request.

'Petero Out: End of an Era' articles blared across the sports pages. I told reporters:

Nobody owes me anything. I don't expect special treatment. I'm a big believer in the honour of wearing the Australian jumper, and I don't think my recent form has earned me the right to wear it in the final. Regardless of what I've done in the past, what the coach has stated right from the start is that form will get you a spot in the team. It's disappointing because I think my form has been great through the season. Unfortunately, for a month I haven't been able to put it together . . . I tried hard to find some form but it didn't happen to me.

Tim graciously said that by standing down I had shown a strong character and put the team before myself. He believed that there was every chance I would wear the green and gold again. At that low point in my career, I doubt too many people believed him.

### BONNIE CIVONICEVA

Scratching himself from the Australian team when it meant everything to him to wear the green and gold was so typical of Petero. Being down on form and feeling so flat was stressing him out. He was always worried that he was keeping a good younger player out of the team and costing him his chance to represent Australia.

I watched the Four Nations final from the grandstands. Could I have done anything to change the result, a 16–12 win to the Kiwis? The way I was playing and feeling, probably not. The Kiwis' backs did the damage, out wide. We were ahead 12–6 with 10 minutes remaining when Benji Marshall chipped through and their winger Jason Nightingale scored. Benji's conversion attempt bounced off the left upright. It was 12–10 to Australia with one minute left. At the death, Nightingale burst clear and threw a looping overhead pass back infield to Benji, who stepped past two defenders and right on our tryline he popped the ball back for Nathan Fien, who picked it up and scored the winning try.

At the end of season 2010 I was burned out in every way. I had never felt like this before. The best thing was to recuperate in the off-season, have good times with my family, and come back refreshed, fit and raring to go for the Panthers, Maroons and Kangaroos in 2011. There was an Anzac Test against the Kiwis on 6 May 2011, and I wanted to be playing in it.

# 11

# Triumph and treachery

In December 2010 and January 2011, large areas of Queensland were devastated by some of the worst floods in Australian history. At least 35 people perished and damage was estimated at $30 billion. In mid-January 2011, the Panthers put our hands up to go to the Ipswich suburbs of Karalee and North Booval to help the locals mop up after much of the region had been inundated. This wasn't a time for swanning around shaking hands and signing balls and jerseys, we wanted to do more than just raise morale. We wanted to help make the place livable again. We stood shoulder to shoulder, heart to heart, with the residents and the volunteers. We were there only a few days, but we were determined to help out physically as much as we could. We ripped down walls and gutted the ruined homes, leaving only the studwork, so the owners could rebuild from scratch. We dragged ruined belongings and furniture from submerged houses and stacked them out the front. The Parramatta, Wests Tigers and Canterbury boys went too, and other NRL teams rolled up their sleeves in other parts of the drowned state.

It was heartbreaking to see a family's precious mementoes strewn all over the yard. One pile of debris included a couple's marriage certificate, and I saw photos, toys, clothes, lifelong possessions, fridges full of food rotting in the hot Queensland sun. Nothing could be retrieved and saved because they were all potentially contaminated. It was like the area had been hit by a bomb. Earthmovers shunted the destroyed belongings from the front yards into the street, where they were piled in the back of trucks by the army and taken away to be burned.

As a Queenslander, as an Australian, I am grateful for the support of the public, and this was a way of paying people back by joining them on the front line in their time of need. If the Ipswich locals got a bit of a buzz by meeting us, then that was good, but I know who the real heroes were. What these people were confronted by, nature at its terrifying worst, was infinitely more challenging than anything football can throw up and they came through the ordeal and today their community is strong again. In the wonderful State of Origin series of 2011, their example inspired the Queensland players.

The floods aside, it had been a relaxed and peaceful off-season. I spent blissful days in Penrith and back home at Redcliffe with Bonnie, Tallulah, Ruby, Kaden and Jacobi and hardly gave rugby league a thought. Then, in January, as the new season loomed, I set my goals. I had three. To lead the Panthers to the semi-finals again and, stranger things have happened, win the premiership. To beat the Blues again in State of Origin and send out the retiring Darren Lockyer on a winning note. And I wanted to reclaim my starting front-row spot with the Australian team that I had lost in the last Four Nations series. Not much to ask for?

I realised that to achieve these goals I would need to pace

myself. Not mentally – my attitude to footy had been revitalised by time away – but I would be 35 in season 2011, years past most players' use-by date, so I had to play and train smarter. I had to compensate for my creaking bones and tired muscles, so Matt Elliott and Carl Jennings and I devised a training plan that would ward off mental and physical burn-out and ensure I was fit and fresh enough to lead the team each week, as well as cope with my representative load. I maintained my cardio fitness on the exercise bike rather than running laps of the oval. I was spared much of the back-breaking pre-season endurance and strength work. They told me I had to recognise when I was fatigued and not try to play through it as I had always done. I would always be in the Panthers' run-on side but play fewer minutes in a match, 40–50 instead of 60–70, coming into the game at strategic moments for maximum impact. Matt put a lot of thought into his prop rotation, using me, Tim, Sam, Matthew Bell and the promising Dayne Weston in bursts. It was also necessary to reduce my off-field commitments as much as possible while still carrying the flag for the club in the community as a captain must do.

I was flattered and humbled, and a little surprised, to be NRL All Stars coach Wayne Bennett's personal pick for the pre-season game against the Indigenous All Stars on 12 February at Skilled Park on the Gold Coast. Locky was our skipper and it was like old home week to be with him again in a team coached by Wayne. Nothing was said about my departure from the Broncos and Wayne and I got on fine.

The annual All Stars match is a wonderful concept that celebrates indigenous culture with traditional music and dance and a game which is always played in a great spirit. It recognises the contribution indigenous players have made and continue to make to our game. Indigenous centre Beau

Champion may not have thought so when he went to tackle me and when rumbling over the top of him my hip accidentally connected with his head and knocked him out. We won 28–12, with brilliant young Canberra Raiders fullback Josh Dugan winning the Preston Campbell award for man of the match. Josh is yet another example of our game's ability to keep producing new stars.

When I heard that Timana Tahu was looking for a team in 2011, I recommended him to Matt. I knew Timana was a fine player who, still bruised from the Andrew Johns scandal of the year before and other off-field worries, would settle in well in the Panthers team and in Penrith because we were a tight little community, an oasis away from the distractions of the city. I called Timana and said I thought we would be a good fit for him and asked him to consider joining us, 'play some good footy and have fun'. He jumped on board for round six. Signing someone of his calibre was a boost for us. There is a wonderful moment captured by the Channel 9 TV cameras that, I promise you, will be in my highlight reel. It's all Timana's doing. In his first game for us, a home match against the Storm, he put the sweetest hit on their big prop Bryan Norrie. Timana's timing and execution were perfect and Norrie went down like he'd been shot. I could not believe it. The cameras caught me with a huge grin on my dial. What a shot! I had seen Timana do that before: zero in from an angle and pick off an unsuspecting victim. How tough is Bryan Norrie? A collision like that would be the end of the game for most. Not him; he dusted himself off and led a rampaging Storm.

Unfortunately, Timana wasn't with us long. He tore his pec a couple of matches later and didn't play again that year. In 2012 he joined the Newcastle Knights under new coach Wayne Bennett. Timana has everything you could want in a rugby league player – speed, size, aggression, and he is a genuine competitor. It's unfortunate his career has been hampered by injuries and controversy. If Wayne can get him fully fit and enjoying his rugby league again he is going to be a terrific acquisition.

I feel it is a captain's responsibility to speak out and as the season got under way, I made it clear to the Panthers board that I believed they should extend the contracts of Matt Elliott and Trent Waterhouse. Matt, I said, was building something special at Penrith, as evinced by our second placing in 2010. He should be given the job security to continue his work instead of always feeling he was standing on the gallows waiting for the trapdoor to open up.

In regard to Trent, 'House' was a tough and experienced forward who was respected by all and I looked forward to playing alongside him for another couple of years. To me, he was Penrith.

As the Rolling Stones said, you can't always get what you want.

I liked Matt a lot as a man and a coach. I didn't want to see him fired, and the spray I gave the guys after our first-round 42–8 thrashing by the Newcastle Knights in front of our home ground fans reflected that. Matt's preparation for the game had been thorough, as usual. It was the players, myself included, who were to blame for our inept and lethargic display. Newcastle out-muscled and out-enthused us. Unless you have strength and enthusiasm, the best game plan in the world is useless. We reverted to our old ways of digging our own grave, making 21 errors and, unforgivably, being penalised three times for players being off-side for kick restarts. It was ironic that one of the Knights' best on the day was powerhouse winger Akuila Uate, around whose neck I'd hung the Petero Civoniceva Medal for 2010's best Fijian player in the NRL at the Australian Fiji Rugby League awards night just weeks before.

We had a slow start to the season, briefly redeeming ourselves after the Knights debacle by beating Parramatta, then copping another belting, 44–12 by the Sharks, in round three. Our old inconsistency was well and truly back. Facing reporters at the post-match press conference, Matt was defiant: 'We are not a bunch of numpties, even though it's been written widely that we are. You guys don't know. We do. We're not numpties. We're better than we showed. We'll get there. We'll be fine.' In the next weeks, we beat the Broncos and the Raiders.

The coach had said we would be fine. He spoke too soon. Penrith chairman Don Feltis suggested in a newspaper article that unless Matt Elliott turned things around within two months he would not be with the club in 2012. 'It's like re-signing a player. You are going to want to see how he plays,' said Feltis. This sat badly with me. Of course club management has the right to decide on the fate of a coach, but Matt had taken us to second spot in 2010 and deserved to remain with us. Besides, surely he could have been put on notice behind closed doors instead of being publicly humiliated in the press.

Suddenly Matt and his players were under enormous pressure. The fun seeped from the joint. It seemed to me that there was hardly a period in my three years at Penrith when Matt's job was not on the line. Such an insecure environment is not conducive to good coaching or contented players. It had long been a case of us and them, but now it seemed to me the players were losing respect for some officials.

Not helping the stand-off was the slashing of $1 million from the football budget over the past years. Our meagre football finances meant we had to make do with a part-time physiotherapist and strapper and antiquated and broken training equipment. I had seen, and trained at, the state-of-the-art set-ups at other clubs and what we had to make do with was neither good enough nor fair. This was in part caused by the Panther parent group's disastrous loss of $20 million.

I gave an interview to Stathi Paxinos of the *Sydney Morning Herald* that could not have endeared me to certain sections of Penrith management. Obviously, the start to the season hadn't helped Matt's cause at the club, I said. It had been difficult with some of the hierarchy at the club coming out and talking about issues that should be controlled within the boardroom and, if anything, it put unnecessary pressure on the team. We were a very tight-knit group. We were close to Matt and 110 per cent supportive of him.

All we hoped, I told the reporter, was that we could get back on track and put all this talk of Matt being terminated behind us. It didn't need to be spoken about, especially out in the media. It didn't do anything for the morale of the team. The threats and scuttlebutt being made were a distraction and counter-productive, but the boys were strong and trying to focus on football. 'Matt has been a huge part of growing this group to where we are. We had a great season last year – to finish second in the regular season was a huge thing for us – and Matt's been an integral part of that.'

After the first third of the season, in spite of our patchy results – we won just two of our first seven games – I had totalled 101 hit-ups for 858 metres, which was more hit-ups than any other forward in the NRL. Not that that counted for much: two from seven games was far from good enough.

•

I REALISED one of my three dreams for the year when I was selected to play for the Kangaroos against the Kiwis in the Anzac Test. Yes! It was deeply satisfying to regain my front-row spot and run out in the starting line-up, and to join with fellow forwards Matt Scott, Sam Thaiday, Ben Creagh, Cameron Smith, Ben Hannant and Paul Gallen in besting the Kiwi pack and laying the foundations for a comprehensive 20–10, four tries to two, victory. I put aside my friendship with my Penrith protégé Sam McKendry in that Test and we gave each other plenty.

IN LATE April, Don Feltis called the Panthers players together at training and announced that Matt Elliott had been sacked. His contract would not be extended beyond the 2011 season, and his replacement was being considered. Tim Sheens, Nathan Brown, Ricky Stuart, Des Hasler, Rick Stone, Ivan Cleary and Steve Georgallis (the Panthers' former under-20s coach and now the Panthers' assistant), were all said to be in contention.

Typically, Matt reacted to his dismissal with class. He said he was disappointed but 'at ease' with the club's decision. Players came and went and coaches did too. He would continue to do his best in the time left to him. 'I have not one ounce of bitterness. I do not have one ounce of anything other than appreciation for the opportunities I've been given.' Matt addressed the players, reminding us of our obligations to the club, to the fans and to each other. He told us to play football and not to obsess about what had happened to him.

As captain, I wasn't going to keep my opinions about something I felt so strongly about to myself. Penrith chief executive Mick Leary insisted that while I had a right to voice my feelings, the board had treated Matt 'with dignity . . . We had a job to do and have come up with what we believe is the right outcome'.

The senior playing group had not been consulted at any time, the decision was handed to us as a *fait accompli*, and I believed we had a right to have our views about Matt known.

Nevertheless, as Matt told me to do, I pledged my and the team's determination to get our season back on course and give him the successful swansong season that he deserved. I told reporters:

> I'm disappointed in the whole process but at the end of the day I'm there as an employee to work, and that means to play football. I don't think my opinions and the players' opinions count for much. The decision has been made by the board and Mick Leary. We just have to get on with it. It's been a tough start to the season, but we're bound to click. The players are all committed to getting out on the field and ripping in for each other and the coach.

There was at least some good news in mid-May. Phil Gould, who had played for the Panthers and coached them to a premiership and New South Wales to State of Origin wins and was now a respected media commentator, was joining us as general manager with overall control of the football side of the club. In my limited dealings with Gus, I had been impressed and I respected his deep knowledge of rugby league. I was confident that his professionalism would transform the club.

I admit that at this time I began lobbying for changes in club management. The board comprised men who had been successful in their careers and at Penrith, but, in my view, time had passed them by and new blood was needed if the club was to progress.

The *Sun-Herald*'s Danny Weidler did some digging around the club and published the following article:

... Penrith captain Petero Civoniceva ... is looming as the man to lead the players in a revolution to save the club from its archaic board. The players are fuming over the conditions they are forced to train under. They are miles behind other clubs in sports science and it's well documented they don't have a full-time physio and have to strap their own ankles and other joints at training.

What hasn't been discussed is that Civoniceva went so far as to instruct players on how to vote for the board elections and there were even suggestions he distributed voting pamphlets – reminding players that their voice could be heard. This earned him a hammering. The board members felt it was out of line. But if Civoniceva is moved to do that, what does it say about the way the players are being treated?

The outgoing coach, Matthew Elliott, was constantly going in to bat for them over financial matters, not always with success. What the next coach needs to know is that Elliott spent a lot of his down-time chasing third-party deals for his players to keep them at the club. The last time I looked there were not too many coaches having to do that ...

The Panthers recently updated their gym equipment, but not with the latest state-of-the-art gizmos. Instead they bought four kettle-balls – basically lumps of steel Russian athletes have been using for years. The cost? A few hundred bucks.

The reason players came to the club and stayed was

Elliott. They lost Frank Pritchard last year through poor management. Pritchard wanted to stay but the club delayed until the Bulldogs had time to pounce.

I thought that having Greg Alexander on the board would have been a plus, but the players say he is too busy with his media commitments to make a difference. I was told he was not at Wednesday's epic board meeting.

It's been pushed to me that the club decided to sack Elliott after the April 17 Melbourne game. The truth is the directors had made up their minds after round one and started the hunt for a new coach then. Elliott naively thought that results might save him. He should be relieved he is getting out of there.

Despite our vow to try to rise above the club turmoil, we were angry and sad when we travelled to Mt Smart Stadium in New Zealand to face the Warriors in the next match and were beaten 26–18.

It CAME as a great relief when I was picked for State of Origin and joined the Queensland boys in camp. It was always a nervous wait to see if your name was read out. Despite how many games I had played, I was another year older and our Queensland young props were firing.

Mal was always reminding us of the Maroons' proud history and getting us to acknowledge where we came from, and one of his innovations this year was to have us train in the jersey of our junior club, presented to us by former Maroon and Canberra grand final hero Steve Jackson and tennis legend Pat Rafter. It was nice to wear a Redcliffe Dolphins jumper again.

I thought I was my usual self in Origin camp. Since

then, however, many who were there tell me I was subdued and super-focused and not quite the happy-go-lucky bloke I normally am. If that was so, I would have been concentrating on proving that I could still cut it at Origin level after last year's Four Nations fizzer, and making sure that our captain Locky didn't exit the Origin arena as a loser. Every Maroon wanted to do it for Darren, because we all owed him so much.

Darren, of course, being a humble bloke, was embarrassed by all the fuss. He made it very clear from the start of the series that this campaign wasn't about him. He told us at Origin I camp that he knew much was being made of this being his last series but that he wanted us to concentrate on having the best possible preparation and playing as well as we had in our past five winning series. We had the chance to win an unprecedented six series in a row. That, and not sending him out a winner, must be our Holy Grail in 2011. We must win for our teammates, for ourselves and for the state that had bred us, a state that was still hurting from the floods.

Going into that first camp was like being reunited with brothers. The three Origin camps each lasted about a week and were held at the Hyatt Coolum Resort on the Sunshine Coast, where they converted the driving range into a footy field for us. There was excellent accommodation and eateries, a pool, a gym, meeting rooms, everything we needed. As usual, Mal drew us into a tight group by firing up our mateship and reminding us of our Maroon tradition and the role of former players in creating our legacy.

Each of us knew his job within the team and what we had to do to beat the Blues, and, as we did every year, we made a pact not to let each other down. Mal's brief to our forward pack was to grind down the Blues in attack and defence. Yes, we trained hard and had tactical talks, but at Origin level, mateship is more important than any game plan. Mal had the best sidekicks: assistant coach Michael Hagan, Alf Langer with his fun-loving attitude and practical jokes, Trevor Gillmeister, Andrew Gee, Chris 'Choppy' Close, Gavin Allen and Mark Hohn, all men who had bled for Queensland and now were demanding that we do the same. From time to time they'd be joined by other former Origin greats. Choppy was Maroons manager when I first came into Origin in 2001. He is passion personified. When he stands in front of the team and tells you what being a Queenslander means to him the hairs on the back of your neck stand up.

People have often asked me how I can smash New South Wales players whom I like and are club and Kangaroo teammates. I tell them that a state of, if not exactly hate, then deep animosity, must exist for the duration of an Origin game. This tradition of course was sparked by Queensland's Arthur Beetson when, in arguably Origin's most famous moment, he whacked his mate, Blues centre Mick Cronin, in the very first Origin game in 1980. If you don't buy into the ethos that the Blues are the enemy, you are wasting your time playing State of Origin and won't be able to lift to meet its ferocity, speed and challenges.

It takes me weeks to recharge emotionally after an Origin game. Coming down off those matches is hard, which explains the post-Origin slumps of club teams with heavy Origin representation.

Always discussed in camp are the thrashings that Queensland regularly suffered at the hands of New South Wales in pre-Origin days that, as the conventional wisdom goes, instilled arrogance in Blues players. Also recalled are refereeing decisions that went against us, and past incidents that demand retribution, like the Blues-instigated brawl in 2009.

The perennial criticism that I was too old for Origin was always excellent motivation and so, in 2011, was an article by the Sydney *Daily Telegraph*'s sports editor-at-large Phil Rothfield saying that Mal Meninga was little more than a figurehead coach and the Maroons' game plans were devised by Neil Henry in past years and in 2011 by Michael Hagan, the defence strategy by Trevor Gillmeister and our attack schemed by Alfie Langer.

This was wrong, and it was cruelly unfair. Mal utilises the expertise of his assistants – of course he does – but the buck stops with him, and it is his man management, pride in his state, and the aura that comes from his great career. Now, as well as for Locky, this series would be about vindicating Mal.

Mal kept his powder dry until the series was over, then fired both barrels at the New South Wales troublemakers who he believed were behind Rothfield's article. He accused 'New South Wales power-brokers . . . faceless men of influence . . . the very rats and filth that tried to poison a monumental team with lies, personal attacks, arrogance and disrespect.' For a time, Mal's friendship with former Canberra and Kangaroo teammate Ricky Stuart – who denied any involvement – was fractured, but happily the two mates made up.

Moments before we ran onto the field in Origin I at Suncorp Stadium on 25 May, I gathered Matt Scott, Ben Hannant and Jacob Lillyman, my fellow front-rowers, around me in a corner of the dressing-room and gave them some simple instructions: run strong, tackle strong and be ruthless. I said that if our backline stars Slater, Boyd, Lockyer and Thurston were to shine we had to roll up our sleeves and lay the platform by playing at a fast tempo and hitting the ball up hard and often, playing the ball fast to get a roll on to win as much yardage as possible and create room for our running second-rowers, Sam Thaiday and Nate Myles, and our brilliant backs. As I looked into each man's eyes I knew we'd do all right that night.

Matt Scott was a man inspired. On top of the emotion of playing in this huge match, just two days before he had lost his old Cowboys' teammate Sam Faust to leukemia. To say that Matt was fired up is an understatement. He went out there and set the standard in attack and defence.

Matt was on the field for 49 minutes, made 15 hit-ups for 154 metres, 21 tackles and two line breaks. He made more ground on his own than the four New South Wales props combined. In my 38 minutes on the field, I made 16 runs for a total of 143 metres (one metre less than the four Blues props), 16 tackles and a line bust. Ben Hannant and Jacob Lillyman also dominated in their stints. On the back of this toil, Locky's, Johnathan Thurston's and Cameron Smith's general play kicking was spot-on, and the team's kick-chase game near-perfect.

Not that we had things all our own way. We hit the Blues with the kitchen sink in the first half but at the break had only a fifth-minute Thurston try (after he'd fallen on a Cam Smith grubber) to show for it, and as that first 40 minutes wore on, New South Wales had been gaining confidence from our inability to convert our many breaks into tries. Then, six minutes into the second half, our new winger Jharal Yow Yeh fell on another grubber, by Cooper Cronk this time, over the Blues' tryline to take the score to 10–0. Still, as you'd expect from any side led by such warriors as coach Ricky Stuart and captain Paul Gallen, the Blues fought back with tries in the 64th and 69th minutes to

Mitchell Pearce (after I'd missed a tackle on Greg Bird) and Michael Jennings.

Unbelievably, although we'd been on top all game we found ourselves behind 12–10 with only 10 minutes to play. As we lined up behind the tryline while Jamie Soward converted Jennings' try, Locky moved among us, telling us to believe in ourselves, and that we could still win if we could get down to the other end of the field and take the chance that would present itself. 'We're Queenslanders,' he said, as coolly as if ordering a coffee, 'we don't fucking give up.' Everyone just nodded.

That's what made Darren a great captain. He was so calm and precise in a crisis. He took the emotion out of it. We *were* Queenslanders and we *didn't* give up. He told us straight up what we needed to do as a team and we did as he said. Our strong culture meant that there wasn't one of us who did not believe that we would snatch victory in the few minutes left in the match. It's hard to defend against such implacable self-belief.

From the kick-off we powered upfield, first I and then Matt Scott with a block-busting 25 metre burst made deep inroads into the Blues' defence. With seven minutes on the clock, the ball went from Smith to Thurston to Lockyer, who found Slater steaming up on the inside. Billy scored, Johnathan converted. We won 16–12.

PROOF THAT I had rid myself of the lethargy of the previous year came in the first club match after Origin, against the Gold Coast, when even though I was battered I notched 19 hit-ups, 162 metres and 16 tackles in my 46 minutes on the field. We won 23-10. I was truly feeling as fit and strong as at any time in my career. I prayed my purple patch would last.

For Origin II at Sydney's ANZ Stadium, Ricky Stuart tried something revolutionary. He chose just two specialist props, Trent Merrin and Tim Mannah. The rest of the pack comprised back-rowers Gallen, Creagh, Beau Scott, Bird, Watmough and Luke Lewis, some of whom, we figured, would have to pinch-hit at prop throughout the game to give Mannah and Merrin a break. Ricky's master-plan was obviously to stack the forwards with fast, agile, lighter men who could run us off our feet and hope that they could hold on in defence when we rumbled up the ball.

Gorden Tallis accused New South Wales of being disrespectful by putting up only two specialist props against me, Matt, Ben and Dave Taylor who had replaced the injured Lillyman. On the other hand, the tactic was endorsed from an unlikely source. Despite our success in Origin I, former great heavyweight prop Glenn Lazarus declared: 'The way the game is at the moment, the Petero Civonicevas, these traditional hard front-rowers, are fading out, unfortunately. We're getting five forwards, all around 100 kilos, all very agile and mobile, running from dummy-half. Guys like myself, where you're 115 or 118 kilos, may be a thing of the past.'

I thought, given our big men's contribution to the Maroons' first-up victory just weeks before, that Glenn's memory was a bit rusty.

What no one in the Queensland camp reckoned on was Paul Gallen's ability to switch from his usual spot at lock or second row and play one of the best prop's games in rugby league history. He wasn't as heavy as our front-rowers, but his strength, speed, work ethic and enormous motor compensated for that. For the full 80 minutes he ran like a truck, hitting the ball up relentlessly, and his tackles stung. He played tight and he played wide and his lightning play-the-balls created irresistible momentum. He grabbed the initiative from us from the kick-off, and we could not reclaim it. His forward cohorts all played an up-tempo game and we were caught out and couldn't match it with them. In defence, they burst off their line fast – too fast, as I kept complaining to the ref – and nabbed us before we had a chance to build up steam.

New South Wales won Origin II 18–8, three tries to one, and that was a fair indication of the difference between the teams. It was a convincing and complete performance, one of their best for many, many years. The Blues' kicking game was superb and their backs had it over ours on the night with young Will Hopoate stamping himself as something special.

Yet all anyone wanted to talk about was how the New South Wales forwards had overwhelmed the Maroon pack. Suddenly pundits were lining up behind Lazo to say that, from what they'd seen in Origin II, big power props grinding out the hard yards over the advantage line to lay the platform for a side's attack had been made redundant by smaller, more mobile forwards. Props such as me, Matt Scott and Ben Hannant were as old hat as dinosaurs. My 29th State of Origin appearance, in which I became the most capped Origin forward, overtaking Steve Price's 28 games, had turned out to be an ignominious occasion.

I didn't despair about our prospects in the series-deciding Origin III. Despite the score in that second match, I was confident we could rise to the occasion and re-establish our dominance over the Blue forwards, making them backpedal, forcing them into making the errors that they had not made in Origin II and nullifying Jamie Soward's and Mitchell Pearce's kicking games. Also, in our loss, uncharacteristically we had been unable to capitalise on opportunities that, had we taken them, would have turned the game our way. On a couple of occasions Billy Slater busted the Blues open but, uncharacteristically for us, the last pass didn't stick.

THAT WEEK, back at Penrith, our new general manager Phil Gould was making his presence felt. Unfortunately one of the first things Gus did, right after we were beaten again by Newcastle, was oust Matt from the coaching role – tearing up the arrangement that he would stay on till season's end – and appoint assistant coach Steve Georgallis as caretaker coach. Matt texted us a message: 'Just wanted you to know that my services are no longer required. Good luck with your footy and your lives.'

I felt bad for Matt and made sure he knew before he left Penrith what I felt about him and the work that he had done at the Panthers. The Sydney Roosters had the good sense to appoint him as head coach Brian Smith's assistant. Good men like Matt are hard to find and because he has so much to offer I know he'll be back at the helm of a first-grade club sooner rather than later.

'Georgie' Georgallis is a fine coach in his own right. His ideas were good and we got right behind him. A lot of the younger boys had won premierships with Steve in the under-20s. We had been tightly behind Matt and now that he was out of the picture we went into a huddle and pledged to give Steve the same level of support.

Steve Georgallis had immediate success. The first match under his coaching was a 30–20 win over the North Queensland Cowboys. This match provided another clip for my end-of-career highlight reel when I reverted to my days as a skinny young centre and scored between the posts after dusting off an outrageous sidestep that Benji Marshall and Freddie Fittler would have envied. Ace tacklers Matt Scott, Aaron Payne and Dallas Johnson were left clutching at air. I cannot say whether they were fooled by my step or stunned into immobility when I produced nifty footwork instead of trying to lumber over the top of them. When someone later asked me when was the last time I showed such a move I replied, 'On the dance floor, many years ago.'

That Cowboys match on 20 June, watched by our best home ground crowd of the year, 14,090, was dedicated to the McGrath Foundation, a charity established by cricketer Glenn McGrath and his wife Jane (who died of breast cancer in 2008), to raise funds for breast cancer research. We wore pink to mark the occasion, and the Pink Panthers raised more than $15,000.

Our caretaker coach's excellent results, the first-up win over the Cowboys and a 20–6 victory against the Bulldogs the following week, did not save Georgie. He had believed, as did the players, that if he kept coaching us to wins he would be named full-time coach in 2012, but Phil Gould announced a couple of days after we'd beaten the Bulldogs that Auckland Warriors coach Ivan Cleary had the job. I registered my disappointment, and that of the players, with Phil. We all thought Georgie had been hard done by, and it was my responsibility as players' leader to say so. Gus welcomed my input but made it clear to me that his decision was final and he expected us to move on and concentrate on football. I learned later that some board members believed my confronting Gus was out of line.

Hot on the heels of Matt Elliott and Steve Georgallis (who saw out the year with us before becoming Tim Sheens' assistant at Wests Tigers), Gus Gould oversaw the departure of chief executive Mick Leary and Trent Waterhouse (who was snapped up by Warrington in the UK).

I was in tears. No, it was nothing to do with turmoil at the Panthers or our State of Origin defeat. On 20 June, at the annual Women in League function at the swish Deckhouse restaurant at Sydney's Woolwich Dock, I was named the 2011 Harvey Norman Women in League's Favourite Son. The award was for 'being a role model to younger players and whose off-field characteristics embody the values of the rugby league community'. I topped a poll of 5000 league women, beating such top blokes as Cameron Smith, Darren Lockyer, Kurt Gidley, Preston Campbell, Nathan Merritt, Alan Tongue and Andrew Ryan. Past years' recipients had been Nathan Hindmarsh and Hazem El Masri, so I was a proud man when I stepped up onto the stage to collect my plaque.

Since becoming captain of the Panthers, I had grown comfortable speaking in public and all was going well as I thanked the Women in League for honouring me, and paid tribute to Bonnie, down in the audience, and Mum for all the sacrifices they had made so I could have a rugby league career. Then I looked at Bonnie and saw that she was crying. That did it. I choked up and couldn't speak. The women burst into applause. Later, when I'd regained my composure, I joked, 'Oh jeez . . . this is going to get me kicked out of the front-rowers' union.'

What I said that day about Bonnie and Mum was completely true. If I'd known I was going to win I would have flown Mum down for the day. I could not have achieved anything like what I have without those two women. Bonnie has been my great support since we got together when we were 16-year-old school kids and embraced all the highs and lows of life, and Mum has always been there for me since I was a kid, even though she rarely saw me play because as a single mum she was working extra shifts at Redcliffe Hospital to provide for me and my sisters. She still works at the hospital, where she is an institution for her spirit and huge heart . . . and she's always up for a chat about footy. (God knows what she's going to talk about now I've retired.)

BONNIE AND the kids and our mothers and fathers and brothers and sisters and their kids were all in the crowd at Suncorp for the third and deciding State of Origin match. I still hadn't made up my mind if it would be my last. In the lead-up, I had been continually asked whether the game would be my swansong in the maroon jersey, as well as Locky's, and I replied, 'Could be, could be, you never know.' I certainly didn't know and, to be truthful, even if I had planned to retire from Origin after the game I would have kept it to myself because I wouldn't have wanted to detract from Darren's parting appearance.

Once more I had something to prove. I wanted to show the world that we were better than the Blues, I wanted to win for Darren, and I wanted to make a statement on behalf of all old-style prop forwards that we hadn't gone the way of the brontosaurus, as our critics had claimed after the smaller, faster New South Wales forwards had got the better of us in Origin II.

No one knows more than me that no one is guaranteed a happy ending in this game. Fortunately Origin III turned out to be one of the great nights of my life.

We were at full strength. Our side was Slater, Boyd, Inglis, Hodges, Yow Yeh, Lockyer, Thurston, Harrison, Thaiday, Myles, Scott, Smith and myself, with Cronk, Hannant,

Lillyman and Corey Parker on the bench. The New South Wales side, a formidable one, was Minichiello, Morris, Hayne, Gasnier, Uate, Soward, Pearce, Bird, Creagh, Glenn Stewart, Mannah, Ennis and Paul Gallen – picked as a specialist front-rower this time – was the skipper. Their bench was Gidley, Galloway, Watmough and Lewis.

Before the match I took Matt Scott aside and told him it was up to us to restore the status quo. I said, 'We have to get back to our natural aggressive, hard-running game. Don't wait for an arm wrestle to develop. Let's blow them away as quickly as possible.'

Suncorp Stadium was electric that 6 July night. When we ran onto the field, a full capacity crowd stood and roared. There were 52,498 there, but we could feel the entire state of Queensland behind us. No ground in the world has the atmosphere of Suncorp on Origin night. The vibe as we burst into the blinding lights of the arena was the most emotional I've experienced at any game. It was wild, off the charts.

Waiting for us were the Blues, grim-faced and focused, with a deadly intent to spoil Locky's farewell party. There were men facing us whom I liked very much. Tonight they were the enemy. I never wanted anything more in my rugby league career than to win this game. Matt Scott took the first hit-up from their kick-off. I took the second, smashing into a swarm of New South Wales forwards and carrying three of them up the field with me. Matt and I took second hit-ups in that first set. It was our way of saying, 'Forget Origin II, this is a whole new ball game.' In their first set, we gang-tackled one of their forwards and he spilled the ball. I took hit-up after hit-up, and in the opening 25 minutes until Mal gave me a rest I carried the ball 12 times for a personal record 125 metres.

All up, in the course of that game my 20 carries took me 206 metres. I don't mind saying it could have been the best I have ever played in the Origin arena. Matt Scott and the other forwards were right alongside me. Matt again was unstoppable. What Paul Gallen and his boys did to us in Origin II, we did to them in Origin III. We rolled easily through the middle of their ruck, getting far over the advantage line with every hit-up. On the back of our go-forward, mistake-free footy and the wonderful kicking games of Locky, Johnathan and Cameron, the Blues were backpedalling, scrambling to contain us.

We had reclaimed control. Total control. We dominated possession. Thirty minutes into the first half, we had had the ball for 69 per cent of the time and spent 80 per cent of the game in Blue territory. Unlike in Origin II, this time it was the Blues who were under siege. And also unlike in Origin II, we turned all our scoring chances into tries. After 20 minutes, Inglis, Thaiday, Smith and Yow Yeh had crossed the New South Wales line and we led 24–0.

Typifying our enthusiasm was the passage immediately after GI's first try. They kicked off and I made two hit-ups in quick succession, making about 15 metres each time, then on the back of this momentum we kicked deep and as Anthony Minichiello gathered the ball behind his tryline he was smashed by Justin Hodges, Greg Inglis, Ash Harrison, Darius Boyd, Cam Smith and Johnathan Thurston.

In the two minutes before half-time New South Wales hit back with tries to Minichiello and Uate. We went to the sheds with the score at 24–12. We knew that the Blues were more than capable of coming back to win the game, but none of us was going to let this happen. Slater and Inglis scored to put the result beyond doubt, then New South Wales produced two consolation tries at the death when,

I have to confess, many of us had turned our thoughts to Locky's farewell celebration later that night. As the siren sounded and we were swamped by our families and fans, the scoreboard read 34–24. Perhaps it was not as decisive as it should have been, but it would do.

I hugged Bonnie and took Tallulah, Ruby and Kaden out onto the field for our slow victory lap. The Queensland players and our loved ones lingered on the field, soaking up that winning feeling. Darren accepted all the accolades with class and modesty. Johnathan Thurston, who had suffered a knee injury and been taken from the field, joined us in a wheelchair. When the boys saw him they mobbed him, and he was in tears. I know that one day, hopefully many years from now, when I'm stockpiling the great times of my life, the events of Origin III 2011 will be in my treasure chest of memories.

Later, amid the cheers and beers, Darren addressed us. In his croaky voice he simply thanked us for our commitment. It was very emotional and more tears were shed. We were as proud as we were happy.

That night, as far as I can remember, we relived every moment of the game. Special for me was the way Matt and I made amends for Origin II when we dominated that fine Blues' pack in the first 25 minutes of the game. Once more Paul Gallen gave it everything he had, making an incredible 50 tackles and running 165 metres in 19 hit-ups, just ahead of Matt Scott, who in his 14 carries recorded 140 metres. There was not a poor player in our side. Locky, Thurston, Inglis and Thaiday were brilliant, as was Cameron Smith, who was calm and steady and made all the right decisions. His dummy-half work and kicking were superb. He was also very, very tough. He was the man of the match and the Wally Lewis Player of the Series. As he mounted the dais to receive his award, he laconically quipped to the vast crowd that had stayed behind for the ceremony, 'What about that, eh? Not too bad?'

Along with a thousand other emotions, I felt how fortunate I was to be part of this group of men. If this *was* to be my last Origin game, what a way to go out.

### GORDEN TALLIS

After Origin II and before Origin III, everyone was saying Paul Gallen was the top prop forward in the game. In Origin III, Pet came out and ate up Paul and the rest of the Blues pack. He ate 'em up in 25 minutes. Destroyed them. We talk about Arthur Beetson coming back to play for Queensland at 35, well, Petero's effort at 35 years of age last year was as good. What Arthur did has sustained our state for 30 years and Petero's effort last year will sustain Queensland for another 30. That game against New South Wales in Origin III 2011 was the best prop's game I have ever seen.

### MAL MENINGA

Origin III 2011 was the best preparation I have ever been involved in since I started coaching Queensland in 2006. The boys were very focused and determined. I knew that they were going to give something very special that night. There was so much at stake. The game would decide the series. The Blues had beaten us in Origin II because Ricky had picked a forward pack of mobile and flexible back-rowers who ran our bigger blokes off their feet. People were saying that the days of the big traditional front-rower were over. This was a direct affront to Petero and Matt Scott, our props. It was a test of their credibility. There was pressure. We responded. We had a good game plan that the guys bought into. Before the match we talked about intensity and controlled aggression. Pet responded by playing one of the great front-rower's games. He was magnificent. Matt Scott was wonderful too and Ben Hannant and Jake Lillyman were ginormous when they came on.

If someone asked me to explain what makes Origin the event that it is, I'd get them to look at a DVD of Origin III in 2011. Origin is as much about emotions as skills and fitness. It's emotion that makes players pull out something miraculous, and to play at a pace 20 per cent higher than club games, and with unmatched intensity. It makes players feel as though they would die before they let down a teammate. It gives the self-belief that makes a man know that he is never beaten, and that there is no situation that he can't, with his mates, get out of. It makes a man put an error behind him and give his all on the next play to make amends. When I walked onto the field after that game, it was one of the finest moments I have ever experienced.

Now that they've retired, I'll be relying on Petero and Darren to remain within the Queensland set-up and be a big part of our camps each year. They'll keep the legacy going, passing on their experience of Origin to the young guys coming through, helping them inherit the Queensland mindset so players can go hard against their club and Kangaroo teammates who are wearing Blue.

Petero always worked hard to get to his standing

in rugby league, at the very top of our game. No
forward worked harder. No prop has ever played
more than 30 games of Origin. It destroys your
body. Petero rolled on. History has recorded that
he is one of Origin's warriors. I expected him to
contribute in camp and, because of the respect in
which they held him, the young blokes hung on his
words. He didn't talk a lot but when he did people
listened.

Origin camp is important. Club games are an
occupation; you get the job done week after week.
Origin should be special, and treated that way.
We try to have fun in camp, and when it's time to
knuckle down, we do and display the necessary
attitude and ruthlessness to win. All players have to
contribute. I have high expectations of my players
and if they stuff up I make them accountable. Unlike
club coaches, I have a long line of Origin-quality
players just waiting for their chance. An incumbent
player's place in the team is something to be valued
and cherished and not relinquished lightly. Being
chosen to play Origin is a privilege, one of the true
vehicles of loyalty that we have in modern sport.
Once selected, a player can remain in the Origin
team for as long as he is doing the job.

Petero and I talked about how long he should play
on at Origin level. All I could ever say to him is what
I said to Locky: 'You are a long time retired, so don't
leave before your time. But know when your time
is up. It happens to us all.' Petero, who is brutally
honest with himself and the total realist, knew when
it was time to say goodbye.

While I was in the Origin III camp, I had a call from Steve Georgallis who said that a rumour was doing the rounds that the Panthers wanted to get rid of me. The whisper was that they wanted me out of the final year of my contract, in 2012, so they could spend the freed-up money on younger players. I needed to concentrate on Origin, so I forced Steve's words out of my head.

Back in Penrith after Origin, gearing up for what we hoped would be the Panthers' surge to the semi-finals, Georgie's warning had wormed its way to front and centre in my mind, so I thought I had better meet with Phil Gould to put the rumour to bed. Gus told me I had nothing to worry about. I was wanted this year, next year and there would be opportunities with Penrith after I retired from football. He even issued a press statement: 'As far as I'm concerned, Petero has a job for life at Penrith as a player and an ambassador for the game.'

I felt conflicted. I was devoted to my Panther teammates and wanted to continue leading them, and I was devoted to our fans; but every time we went to Brisbane and the children, now aged from two to seven, were reunited with their cousins, and Bonnie with her parents and siblings, it was increasingly difficult to wrench ourselves away to return to Sydney. Our eldest daughter, Tallulah, is a sensitive girl who feels a strong connection to family. She broke our hearts when she wrote us a letter: 'Please, can we go back to Queensland?' She and her siblings were sad at being apart from our big noisy happy extended family.

So Bonnie and I had a heart-to-heart and we decided that in 2012 she, Tallulah, Ruby, Kaden and Jacobi would return north to our house, which we'd rented out, in Redcliffe, and I would remain in Penrith to fulfil my contract. Then, at the end of 2012, I would join them in Redcliffe, and see if I could get a game with the Broncos or perhaps a new Brisbane franchise that people were saying may kick off in 2013. I figured that one year was not forever and I could make that arrangement work, although I knew I'd be a lonely mess without Bonnie and the little ones.

I felt justified in assuring the Penrith players and the fans that I would be around in 2012.

I soldiered on in the second half of the season, as we suffered some losses and had some good wins. Meanwhile the rumour mill kept grinding out the story that the club was about to move me on.

In late July, at this low ebb, the Broncos' football manager, my old friend and teammate Andrew Gee, called to enquire about my contract situation at Penrith. I told him I was contracted to remain at Penrith for season 2012. He told me that Broncos were keen for me to return to them. However, it was at this time that several Panther players had found themselves in contract limbo because of salary cap constraints at the club. I had a few discussions with the boys in question. I weighed up the fact that these players, who were the future of the club, looked like having to leave the Panthers because there was no room under the cap for them, and I considered the strengthening rumors that I would be told there was no place for me in 2012, and I made a decision. I would ask for a release from my contract so the money would become available to retain the players with their careers ahead of them. I now wanted to return to Queensland with my family, and I knew there was a spot for me at the Broncos. It seemed like a win-win situation to me. On 26 July, I went to Gus Gould and asked to be released from my contract for 2012 on the grounds that I did not want to be separated from my family and that my leaving would free up salary cap money that could be better spent on player retention and recruitment. He granted me my wish and released a statement:

> Petero has indicated his desire to return home to Brisbane to be with his family. The Panthers . . . feel it would be unwise to stand in his way. Petero has given tremendous service to the Panthers club, the community, not to mention outstanding leadership to our team. His influence at Penrith will be evident long after he's gone.

I gathered together the players and coaching staff and, although the huge lump in my throat made it hard for me to do so, I announced that I would not be with them in 2012. I told them I was so proud of them for sticking tight through what had been a tough season. I promised that I would give the team my best in the final six weeks of the competition and emphasised that, with making the semis still a possibility, we must not drop our heads. Some of the players became a bit emotional, then disguised their feelings by telling me what they were going to do to me the first time I faced them in a Broncos' jersey. I released a statement to the fans, apologising if they felt I had lied to them when I said I'd be staying. When I'd told them that, I had every intention of doing so. I thanked everyone who had made me welcome, and I praised the players. It had been a privilege to lead them.

Of course, the smarties reckoned that the club wanted to get rid of me because I had supported Matt Elliott and Steve Georgallis, and that Gus and I couldn't stand the sight of each other. I had an inkling that I was on the outer with some officials, but I could live with that. What was not true was that Phil Gould and I had fallen out. I can honestly say that my dealings with Gus were straight-up and cordial, although he disagreed with some of the things I had said to him. With Gus in charge, the Panthers are in the best of hands.

No matter how hard we tried to buckle down, there had been too much damage done and the players found consistent success on the field elusive. No player rose to the challenge better than Luke Lewis. He dispelled any doubt that he was the man to lead the Panthers in 2012 by playing his heart out even as our season disintegrated around him. A Penrith junior, he is a rugby league footballer to his boots who has distinguished himself in pretty much every position on the field and represented New South Wales and Australia. He can play it tight or win you a game with individual brilliance.

Luke missed many games to injury in 2011 and that hurt us, as did Michael Gordon's season-ending anterior cruciate ligament injury. Six rounds out from the semis, we looked likely to sneak into a lower semi spot, then the accumulated injuries and the internal strife that had dogged us all year ganged up on us and, despite the gallant efforts of such players as Luke Walsh, Travis Burns, Brad Tighe, Tim Grant and Sam McKendry, we lost our last five games and finished 12th.

I was injured in the final competition round, a 32–12 loss against the Dragons. In an innocuous 22nd-minute tackle I ripped my pectoral muscle. That was my season and my October–November Four Nations Kangaroo tour to England gone. While my teammates were celebrating Mad Monday, I was off having scans done. That was probably a good thing.

I had achieved two of my three aims for 2011 – reclaiming my Kangaroo jersey and being part of a winning Queensland State of Origin team. But my third dream, of leading the Panthers to the semis and a premiership, sadly went unrealised.

As MY time in Penrith wound down, I was determined to have my say about the problems at the club and what I felt needed to be done to solve them. I planned to do so in my column in the *Panther News*, the club's journal that was distributed at games. In my final message to the fans, I would give thanks for all the support and good times I'd had at Penrith, and I would also have a shot at the officials who I felt were not up to the job.Obviously I would not have been able to speak my piece if head office had got wind of my intention, so I surprised them. Here's what happened. Through the years, my captain's column in the *Panther News* had been ghost-written by media manager Andrew Farrell. We'd get together and Andrew would note down my thoughts and they'd be published in the journal. But Andrew left the club at the end of the 2011 season, and the new media manager ghost-wrote my column and gave it back to me to make any final changes and then I sent it on to the editor who sent it straight to the printer without realising how critical of the club hierarchy and how political my column now was thanks to the changes I had made to it. The newsletter was printed and distributed at the last home game.

What I said in my column resulted in my being accused of treachery, subversion and guerrilla tactics. I wrote:

We have seen many changes to the football department over recent months. Fans and supporters, you have the chance to further that change by electing a new board later in the year. We need a passionate, successful and driven board who can give Phil Gould the backing and support he needs . . .

I called for people who loved the club to decide who they wanted in power at board level. I believed that the Panthers needed new blood, new faces with fresh ideas to help Gus drive the club into the future and help it realise its full potential as an NRL powerhouse. Penrith needed to attract and hold men who were good players and citizens. They had to have infrastructure at least the equal of other clubs. They had to have more of a presence in the community, with players getting out to schools, shopping centres and workplaces to make the people of Penrith feel they were a part of the team, and also counter the cashed-up encroachments of AFL. (Images of my old mate Israel Folau in his orange GWS Giants strip were popping up everywhere.) The club had to put its finances in order and stop haemorrhaging money. I said I believed that these were all initiatives close to Phil Gould's heart.

Some were horrified by my column, although nobody said anything to my face. Others supported me, reckoning that I was only saying what many were thinking. Whatever, I had been captain of the Panthers first-grade side for four years and I was entitled to my opinion.

At the end-of-season function at Panthers Leagues Club I was not invited to make a speech to farewell the players, staff and fans. I understand that the powers-that-be feared that if I was given such an opportunity I might publicly criticise them after what I'd written in my column. This was never going to be the case. If I'd been allowed to speak at the function I would have thanked the players, football staff and fans for four great years.

I will always believe my days at the Penrith Panthers, despite, or because of, all the ructions and never winning the competition, matured me as a footballer and as a man.

# 12

# Endings and beginnings

Arthur Beetson died on 1 December 2011, soon after I returned to Redcliffe. He was riding his pushbike near Paradise Point on the Gold Coast when, around 9 am on a sparkling summer morning, he had a massive heart attack and pitched onto the street. By the time paramedics arrived, Big Artie, who was only 66, had left us. He had been in my thoughts now and then since I had arrived back in Redcliffe a couple of weeks before. As it was for me, the mighty Redcliffe Dolphins rugby league club was where Arthur learned his skills.

I would never compare myself to Artie, who is an Immortal of rugby league and the benchmark by which front-row forwards are measured, however we had a few things in common. There was the Redcliffe connection, and we both ended up in the front row after playing in the centres. We both represented Australia and played for Queensland well into our thirties. It was Artie who took a keen interest in me when I was a kid and later tried to lure me to the Roosters. He supported me my whole career and always had my back when the critics came for me.

Just before he died, he filmed an interview in which he remembered my ball skills as a youngster, and wished that the modern game had given me more opportunities to be a ball-player. In Artie's era, front-rowers mixed skill with power, whereas in the modern game, by and large, a front-rower's primary role is as a battering ram. If I'd played in Artie's time I'd have been using my ball skills and if he was playing in mine, he'd be hitting it up, buckling the defensive line and playing the ball quickly. He had passed away by the time I saw that interview clip, and I was humbled that he'd taken the trouble to mention me.

I went to Redcliffe's home ground, Dolphin Oval, for Arthur's funeral – or celebration, as it turned out. I thought about him that day and I remembered his exploits on the field – his astonishing turn of speed for one so big, his magical ball skills, his ability to stand like a colossus in tackles and offload. I remembered his huge hand that engulfed mine when we shook hands when I was a boy, and he said, 'G'day son, how you travellin'?'

It's rugby league folklore, and my own personal folklore, that Artie ignited Origin and made it the event it is today when, a few kilos overweight and wearing a jersey with cut-off sleeves and chalk marks all down the front, he threw caution to the wind in the first State of Origin match in 1980. This was the genesis of mate against mate, state against state. Since then, for the 80 minutes of an Origin match, the gloves have always been off.

I watched that game on TV as a kid and couldn't believe what I was seeing. This transcended sport. It was deadly serious. It was war – a sporting war. Artie's presence was enormous and I was in awe of him, just as I was of Mal Meninga and my dad.

I attended Arthur's funeral with my dad. It was a touching and emotional occasion. There were a lot of funny stories told and memories shared, and I have it on good authority that afterwards at the club a lot of beer was consumed. His sons and his great mates Mick Cronin, Tommy Raudonikis, John Quayle, Ron Coote and Johnny Peard spoke from the heart. Wally Lewis read out a message from every member of the 1980 Queensland State of Origin team. There on the field and around the ground was a who's who of rugby league. Artie's Eastern Suburbs Roosters teammates, whom he captained to the premiership in '75, flew up to pay tribute to their fallen leader.

Eight straining pallbearers carried Arthur's white casket from the Dolphins dressing-room to a marquee in the middle of the ground for the service, and then they bore it on their shoulders before they gently laid his coffin in the hearse for a last lap of honour of the oval. Well over a thousand were there to say goodbye and every soul cheered and clapped and many of us shed a tear or two for Artie, who was as good a bloke as he was a player, and that's saying something.

Later, as I drove home, I thought that if I was lucky enough to make State of Origin in a few months' time, I would think of Artie and his legacy as I ran onto the field.


ARTIE'S DEATH made me realise how much we have to celebrate in our game. I look forward to the day when the Australian Rugby League has its own museum, honouring the great players and games and commemorating our code with mementoes, photographs, film and audio. If we fail to preserve our heritage in such a place, then it will be lost when those who lived it pass away. There is a tremendous British rugby league museum at rugby league's birthplace, the George Hotel in Huddersfield in the north of England, and other sporting codes have their museums. We should too.

Now I've called it quits, I plan to repay the game that has given me and my family everything. It's my dream to help make rugby league the number one football code in Australia. My role as general president of the Rugby League Players' Association ended when I ceased to be an active player, but I plan to remain a servant of the game, taking on challenges to ensure that rugby league matches it with AFL, soccer and rugby union into the future.

Most pressing, as I see it, is establishing a fair Collective Bargaining Agreement for the players to ensure their rights, such as an increase in minimum wage, income protection insurance and improved player retirement accounts. There should also be an increase to the salary cap flowing from the lucrative new TV rights deal. I want salary cap dispensations to allow clubs to keep players they nurtured from rookie to champion, and allow clubs salary cap exemptions to retain long-serving players. RLPA boss David Garnsey told me he hoped my involvement would encourage other players to become more active in the Players' Association – not sit back passively and accept whatever is dealt to them by the NRL.

Also close to my heart are academic and trades schemes to prepare players for life after footy. I'd like to liaise with NRL Welfare Officer Nigel Vagana on formulating player welfare and education programs aimed at the ever-increasing numbers of Polynesian and Melanesian players in our game. After all, they make up 30 per cent of all NRL players now and 35 per cent of the National Youth Competition (Toyota

Cup) players. Having experienced it at close hand, I will also do whatever I can to stamp out racism in rugby league.

Another program close to my heart is Men of Honour, a scheme to help young rugby league players grow into good men, helping them make good life choices and embrace their masculinity in the best way. Nigel Vagana linked with an old Redcliffe mate of mine, Glen Gerreyn, a former champion runner whose brainchild Men of Honour is, and introduced the program to the NRL. Basically, Glen talks to young players from all 16 clubs about what it is to be a real man.

Things on the agenda include being responsible and doing what you say you are going to do; developing a mature attitude towards drugs and alcohol; being yourself – having your own code of good behaviour and not falling prey to peer pressure; and planning for a financially secure future. Glen and Nigel believe that young blokes need good role models, and I've offered to make myself available to talk to the players whenever they feel I can be of use.

I am the sum of all the wisdom I have been offered by others in my life, and if I can pass on the flame, that will be the least I can do.

I STARTED what would be my last NRL season behind the pace because of the surgery to reattach my torn pectoral muscle to the bone. The operation and its aftermath knocked me around more than I expected. I had to wear a sling until the start of the season, which stopped me doing strength and skill work with my teammates, and for the first month of games I wore a shoulder harness to restrict movement and avoid tearing the muscle again. First I had to make the pec strong again, and then get used to the collisions. It was frustrating not to be able to hit the ground running.

Early on, I hadn't decided whether this would be my final season, or if I would make myself available for Queensland and Australia. I figured I'd make up my mind as the season played out. I felt strongly that I did not want to outstay my welcome, especially at a time when Australian rugby league was blessed with fine front-rowers, such as Matt Scott, Paul Gallen, Ben Hannant, Tim Mannah, Keith Galloway, David Shillington, Michael Weyman and the up-and-coming Trent Merrin, Josh McGuire, Aaron Woods and James Tamou. I wanted to go out on top, not as a has-been who hung around a year too long.

I was feeling the pinch. I would be 36 in April. In past seasons it had taken me a day or two to get over the bumps and bruises of a game. Now I hurt all week long. Mentally, I felt a little jaded, and the long drive from Redcliffe to Red Hill for training each day began to be a bit of a burden. These were bad signs.

I was underdone for our first trial match, against the Melbourne Storm. Tackling their second-rower Ryan Hinchcliffe, my mis-timing saw me collect him high. He went down and I was placed on report for a careless high tackle and suspended for the opening match of the season, an 18–6 away win over Parramatta.

I felt bad, because the Broncos had brought me back to support new skipper Sam Thaiday – who had taken over from Darren Lockyer – and I wasn't much use to anyone on the sideline. However, the young Bronco forwards stepped up. Ben Hannant, Corey Parker, Josh McGuire, Matt Gillett, Andrew McCullough, Alex Glenn, Scott Anderson and Ben Te'o more than held the fort until my return. The backs – Peter Wallace, Corey Norman, Justin Hodges,

Jack Reed, Jharal Yow Yeh, Gerard Beale and Josh Hoff-man – ran riot. Their skill and athleticism astounded me. Their form ensured that I'd need to be at or very near my best to make it back into the team. As it was, because of my lack of game time, I spent two weeks on the bench after my return from suspension before I was reinstated to the run-on team.

Coach Anthony 'Hook' Griffin dispelled any notion that I was back as a Bronco for sentimental reasons, or to be some cosseted elder statesman dispensing wisdom to the young blokes. 'We don't need any guardians or teachers in here, we need footballers, and if they can be a guardian or a teacher after they get their job done, that's great. We signed Petero because he is a front-rower who was the best prop in last year's State of Origin series. That's the attraction. I expect him to play to the highest standards every week.'

We were narrowly beaten 28–26 by the Cowboys in round two, then downed the Knights 24–10 and the Rab-bitohs 20–12 in the next two games. By the fourth round, I had regained match fitness and, in spite of being strapped up like a mummy during a match, I was feeling strong and happier with my form. Hook used me for 35 minutes in our win against Souths, whose formidable forwards Sam Bur-gess, Roy Asotasi and Dave Taylor gave my pec and match fitness a good workout.

Whereas in 2011, with the Panthers, I played around 55 minutes a game, now Hook typically played me for the open-ing 20 minutes, and the final 20, with Josh McGuire – who is very close to Queensland and Australian selection – com-ing off the bench to do his damage in the middle section of the game.

It was in the Souths match that our Queensland and Kangaroo winger Jharal Yow Yeh suffered a compound fracture and dislocation of his ankle. You could hear the blood-chilling snap around the ground. Jharal lay on the ground writhing in agony with his bone sticking through his skin. The horrific injury required several surgical procedures and skin grafts. It was a tragedy for Jharal, who had the world at his feet before the injury and would now be out for all of 2012. Being at the Broncos meant he would be taken care of and given every opportunity to come back as good as ever in 2013.

While not yet playing as well as I would need to if I was to have a chance of making the Test and Queensland Origin sides, I felt I was making a strong contribution to the team. I knew my role and performed it. What made everything easier was being just a cog in a well-oiled machine where everyone, from the players to the coaching staff to the administration, knew precisely what was expected of them and had the talent to do it well. Unlike at Penrith, at the Broncos I didn't have to be a peacemaker, politician and team leader.

Hardly a day went by when a journo didn't call me and ask if this year would be my last in the NRL and if I was putting my hand up to play for my state and country again. I told them the truth: I just didn't know. All would depend on my form and state of mind as the season progressed.

For me, the game when I knew that there really was life for the Broncos after the retirement of our playmaker Darren Lockyer was our 28–20 victory over St George in round five. The hot youngsters in our team, who had been eased into the big-time by coach Anthony Griffin and his staff, were about to launch the Broncos into an exciting new era. Against the Dragons, we fielded 10 players who were under 23. I had no doubt that Corey Norman – who was making Locky's five-eighth spot his own – Matt Gillett, Jack Reed,

Josh McGuire, Josh Hoffman, Andrew McCullough, Alex Glenn, Ben Hunt and Dale Copley were on the verge of great achievements. There's a way to go, and potential still to be tapped, but the signs are there that these young guys have the strong self-belief and desire that you need – in addition to football talent – to win premierships.

The challenge for the Broncos would be holding on to these young stars as they became superstars. Already winger Gerard Beale had announced he would be with the Dragons in 2013. This brings me back to my gripe – mentioned before in relation to the Players' Association – about the need for a salary cap dispensation to assist a club which identifies, signs and then nurtures players to hang on to them.

The Broncos continued their season by beating the Tigers, the Raiders and the Titans, before losing to the Warriors and Manly. I thought I gave probably my best performance of the year in the game against the Gold Coast. So, after 10 rounds, just before Origin I, with seven wins and three losses, we were running second behind the undefeated Melbourne Storm. Despite the good form of the Storm, the Sea Eagles, the Cowboys, the Tigers and the Rabbitohs, we were a lot of people's pick as likely premiers.

IN MID-APRIL, shortly before the Kangaroos side was named to play the Kiwis in the Anzac Test, I declared myself available for the Kangaroos and for State of Origin, if picked. However, the Australian selectors believed that I was still underdone, and opted for Ben Hannant, Dave Shillington, Paul Gallen and James Tamou as the Test front-rowers.

I accepted being left out of the Australian side because I knew in my heart that I had not really done enough to earn my inclusion. I realised I'd been very lucky to have had such a long run in the green and gold and, if this was to be the end, so be it. I was happy to let the selectors decide my representative future. They know what they're doing and if you deserve to be there, you usually get picked. If anything, missing the team increased my determination to play well enough that Mal would have to pick me for my final Maroons State of Origin campaign.

But not everyone thought I should declare myself a starter for this year's Origin series. Shane Webcke earlier in the year had tried to talk me out of it. He said I had nothing more to prove and should make the Broncos my first and only priority and be in the best mental and physical shape to help steer the team through any post-Origin slump.

Greg Dowling also said it was time for me to make way for the young brigade:

> I think it's time for Petero to go. I don't say that as criticism. Petero's had a bloody glorious Origin career – I simply can't see any forward matching it – but the time has come for Petero to say goodbye. He has been an absolutely wonderful servant for Queensland and Australia and not for a second would I deny the magnificent contributions he has made. But it's the old story – you can't beat youth and enthusiasm. Eventually young blokes who have come through are ready to take on more . . . and I feel it's that time for Queensland. At age 36, this will be Petero's hardest-ever year in the game. Without Darren Lockyer, he has a huge leadership role to play at the Broncos and I think he should just focus his energies on them.

For their part, the Broncos' playing and coaching staff said that if I wanted to make myself available for State of

Origin, they would back me. I had a number of discussions with Hook on making the right decision, but to have his backing meant a lot to me.

THERE WAS one issue that needed addressing, for it had been on my mind for quite some time. Retirement. I was always adamant that I wanted to make the right call at the right time. That time was now.

I broke the news to Hook, football manager Andrew Gee and Sam Thaiday in the first week of May. I then told the team. Unlike when I left the club at the end of 2007 and when I departed the Panthers in 2011, I wasn't sad this time. I simply felt thankful that I'd had a good and long career. Retirement is something we all must face and now it was my turn.

On 8 May, the club called a media conference at Bronco Headquarters at Red Hill. Hook and our CEO Paul White were at my side when I told reporters that after 45 appearances for Australia, 30 games for Queensland and 297 NRL matches for Brisbane and Penrith, I'd had my time as a top-flight rugby league player. My head, heart and aching bones and muscles were all telling me it was approaching time to retire. I would devote myself to helping Queensland win a record seventh State of Origin series and the Broncos the premiership, then I would be gone.

There, I'd done it. For months I had been weighing up my options, trying to figure out what I should do, and now it was all clear. Coming out and saying it lifted a weight from my shoulders. I told the gathering:

It's a decision that has been hanging over my head for a little while now. I'm just grateful for the club allowing me the opportunity to come back and play in these colours.

You'd love to think you can go on forever, but I think the time is right for me to step into the next stage of my life.

One journo said that while everyone was talking about the Broncos handing me a fairy-tale ending with a premiership, he suspected that the real fairy-tale was that I could finish my career at the club where I belonged. He was right. I concluded: 'I don't have any regrets. I just feel so lucky with the career that I've had and the opportunity to finish up wearing these proud colours . . .'

Sam Thaiday said the best way he could thank blokes like Locky and me for our long service was not with words but by deeds. 'Playing good footy, giving them our all, the way they've done that for us for so many years. Having Locky retiring last year was such a huge event at the club. Now that we know Petero is leaving at the end of this year, we can get through this next period pretty well, having dealt with it last year with Locky. We never want to [win the premiership] for just one individual player; it's a goal for everyone in the team and we've all been working hard for that goal.'

Coach Griffin concurred. 'It's important now that Pet has made his decision that we not so much talk about it anymore, but get on with it on the field and try and make it as good a year as it can be for him for his last year.'

Once my announcement was made, it was humbling to get so many emails and text messages from friends and family congratulating me on my decision. There was one article I have kept that was published in *The Australian* to mark the announcement of my retirement. It meant a lot to me because it was written by a man for whom I have enormous respect, Craig Bellamy.

As a proud New South Welshman involved with State of Origin, it was something I never wanted to say publicly but I kept thinking: 'Next year Petero Civoniceva can't possibly be as good as he was this year.'

But every year he seemed to get better and better. Let's go back to Game II of the 2009 series, when I was coaching New South Wales. The game was close and we had Queensland pinned down at its end during the second half. It was just remarkable that in a 15-minute period, every run Petero made he gained 10 or 15 metres, getting Queensland out of trouble in the process. We kept kicking the ball down their end, trying to build pressure, and he kept bringing it back. All of a sudden the tide turned. Sam Thaiday won the man-of-the-match award that night but Petero was the guy in my eyes who won that Origin game for Queensland.

I heard later he picked up the players' player award for his side but I will never forget how he kept ploughing into our defence, making inroads with every stride.

He was 33 years old that year. And I'm sure a lot of people thought he could not be as effective that year or the next.

But here he is at 36 and he's still a classic Origin player. And from what I've seen so far he deserves to be there again in 2012 as much as he did back in 2009 and when he first made his Origin debut in 2001.

I thought he would slow down at 34 or 35 but he hasn't. Far from it. He's never let Queensland down before and he's not about to do it now. You know he will always rise for Origin. And Mal Meninga doesn't need me to tell him how all the guys in the team trust him and really look up to him. I know my three guys (Cooper Cronk, Cam Smith and Billy Slater) do, along with former Storm players Greg Inglis, Dallas Johnson and Mick Crocker.

Last year New South Wales had to battle against the 'Do it for Locky' factor and this year it will be another sentimental cry of 'Win it for Petero'. It will be a genuine war cry and not a slogan made up out of any sense of obligation.

So hearing about his decision to retire is obviously sad news but it had to come. Quite honestly, given the position he's played all these years and the level of performance he's played at, I'm surprised it hasn't come sooner. Prop forward is one of the toughest positions of any team sport. It's virtually running into brick walls each week for nine months of the year.

How highly he should be regarded is shown in some of the figures he's produced – the most Tests for Australia for a forward (45); the most Origin games for a forward (30). And he's soon to reach the NRL's 300-game club.

I started on the coaching staff at the Brisbane Broncos in 1998, the same year as Petero made his NRL debut a couple of days after his 22nd birthday. I remember him as a regular first-grader, but he came off the bench mostly in those days. He won a premiership with the Broncos that year, as an interchange player in the grand final. But it wasn't an easy road for him. He was a late developer, although front-rowers are often like that. He wasn't one of the superstar kids earmarked for first grade at 17 or 18. He had to work hard and convince a few people that he wasn't just the perfect size for a prop, he had the skills too.

Petero is one of those guys who, when he crosses that white line, he's hard, courageous, and ruthless – all the things you want. But off the field, he's quietly-spoken, very caring about people and just a very humble and lovely bloke. You wonder how the two types fit into that one body, but they do . . .

•

A WEEK out from the selection and announcement of the Queensland State of Origin team, Mal Meninga called. He wanted to know if I was really serious about saddling up again for Origin, especially in the light of my missing out on Kangaroo selection. I acknowledged I'd had a slow start to the season, but that my form and confidence were definitely starting to pick up. I told him I was up for Origin, for sure.

'If you and [chairman of selectors] Des Morris want to pick me, then I would love to play, but I don't want to be picked on past performances. I don't want to be included on sentiment. We've got plenty of excellent props and none of them would let the state down.'

Mal wished me a long and happy retirement. But first I had a job to do: help Queensland win Origin this year.

I said, 'Then I'm in the side?'

'Mate,' he said, 'of course you're in the side.'

On 23 May, when Queensland ran out against New South Wales at Melbourne's Etihad Stadium for Origin I, I would be 36 years and 32 days old, the oldest-ever Origin player. Allan Langer was 35 years and 331 days when he played his final game; Arthur Beetson was 35 and 168 days and Steve Price 35 and 125 days. Origin I would be my 31st game, putting me on level pegging with Brad Fittler and Wally Lewis and behind only Locky, who played 36 Origins, Alfie Langer (34) and Mal Meninga (32). Of current State of Origin players, I was now the only one who was already born when State of Origin came into being in 1980.

Was I making a dumb mistake taking on Origin duty again? Was I in denial about my ability to play at that standard again? Was I past my Origin use-by date? I was sure I wasn't. I had stepped down from the Test side in 2010 when I doubted my form was good enough to play a Test, but now I felt fit and focused. I wouldn't have taken it on if I'd thought I would let Queensland or myself down. Time would tell. If I was past my prime, Origin would find me out. All I could do was what I had always done: prepare meticulously and, in the game, do my very best.

On Monday 14 May, the team for the first State of Origin match was named, and I was in the run-on side, wearing my No. 10 jersey. The rest of the side was: Billy Slater, Darius Boyd, Brent Tate (replacing Jharal Yow Yeh), Greg Inglis, Justin Hodges, Johnathan Thurston, Cooper Cronk, Matt Scott, Cameron Smith (c), Sam Thaiday, Nate Myles and Ashley Harrison, and on the bench were Ben Hannant, Dave Taylor, Dave Shillington and Matt Gillett. It was a strong side, with Inglis, Taylor, Slater, Thurston and Gillett in particular enjoying purple patches of form.

The Blues would be led by the inspirational Paul Gallen and have a share of players in brilliant form as well, including Glenn and Brett Stewart, Robbie Farah, Todd Carney and Mitchell Pearce. My old Penrith teammate Michael Jennings had not been playing first grade – having issues at the club – and was plucked from the Panthers' feeder team the Windsor Wolves; and Jarryd Hayne had been struggling in a disappointing Parramatta team. But nobody in the Queensland camp was fooled. These guys were tremendous players and they would lift when they pulled on that sky blue jersey. They had been roundly criticised and had plenty to prove and nobody knows as well as me how motivating that can be. This was going to be one hell of a series.

I was under no illusions. I had to play well or I would not be in the side for Origin II. I told reporters after the side had been named, 'I have to perform or perish.'

Once the Maroon squad arrived in chilly Melbourne, we trained at Simonds Stadium, home ground of the Geelong

Cats AFL side. The formidable ghost of Arthur Beetson was with us. Queensland players have always had a war cry that we yell to each other when things get tough in a match and we have to pull out all stops. For years it was 'Queenslander!', then 'Tonga', in tribute to Willie Tonga who played on with a dislocated shoulder. In 2012, our battle cry would be 'Artie!' The great man's name rang out at Simonds Stadium as we prepared for our big showdown with the boys of New South Wales. Artie was gone now, but he was inspiring us just as he did when he led the Maroons to glory as a player and captain.

It was a focused and emotional camp and, as usual, a lot of fun. Our mateship kicked in from the word go. Once more we embraced our Maroon heritage, remembered the great games and the men who played them. Former Origin stars joined us, and inspired us with their tales, and it was good to see Jharal Yow Yeh, who surely would have been in the team if not for his injury, invited to be part of the group. We acknowledged how much victory means for the people of Queensland. We talked about Artie, of course, and two other former Queensland Origin stars who had passed away, Peter Jackson and Ross Hendricks. We were presented with our Queensland jerseys. The first, our team training jersey, was maroon with every Queensland player's name and number on a white V across the chest. The second, our game jersey, was emblazoned with the names of Arthur, Peter and Ross on the sleeve. That was very special.

Mal drilled into us that talent alone is not enough to win a State of Origin match. Respect for our history, ferocious commitment, courage, a love for each other manifesting in a do-or-die refusal to let a teammate down – all these things would be needed on game night.

There was an edge to our mental preparation because we

knew how desperate Ricky Stuart and his men would be to avoid being beaten in seven straight State of Origin series. The day before the match, a reporter in the Blues' camp asked Ricky how he felt about Queensland's domination of New South Wales and he replied, 'I fucking hate it.' There would be no prisoners taken, and nobody in a Maroon jersey would have it any other way.

As we always did before the match, we forwards came together and acknowledged that the Blues saw our backs as our strength and us as the weak link, and that the role of their huge men – 113 kilogram James Tamou, 110 kilogram Trent Merrin and 118 kilogram Tony Williams – would be to smash us, and then their smart hooker Robbie Farah would direct the smaller, fleet-footed men Gallen, Glenn Stewart, Luke Lewis, Ben Creagh, Greg Bird and Jamie Buhrer at Matt Scott, Dave Taylor, Dave Shillington, Ben Hannant and myself, trying to catch us flat-footed. To a man, we welcomed the attention. This tactic had worked well for New South Wales in Origin II in 2011, but by increasing our pace, power and intensity in Origin III we had blown them away.

The Blues planted stories in the media to unsettle us. Paul Kent of the *Daily Telegraph* claimed sacrilegiously that Artie Beetson was more a New South Welshman than a Queenslander because he had worn a blue jersey in the pre-Origin days. We all had a laugh at that. Then stories kept appearing about how my 'lack of mobility and ageing legs' would be found out by the Blue forwards. I kept quiet and concentrated on my preparation, leaving Alfie Langer to return serve:

The forward battle will be vital in deciding the winner. I know they tried to run Petero around last year and he came out on top. He's going to be up against it again because they're very mobile and they're going to try and tire us out. They'll throw the ball around, run their big guys at us; they've done it all before. We've got to make sure we're defending well. In Origin, you have to get your defence right and your attack will come. The game is going to be won up front. It all starts with defence. We can throw the ball around, but if we're giving away a lot of ground we'll be constantly working out of our own half and getting very tired.

Ten minutes from game time we moved nervously around our dressing sheds. The team talk was over, and now all there was to do was absorb the tension, encourage each other, go over our game plan. Mal passed calmly among us, shaking our hands, revving us up.

For a few moments I dared to think beyond tonight, to Origin II and III, to the Broncos' premiership campaign, to taking Bonnie for a New York holiday as I'd long promised I would when I retired from football and our life was our own. After that? God willing, health, happiness, good family times, new challenges . . .

A bang on the dressing-room door snapped me back to the here and now. 'Queensland, let's go!'

I reined in my thoughts and thought only of the job at hand. There was the rest of my life to think about the future. Tonight there was a game to win. I pulled on my jersey, as usual the very last thing I did, and joined my teammates as we filed out of the dressing-room into the blaze of the floodlights and the roar of the crowd.

# EPILOGUE

## New Horizons

On 4 July 2012, when Queensland captain Cameron Smith called me up onto the podium at Suncorp Stadium after we had won the third and series-deciding State of Origin game, I was humbled by the cheers of my team-mates and the vast crowd. I raised my arms above my head and returned the applause. With my gesture I was thanking my Queensland teammates who, in winning a seventh straight State of Origin series, had helped me to end my Origin career in the best possible way. I was acknowledging my Queensland and Bronco coaches, Mal Meninga and Anthony Griffin, who encouraged me to play Origin in 2012 when my instincts – and 36-year-old body – were warning me that I just may not be up to it anymore. I was clapping the fans in the grandstands, whose display of affection moved me deeply. I was showing my appreciation for the New South Wales boys who gave their very best and made Origin 2012 one of the finest and most closely-contested series ever.

There at Suncorp on that wonderful night as I put my hands together, I was expressing my love for Bonnie, and for Tallulah, Ruby, Kaden and Jacobi, who later joined me in a lap of honour. I was reaching out to my mother, Tima, for whom no sacrifice was too great when I was growing up with a head full of footy dreams, and my father, Petero Snr, who taught me what it took to be a good footballer. My sisters Lusi and Lily, too. And I was acknowledging the love and kindness of Bonnie's parents, Terry and Peter Chisholm, who had welcomed me into their life.

That post-Origin salute was also my way of sending out my thanks to the teammates and opponents, wherever they were, whom I'd encountered in my 15 years of football at the top level. Without players, there's no game. Boys, it's been a pleasure. Rugby league players are a special breed, and in the years ahead I'll have your back, be it in an official or unofficial capacity.

As well, I was recognising the coaches, staff, mentors, administrators, managers and fans who supported me through the highs and lows and made possible my long career in the wonderful game of rugby league. I can remember bursting with pride when I played my debut first grade match. And on 22 June 2012, when I racked up my 300th game and Darren Lockyer and Shane Webcke presented me with my jersey before the match, I was more proud than I can express. I am awed to now be in the company of such great players as Locky, Terry Lamb, Steve Menzies, Steve Price, Ruben Wiki, Nathan Hindmarsh and Hazem El Masri, who also achieved the 300-game milestone. My 300th match was on 22 June against the South Sydney Rabbitohs in the Women in League round. When the game was safely in our grasp, our regular kicker Peter Wallace tossed me the ball to convert our final try. I missed, but at least the ball left the ground.

After Origin, Anthony Griffin paid me a compliment

when he spoke of the role he wanted me to play for the Broncos in the remaining competition rounds and the finals series, and likened me to an old bus, determined to make it to the finish line. At least I think it was a compliment.

Well, as I write these final words and that finishing line looms, I *am* feeling good. After a slow start to the season, I feel that I have regained form and, at the risk of sounding greedy, am certainly up for one last hurrah. The Broncos are capable of making the grand final and we are capable of winning it. In such a wonderful farewell year as this has been, I believe that anything is possible. Yet win or lose, come October, a new phase of my life will begin. I will have to learn to live without rugby league. This old bus is bound for new horizons.

18 July 2012